ISBN 978-0-282-31152-0
PIBN 10847105

1 MONTH OF
FREE
READING

at
www.ForgottenBooks.com

By purchasing this book you are eligible for one month membership to ForgottenBooks.com, giving you unlimited access to our entire collection of over 1,000,000 titles via our web site and mobile apps.

To claim your free month visit:
www.forgottenbooks.com/free847105

English
Français
Deutsche
Italiano
Español
Português

www.forgottenbooks.com

Mythology Photography **Fiction**
Fishing Christianity **Art** Cooking
Essays Buddhism Freemasonry
Medicine **Biology** Music **Ancient
Egypt** Evolution Carpentry Physics
Dance Geology **Mathematics** Fitness
Shakespeare **Folklore** Yoga Marketing
Confidence Immortality Biographies
Poetry **Psychology** Witchcraft
Electronics Chemistry History **Law**
Accounting **Philosophy** Anthropology
Alchemy Drama Quantum Mechanics
Atheism Sexual Health **Ancient History**
Entrepreneurship Languages Sport
Paleontology Needlework Islam
Metaphysics Investment Archaeology
Parenting Statistics Criminology
Motivational

F. Ranger

the Gift of his Aunt S

30th Octr 1828

C. Pannett

B Lawrence

The Waterman.

THE BOOK

OF

ENGLISH TRADES,

AND

𝔏𝔦𝔟𝔯𝔞𝔯𝔶

OF

THE USEFUL ARTS.

WITH EIGHTY-SIX WOOD-CUTS.

A NEW EDITION.

═══

LONDON:

PRINTED FOR C. & J. RIVINGTON,

Booksellers to the Society for Promoting Christian Knowledge;

Printed by R. GILBERT, St. John's-square, London.

CONTENTS.

Description of Machines.

The Apothecary.

BOOK OF TRADES.

THE APOTHECARY.

THE office of an *Apothecary* is to attend on sick persons, and to prepare and to give them medicines, either on his own judgment, or according to the prescription of the Physician.

It is well known that the word *Apotheca*, signified originally any kind of store, magazine, or warehouse; and that the proprietor or keeper of such a store was called *Apothecarius*. We must not, therefore, understand by the word, when mentioned in writings two or three hundred years old, Apothecaries such as ours are at present. At those periods, persons were often called Apothecaries who, at court, and in the houses of great people, prepared for the table various preserves, particularly fruit incrusted with sugar, and who, on that account, may be considered as confectioners. Hence, perhaps, we see the reason why Apothecaries were in this country combined with the *grocers* till the reign of James the First. They were then separated, and the Apothecaries were incorporated as a company: the reason assigned for this was, that medicines might be better prepared, and that unwholesome remedies might not be imposed on the sick.

From this period, Apothecaries were distinguished for selling drugs, used in medicine, and preparing from them different compounds, according to the prescriptions given by physicians and others. Prior to this, it is probable, Physicians usually prepared

B

their own medicines; and it has been thought that they gradually became accustomed to employ Apothecaries for the sake of their own convenience, when they found, in their neighbourhood, a druggist in whose skill they could confide, and whose interest they wished to promote, by resigning in his favour that part of the occupation.

Such an employment as that of an Apothecary is, however, mentioned at a much earlier period of our history; for it is said, that King Edward the Third gave a pension of sixpence a day to Coursus de Gangeland, an Apothecary in London, for taking care of and attending his majesty during his illness in Scotland; and this is the first mention of an Apothecary.

In the year 1712, the importance of this profession was acknowledged by an Act of Parliament, which exempted, for a limited time, Apothecaries from serving the offices of constable, scavenger, and other ward and parish offices, and from serving upon juries; which act was, a few years afterwards, made perpetual.

The Apothecaries, as a body, have a hall near Bridge Street, Blackfriars, where there are two magnificent laboratories, out of which all the surgeons are supplied with medicines for the British Navy. Here also, drugs of all sorts are sold to the public, which may be depended upon as pure and unadulterated. They are obliged to make up their medicines according to the formulas prescribed in the Dispensary of the Royal College of Physicians, and are liable to have their shops visited by censors of the College, who are employed to destroy such medicines as they think not good. But as almost all persons who practise in this profession are men of liberal education, and acquainted with the theory and practice of chemistry, there are very few of them who do not prepare their own drugs, either wholly or in part.

In many places, and particularly in opulent cities, the first Apothecaries' shops were established at the public expense, and belonged in fact to the magistrates. A particular garden also was often appropriated to the use of the Apothecary, in order that he might rear in it the necessary plants, and which was therefore called the Apothecaries' garden.

In conformity to this principle Sir Hans Sloane, in the year 1721, presented the Apothecaries' company with a spacious piece of ground at Chelsea, for a physic-garden, on condition of their paying the small ground-rent of 5*l.* per annum; of continuing it always as a physic-garden, and of presenting to the Royal Society fifty samples of different sorts of plants grown there, till they amounted to two thousand. The latter of these conditions has been long since more than completed.

In this garden there are two very magnificent cedars, which were planted in 1683, and were then about three feet high. The pine-tree, the coffee-tree, the tea-shrub, and sugar-cane, are amongst the curiosities which may be seen at this place.

This is a very genteel business; a youth intended to be an Apothecary should be a good scholar, at least he should know as much Latin as to be able to read the best writers in the various sciences connected with medicine. Indeed, the late Act of Parliament renders it more necessary than ever for a person to be well acquainted not only with the classics, but with *Botany,* the *Materia Medica, Chemistry, Anatomy,* and the outlines of *Medicine:* for by that Act, passed in 1815, a Court of Examiners is appointed by the Apothecaries' Company to examine into the qualification of every person applying for a certificate to practise as an Apothecary in *England* and *Wales;* for which certificate, when obtained, 10*l.* 10*s.* are to be paid for every Apothecary practising in London or within ten miles of it; and for a certificate to practise in the country,

6*l.* 6*s.* are to be paid. Even *Assistants* to Apothecaries must now undergo examination. The price of a certificate for an Apothecary's assistant is 2*l.* 2*s.*—The penalty of practising without a certificate is 20*l.*—Assistants' penalty 5*l.*

There is also a numerous class of medical men in London, and various parts of England and Wales, called *Surgeon and Apothecary,* to which is commonly added the designation of *Man-midwife;* and to such persons, in the country more especially, are the lives and health of by far the greater part of the community intrusted, by those whose finances will not enable them to consult a regular Physician. These of course must undergo an examination not only at Apothecaries' Hall, but at the College of Surgeons.

All persons applying for a certificate to practise as an Apothecary, must produce testimonials of having served at least five years Apprenticeship to an Apothecary; and, in general, five years are the usual number for which Apprentices are bound. The premium is very various: sometimes two hundred guineas have been given.—An assistant or journeyman to an Apothecary will sometimes have from forty to eighty pounds per annum, or more, exclusive of his board; but in general the salaries are much lower, often not exceeding twenty-five. The principal expense in establishing a young man as an Apothecary is his education, certificate, &c. His whole stock in trade, exclusive of books, does not often exceed the value of one hundred pounds.

In China they have a singular mode of dispensing their medicines. In the public squares of their cities, there is a very high stone pillar, on which are engraven the names of all sorts of medicines, with the price of each; and when the poor stand in need of such assistance, they go to the treasury, where they receive the price each medicine is rated at.

THE ATTORNEY.

———

An Attorney primarily signifies any one who is appointed by another to transact any business for him in his absence: but an *Attorney-at-Law,* of whom we are now to speak, is a person who manages the *Law* business of another, for whom he is retained; the term being analogous to the procurator or proctor of the civilians and canonists in the ecclesiastical courts.

Anciently, according to the old Gothic constitutions, every suitor was obliged to appear and prosecute or defend his suit in person, unless by special license from the king; and this still continues to be the rule in criminal cases. But by sundry old statutes from that of Westm. 2. c. 10, permission was granted to Attornies to prosecute or defend any civil suit in the absence of the parties. An idiot, however, cannot at this day, prosecute or defend by his Attorney, but must appear in person.

Attornies are admitted to the execution of their office, by the superior courts at Westminster Hall. They are considered as officers of the respective courts in which they are admitted; on which account, they enjoy many privileges; and are peculiarly subject to the censure and animadversion of the judges. In order to enable a person to practise as an Attorney, in any of these courts, he must be admitted and sworn an Attorney of that particular court: and an Attorney in the court of King's Bench cannot practise in the Common-Pleas, nor can an

Attorney in the Common-Pleas, practise in the court of King's Bench. To practise in the court of Chancery, it is also necessary to be admitted a Solicitor therein.

The business of an Attorney is one of the most important occupations which can engage the attention of a conscientious man, in the present state of society. To him, the oppressed repair to learn by what means the oppressor is to be resisted; to him, the orphan and the friendless look, as to one who knows how to direct them to recover their property or their rights. The Attorney it is to whom, as a *Conveyancer* in preparing deeds, bonds, mortgages, marriage settlements, &c. we confide the transfer and security of our monies, our goods, and our estates. It is the Attorney before whom we lay those documents, upon his opinion of which we buy and sell land, houses, and a variety of other property depending more especially upon what is usually called, the *Title* to their possession. By these means, it is the Attorney who has an opportunity of knowing the most intimate affairs of individuals in every relative situation in life; and it is the Attorney, thus invested with so much power, who has an opportunity of becoming either a blessing or a curse to the neighbourhood in which he resides: for such is now the complexity of our laws, that it is scarcely possible for a plain and simple-minded man to meddle with them without having his Attorney at his elbow, unless he choose to run the great risk of being overthrown and defeated, even in the best of causes.

If, therefore, instead of that manliness and integrity, which should dignify an Attorney, he abuse the confidence reposed in him, and descend to the low and petty arts of fomenting litigation and strife between contending parties, for the mere purpose of filling his own pocket, or to gratify the malignity of some tyrant of power, it is evident that there is no term in language sufficiently strong to designate the man. If, on the contrary, an upright man, well acquainted with the laws and their forms, but knowing the fallibility of human nature, and the fallible nature of testimony too, if such a man should be an Attorney, how much strife can he not prevent, how much misery and distress can he not cure!

The legislature has, from time to time, passed various acts relative to the conduct and powers of Attornies, who are liable to be punished in a summary way, either by attachment, or having their names struck off the roll, for ill practice, attended with fraud and corruption, and committed against the obvious rules of justice and common honesty; but the court will not easily be prevailed on to proceed in this manner, if it appears that the matter complained of was rather owing to neglect or accident, than design; or if the party injured, has other remedy by act of Parliament, or action at law.

Attornies have the privilege to sue, and be sued, only in the courts at Westminster, where they practise.

Besides the obligations of fidelity to his client the Attorney owes him secresy; and in certain cases, an action lies at the suit of his client for neglect of duty: but such actions are extremely rare.

Persons who are bound clerks to Attornies or Solicitors, are to cause affidavits to be made and filed of the execution of the articles, names and places of abode, of Attorney or Solicitor, and clerk, and none are to be admitted till the affidavit be produced and read in court; no Attorney having discontinued business, is to take a clerk. Clerks are to serve actually during the whole time, and make affidavits thereof. Persons admitted sworn clerks in Chancery, or serving a clerkship to such, may be admitted *Solicitor.* By the stat. 23 Geo. 2. c. 26, any person duly admitted a Solicitor, may be admitted an Attorney, without any fee for the oath, or any stamp to be impressed on the parchment whereon his admission shall be written, in the same manner as, by stat. Geo. 2. c. 23. § 20, Attornies may be admitted Solicitors.

Every Attorney and Solicitor must annually take out a certificate from the courts in which they practise: if the Attorney resides in London, and has been admitted three years or upwards, the stamp duty, for his certificate, is ten pounds; if less than three years, five pounds: if he reside *elsewhere,* and has been admitted three years or more, the stamp for his certificate is six pounds; less than three years, three pounds.

The stamp duty for the articles for an Attorney's clerk, in order to have admission to the courts of law, is one hundred and ten pounds.

The late acts of parliament having made it more expensive to become an Attorney, it is presumed that incompetent, vulgar, and illiterate persons, must have more difficulty to get into the profession, and in consequence, the respectability of the Attorney ought to be increased.

The expense of establishing a young man as an Attorney, consists in an apprentice fee of sometimes three, or even five hundred guineas, the expenses afterwards, in admission to the courts of law, the stamp duties and books; which, if properly selected, amount in value, to many hundred pounds. Some young men who are desirous of excelling as Attornies, will, after the expiration of their clerkship, place themselves in the office of some eminent Attorney in London, to obtain experience, or become pupils to a Barrister for a limited time.

Baker.

THE BAKER.

The business of the BAKER consists in making bread, rolls, and biscuits, and in baking various kinds of provisions.

Man, who appears to be designed by nature to eat of all substances that are capable of nourishing him, and still more of the vegetable than the animal kind, has, from the earliest times, used farinaceous grains as his principal food; but as these grains cannot be eaten in their natural state without difficulty, means have been contrived for extracting the farinaceous part, and of preparing it so as to render it a pleasant and wholesome aliment.

Those who are accustomed to enjoy all the advantages of the finest human inventions, without reflecting on the labours it has cost to complete them, think all these operations common and trivial; and it is not to be wondered that, to such, there should appear nothing more easy than to grind corn, to make it into paste, and to bake it in an oven.

It is however certain that, for a long time, men did not otherwise prepare their corn than by boiling it in water, and forming viscous cakes, which were neither agreeable to the taste, nor easy of digestion. To make good bread, it was necessary to construct machines for grinding and separating the pure flour with little labour and trouble; and inquiries, or perhaps accident, of which some observing person availed himself, discovered that flour, when mixed with a certain quantity of water, and moderately heated, would ferment, by which its viscidity might be nearly destroyed, and bread might be made more pleasant to the taste, and easy of digestion.

No great care was taken in ancient times to bake bread: the hearth of the fire was commonly used for the purpose. This method is still adopted by the poor and lower class of farmers, in many parts of England. The ancients laid upon the hearth a piece of flattened dough, and covered it with hot ashes, under which it remained until it was sufficiently baked. In England, at the present time, an iron pot is inverted over the loaf intended to be baked, and placed upon the hot hearth, and hot ashes are placed around and upon the pot. The invention of ovens is, however, very ancient. They are spoken of in the time of ABRAHAM. Some writers give the honour of their discovery to a person named *Annus,* an Egyptian, but who is wholly unknown in history. There is, however, reason to believe that the ovens of the ancients were very different from ours; being, as far as we may judge of them, made of a kind of earthen pan, which could be easily carried from one place to another: indeed, this mode of baking still subsists in the East.

It is not known when this very useful business first became a particular profession. Bakers were a distinct body of people in Rome, nearly two hundred years before the Christian æra, and it is supposed that they came from Greece. To these were added a number of freemen, who were incorporated into a *college,* from which neither they nor their children were allowed to withdraw. They held their effects in common, without enjoying any power of parting with them. Each bake-house had a *patron,* who had the superintendency of it; and one of the patrons had the management of the others, and the care of the college. So respectable were the bakers at Rome, that occasionally one of the body was admitted among the senators.

Even by our own statutes, the bakers are declared not to be handicrafts.

Bread is made of flour, mixed and kneaded with yeast, water, and a little salt; the salt making the bread more perfect by being dissolved in water, the fluid penetrating the flour in the most intimate manner; by which the bread becomes more light, better tasted, and will keep a longer time. It is known in London under two names, the *white*, or *wheaten*, and the *household:* these differ only in degree of purity; and the loaves must be marked with a W, or H, or the baker is liable to suffer a penalty.

The process of bread-making is thus described; to a peck of flour are added a handful of salt, a pint of yeast, and three quarts of water, cold in summer, hot in winter, and temperate between the two. The whole being kneaded, as is represented in the plate, will rise in about an hour; it is then moulded into loaves, and put into the oven to bake.

The oven takes more than an hour to heat properly: the time of baking is regulated by the quality of the flour, of the dough, hard dough requiring more time than soft, and by the bigness and form of the loaves. Half an hour is sufficient for soft and spongy loaves of one pound weight, when there is no milk in them, because water evaporates quicker than milk. A loaf of twelve pounds should remain about three hours in the oven; of eight pounds, two hours; of six pounds, one hour; of three pounds, fifty minutes; of two pounds, three quarters of an hour; one pound and a half, thirty-five minutes; of one pound, half an hour. In general, the more surface the loaves have, the sooner they are baked, whence it arises that small loaves remain a less time in the oven, in proportion to their form and weight, than large ones.

Most bakers make and sell rolls in the morning; these are either *common*, or *French* rolls: the former differ but little from loaf-bread: the ingredients of the latter are mixed with milk instead of water, and the finest flour is made use of for them. Rolls require only about twenty minutes for baking.

The life of a baker is very laborious; the greater part of the work being done by night: the journeyman is required always to commence his operations about eleven o'clock in the evening, in order to get the new bread ready for admitting the rolls in the morning. His wages are, however, but very moderate, seldom amounting to more than ten shillings a week, exclusive of his board.

The price of bread is regulated according to the price of wheat; and bakers are directed in this by the magistrates, whose rules they are bound to follow. By these the peck-loaf of each sort of bread must weigh seventeen pounds six ounces, avoirdupoise weight, and smaller loaves in the same proportion. Every sack of flour is to weigh two hundred and a half (*i. e.*) 280 lbs. and from this there ought to be made, at an average, twenty such peck loaves, or eighty common quartern loaves.

If bread were short in its weight only one ounce in thirty-six, the baker formerly was liable to be put in the pillory; and for the same offence he may now be fined, at the will of the magistrate, in any sum not less than one shilling, nor more than five shillings for every ounce wanting; such bread being complained of, and weighed in the presence of the magistrate, within twenty-four hours after it is baked, because bread loses in weight by keeping.

The process of biscuit-baking, as practised at the Victualling Office at Deptford, is curious and interesting. The dough, which consists of flour and water only, is worked by a large machine. It is then handed over to a second workman, who slices it with a large knife for the bakers, of whom there are five.

The first, or the *moulder*, forms the biscuits two at a time; the second, or *marker*, stamps and throws them to the splitter, who separates the two pieces, and puts them under the hand of the chucker, the man that supplies the oven, whose work of throwing the bread on the peel must be so exact that he cannot look off for a moment. The fifth, or the depositor, receives the biscuits on the peel, and arranges them in the oven. All the men work with the greatest exactness, and are, in truth, like parts of the same machine. The business is to deposit in the oven seventy biscuits in a minute; and this is accomplished with the regularity of a clock, the clacking of the peel operating like the motion of the pendulum. There are twelve ovens at Deptford, and each will furnish daily bread for 2040 men.

By referring to the plate, we see the baker represented in the act of kneading his dough: the bin, upon which he is at work, contains the flour: on his right hand is the peel, with which he puts in, and takes out, the bread: at his back we see the representation of the fire in the oven, and in the front is the pail in which the yeast is fetched daily from the brew-house; and by the side of the flour-bin, on the ground, is the wood used to heat the oven.

It is said that scarcely any nation lives without bread, or something as a substitute for it. In Lapland, where there is no corn, a kind of cake is made of dried fishes, and the inner bark of the pine; this mixture would lead us to suppose that they did not expect nourishment from it, but only a dry substance which should be eaten, and would distend the stomach and bowels. The Norwegians make a bread that will keep thirty or forty years; and the inhabitants esteem old and stale bread far beyond that which is new; so much so, that particular care is taken to have the oldest bread at their great feasts. It frequently happens at the christening of a child,

that their guests are supplied with bread which has
been baked at the birth of a father, or even grand-
father.   This bread is said to be made of barley and
oats, and baked between two hollow stones.

The Basket Maker.

THE BASKET-MAKER.

THE ancient Britons have been celebrated for their skill in the manufacture of baskets, from the time of the Romans; and so much were the baskets of this country valued by that people, that immense quantities of them were exported to Rome, where they were held in great estimation, and bore so high a price, that they are mentioned by Juvenal, among the extravagant and expensive furniture of the Roman tables of his time.

Baskets are made either of rushes, splinters, or willows, which last are, according to their growth, called osiers or sallows. They thrive best in moist places; and the proprietors of such marsh lands generally let what they call the willow-beds to persons who cut them at certain seasons, and prepare them for basket-makers. To form an osier bed, the land should be divided into plots six, eight, or ten feet broad, by narrow ditches, and if there is a power of keeping water in these cuts, at pleasure, by means of a sluice, it is highly advantageous in many seasons. Osiers planted in small spots, and along hedges, will supply a farmer with hurdle-stuff, as well as with a profusion of all sorts of baskets. The common osier is cut at three years, but that with yellow bark is permitted to remain a year longer.

When the osiers are cut down, those that are intended for white-work, such as baskets used in washing, are to be stripped of their bark or rinds while green. This is done by means of a sharp instrument fixed into a firm block: the osiers are passed over this, and stripped of their covering with great velocity. They are then dried and put in bundles for sale. Before they are worked up, they must be previously soaked in water, which gives them flexibility. The mode of operation is very well displayed in the print: the basket-maker usually sits on the ground to his business, unless when the baskets are too large for him to reach their upper parts in that position.

Hampers and other coarse work are made of osiers without any previous preparation except soaking. Some expert workmen make a variety of articles of wicker manufacture, as work-baskets of different descriptions, table-mats, fruit baskets for desserts, &c. Even in the coarser articles, a man well skilled in his trade, will earn three or four shillings a day. On the right and left of the plate we see bundles of osiers ready for use; on the ground by the side of the workman there are some with which he is at work, and round about him are a variety of different kinds of baskets upon which he has shown his skill.

By some accident it once happened that a rich man and a poor pennyless basket-maker were thrown on a distant island, inhabited only by a savage race of men. The former seeing himself exposed to apparent danger, without the means of assistance or defence, and ignorant of the language of the people in whose power he was, began to cry and wring his hands in a piteous manner: but the poor man, ever accustomed to labour, made signs to the people, that he was desirous of becoming useful to them; on which account they treated him with kindness, but the other they regarded with contempt.

One of the savages found something like a fillet, with which he adorned his forehead, and seemed to think himself extremely fine. The basket-maker, taking advantage of his vanity, pulled up some reeds, and, sitting down to work, in a short time finished a very elegant wreath, which he placed upon the head of the first inhabitant he chanced to meet. This man was so pleased with his new acquisition, that he danced and capered about for joy, and ran to seek his companions, who were all struck with astonishment at this new and elegant piece of finery. It was not long before another came to the basket-maker, making signs that he also wanted to be ornamented like his companion, and with such pleasure were these chaplets received by the whole tribe, that the basket-maker was continually employed in weaving them. In return for the pleasure which he conferred upon them, the grateful savages brought him every kind of food which their country afforded, built him a hut, and showed him every demonstration of gratitude and kindness. But the rich man, who possessed neither talents to please, nor strength to labour, was condemned to be the basket-maker's servant, and cut him reeds to supply the continual demand for chaplets. Such are the advantages of industry and ingenuity.

The business of a basket-maker requires but a small capital, either of money or of ingenuity, in consequence of which, it has been fixed upon as one of the most proper occupations for that class of our suffering fellow-creatures, the indigent blind, for whom asylums are established in different cities of the empire, and where the art of basket-making is carried to a surprising degree of perfection. Besides affording the pupils instruction gratis, these asylums allow them a weekly sum, proportioned to the nature of their work, and the proficiency made by them, thereby relieving them, in some degree at least, from the painful idea of absolute dependence on the bounty of others; and, which is of scarcely less importance, affording them an active employment for those hours which would be otherwise spent in despondency and gloom.

Baskets have, of late years, been introduced by
coach-makers, to form the bodies of gigs, for which
purpose they are particularly well calculated, as we
know of no other means, whereby so much strength
can be obtained with so little weight. The mail
carts in London are baskets, and many of the stage
coaches have baskets placed behind them, for the
purpose of carrying parcels; and we are convinced
that the principle of basket-making might be extended with good effect, to many other purposes,
where the three qualities of strength, lightness, and
elasticity are required.

On the shores of North America, is found a remarkable fish, called the BASKET-FISH. Its body
resembles that of a star-fish, and it is furnished with
numerous arms to catch its prey. When caught
with a hook, it clasps the bait, and encircles it with
its many arms, coming up in the form of a *wicker
basket*, whence it has its name.

The Bleacher.

THE BLEACHER.

———

BLEACHING is the art by which those manufactures, which have vegetable substances for their raw material, are freed from the colouring matter with which such substances are naturally combined, or accidentally stained; and the pure vegetable fibre, deprived of these coloured matters, is left to reflect the different rays of light in due proportion, so as to appear white.

Besides the spoils of animals, mankind, to supply their natural want of covering, have, in all countries, had recourse to vegetable substances, preferring those whose fibres excelled in strength, durability, and pliancy; and experience having proved, that flax and cotton were well adapted to such purposes, these substances have been very generally adopted, and formed into such cloths as the skill and industry of the weavers could execute.

It would soon be observed, that the action of water, together with that of the sun and air, rendered those rude cloths whiter than they were at their first formation; and since the first step towards refinement is to add beauty to utility, as the state of society improved, a desire to give them a pure and spotless white would naturally arise. The idea of white raiment being the emblem of innocence and peace, which seems to have been very early entertained, would make every means for facilitating the removal of natural or adventitious stains more earnestly studied.

, Accident would probably discover, that a certain degree of putrid fermentation carried off colouring matter from vegetable fibres. Hence the practice of macerating cloth in water, mixed with putrid urine and the dung of domestic animals, which has been continued to our days.

From the earliest accounts we have of India, Egypt, and Syria, it appears that these enlightened nations knew the efficacy of natron, (the nitre of scripture,) an impure mineral alkali, found in these countries, for combining with, and carrying off, the colouring matters with which cloth is stained; and it is still found in great abundance by the present inhabitants, and used for the same purpose. We are also informed by Pliny, that the ancient Gauls were acquainted with the use of a lixivium, extracted from the ashes of burnt vegetables, as a detergent, and knew how to combine this lixivium with animal oil to form soap.

But though these nations appear to have early acquired some knowledge of the art of bleaching, the progress of improvement which they made in it, when compared to the advantages which some of them enjoyed, was very inconsiderable. The same practices seem to have been handed down from one generation to another, without any material improvement. In India it would appear, that the art of bleaching, as well as that of staining of cloths of various colours, are not in greater perfection at present, than they are described to have been in the days of Herodotus. Even in Europe, when the arts, after they have been once introduced, have generally made rapid progress, the art of bleaching made very slow advances, till towards the end of the eighteenth century.

At this period the oxymuriatic acid, and its effects, were discovered by Scheele; and its application to the art of bleaching, by Berthollet, has given it an impulse towards perfection unknown in the history of any other art. It now became evident that oxygen had an affinity with the colouring matters with which cotton and linen manufactures are stained; and that, by a proper use of the alkalis, along with the oxymuriatic acid, these colouring matters could be removed, and the goods rendered white, in a space of time almost instantaneous, when compared with the former method of bleaching.

Upon these discoveries the present improved state of bleaching is founded. The machinery and utensils used in bleaching are various, according to the business done by the bleacher. Where linen or heavy cotton cloths are whitened, and the business is carried on to a considerable extent, the machinery is both complicated and expensive. It consists chiefly of a water-wheel, sufficiently powerful for giving motion to the wash-stocks, dash-wheels, squeezers, &c. with any other operations where power is required.

After the process of washing by the dash-wheel, the water is compressed from the cloth by means of squeezers. The boilers used in bleaching are of the common form, having a stop-cock at bottom for running off the waste ley. They are commonly made of cast iron, and are capable of containing from three hundred to six hundred gallons of water, according to the extent of the business done.

The substances used in bleaching, are chiefly pot and pearl ashes, soda, soap, oxymuriate of potash, oxymuriate of lime, manganese, muriatic acid, and sulphuric acid.

The common operations of bleaching, consist of steeping, bucking, boiling, immersion in the oxymuriatic acid, souring, washing, &c.

Steeping, is a process made use of for cleansing the cloths designed to be bleached, from the substances used by the weavers in their manufacture, and is principally effected by means of an alkaline ley at a blood-heat.

8

Bucking is one of the most important operations in the bleaching of linen goods: it consists in boiling the cloths in caustic alkaline ley, by a heat gradually raised, and thereby dissolving, and taking off their colouring matter.

Boiling, in the bleaching of linen cloth, is only used when the goods are nearly white with pearl ashes alone, or with pearl ashes along with soap, towards the end of the whitening process.

Immersion in the oxymuriate of potash. The linens, after being clean washed, are steeped in it for twelve hours, then drained, and washed for being further bucked or boiled.

Souring is, in general, the last or finishing process in bleaching, as afterwards the linens are only further washed in spring water, in order to their being blued and made up for the market.

In preparing the sour, into a large fir tub, lined with lead, as much sulphuric acid is added to water as will give it the acidity of strong vinegar. The acid and water must be well mixed together before immersing the linens, which are generally steeped in it for twelve hours.

Where washing is mentioned, it must be always understood that the linen is taken to the washstocks, or dash-wheel, and washed well in them for some hours. This part of the work can never be overdone; and on its being properly executed, between every part of the bucking, boiling, steeping in the oxymuriatic acid, and souring, not a little of the success of bleaching depends. By exposure, is meant that the linen cloth is taken and spread upon the bleach-green, for four, six, or eight days, according as the routine of business calls for the return of the cloth, in order to undergo further operations.

There are a variety of processes adopted for the bleaching of goods of different degrees of fineness: muslin, for instance, requiring a process varied from that adopted for coarse linen; and more delicacy is still necessary in bleaching coloured cottons and pulicates into which permanent colours are woven.

The plate represents the bleaching of cloth, as it is now sometimes practised, by pouring water upon it, as it lies exposed in the bleaching-ground, to whiten, by the united operations of the sun, the air, and moisture, the cloths having previously passed through proper alkaline leys: this is called the *old* method of bleaching, the *new* is by the more expeditious process of oxymuriatic acid, &c.

THE BOOK-BINDER.

BOOK-BINDING is the art of sewing together the sheets of a book and securing them with a back and side boards. Binding is distinguished from *stitching*, which is merely sewing leaves, without bands or backs; and from *half-binding*, which consists in securing the back only with leather, the pasteboard sides being covered with blue or marbled paper; whereas, in binding, both back and sides are covered with leather.

At what time the art of BOOK-BINDING was first invented it is impossible to ascertain; but Phillatius, a learned Athenian, was the first who pointed out the use of a particular kind of glue for fastening the leaves of a book together; an invention which his countrymen thought of such importance as to entitle him to a statue. The most ancient mode of binding consisted in gluing the different leaves together, and attaching them to cylinders of wood, round which they were rolled. This is called Egyptian binding; and continued to be practised long after the age of Augustus. It is now wholly disused, except in oriental countries, and in Jewish Synagogues, where they still continue to write books of the law on slips of vellum sewed together, so as to form only one long page, with a roller at each extremity, furnished with clasps of gold or silver. The square form of binding which is now universally practised, at least in Europe, is said to have been first invented by one of the kings of Per-

Book Binder.

gamus, the same to whom we owe the invention of parchment.

Modern or square binding is of two kinds: the one particularly adapted to printed books where leather forms the general covering, and the other more immediately applied to account books, where parchment or vellum is made use of as the outside covering.

In this business the first operation is to fold the sheets according to the proper form; that is folios into two leaves, quartos into four, octavos into eight, and so on; this is usually the work of women, who perform it with a slip of ivory or box-wood, called a folding-stick: in this they are directed by the catch-words and *signatures*, which are the letters with the numbers annexed to them, at the bottom of the pages of the first one or more leaves in each sheet.

The leaves thus folded and laid over each other in the order of the signatures, are beaten on a stone with a heavy hammer, to make them solid and smooth, and then they are pressed. Thus prepared, they are sewed in a sewing-press, upon packthreads or cords, which are called bands, at a proper distance from each other; which is done by drawing a thread through the middle of each sheet, and giving a turn round each band, beginning with the first, and pro-ceeding to the last. The common number of bands is six in folios, and five in quartos and octavos. In neat binding a saw is made use of, to make places for the bands, which are sunk into the paper, so that the back of the book, when bound, may be smooth, without any appearance of bands. After this the backs are glued, the ends of the bands being opened with a knife, for the more convenient fixing of the pasteboard; then the back is turned with a hammer, the book being fixed in a press between boards, called backing-boards, in order to make a groove for admitting the pasteboards. The boards being then applied, holes are made for drawing the bands through, the superfluous ends being cut off, and the parts hammered smooth. The book is then pressed, in order for cutting, which is performed by a machine called a plough. After this the book is put into a press, called the cutting-press, betwixt two boards, the one lying even with the press, for the knife to run upon, the other above, for the knife to cut against.

The book being cut, the pasteboards are squared with a proper pair of iron shears, and it is then ready for sprinkling, gilding, blacking, or marbling the leaves. If the leaves are to be gilt, the book is put between two boards into a press, and when the leaves are rendered very smooth, they are rubbed over with size-water, the gold leaf is then laid on, dried by a fire, and burnished off.

The head-band is now to be added, which is an ornament of thread or silk, placed at the extremities of the book across the leaves, and woven or twisted about a roll of paper.

The book is now fit for covering : calf-skin is the most usual cover; this is moistened in water, and cut to the size of the book; the edges are then pared off on a marble stone. The cover is next smeared over with paste, then stretched over the pasteboard on the outside, and doubled over the edges within-side. The book-binder then fixes it firmly between two boards to make the cover stick the stronger to the pasteboards and the back; on the exact per-formance of which depends the neatness of the book. The back is now to be warmed by the fire to soften the glue, and the leather of the back is rubbed down with a folding-stick or bodkin, to fix it close to the back of the book. After this, it is washed over with a little paste and water ; two blank leaves on each side are then to be pasted down to the cover, and when dry, the leaves are burnished in the press, and the cover rolled on the edges. The cover is now glazed with the white of an egg, and then polished with a polishing iron. If the book is to be lettered, a piece or pieces of red morocco are pasted between the bands, to receive the title, &c. in gold letters.

The letters or other ornaments are made with gilding-tools, engraved in *relievo,* either on the points of puncheons, or a round little cylinder of brass. The puncheons make their impressions by being pressed flat down, and the cylinders by being rolled along by a handle, to which they are fitted on an iron stay, or axis.

To apply the gold, the binders glaze the parts of the leather with a liquor made of the white of eggs diluted with water, by means of a bit of sponge; and when nearly dry, they slightly oil them and then lay on pieces of gold leaf, and on these they apply the tools, having first warmed them in a charcoal fire. When the gilding is finished, they rub off the superfluous gold, and polish the whole.

The business of the book-binder, in general, requires no great ingenuity, nor any considerable strength of body. Journeymen can earn thirty shillings a week; and much more if they are good workmen, and are intrusted with very fine work. Formerly book-binding was not a separate trade, but it was united with that of the stationer: it is now, however, carried on alone, and book-binders are generally employed constantly throughout the year.

All *stationery* work is sewed with strong waxed thread, and as the vellum or parchment is never attached to the back like leather, but lies hollow and loose, when the book is open, it cannot, of course, afford that security to the back which leather does; it is therefore common to line the back, between the slips, with coarse canvass or slips of leather, letting them come as much over the sides, as to paste down with the boards and slips. The boards for stationery are not so thick in proportion as for printed work, and when put on, are placed at least half an inch from the back, on each side of the parchment slips which books are sewed upon : you must cut with scissars a very narrow strip, which is not to be pasted down, but left for the purpose of drawing through the parchment when the cover is applied, serving to attach the cover, before it is pasted to the boards. Parchment or vellum covers should always be lined before they are put on, and applied before they are quite dry.

Different kinds of bindings are distinguished by different names, such as *law binding, marble binding, French binding, Dutch binding,* &c. In Dutch binding, the backs are of vellum. In French binding, a slip of parchment is applied over the back between each band, and the ends are pasted on the inside of each pasteboard. This indorsing, as it is called, is peculiar to the French binders; who are enjoined, by special ordonnance, to back their books with parchment. The parchment is applied in the press, after the back has been grated to make the paste take hold. The Italians still bind in a coarse thick paper, and this they call binding *alla rustica.* It is extremely inconvenient, as it is liable to wear without particular care.

The price of binding is regulated by certain printed lists agreed on between the bookseller and the bookbinder.

In the plate the man is represented in the act of cutting the leaves of the book ; on his right, on the floor, are his glue-pot and paste-tub; behind him are his tools for gilding; and on his right is the press for bringing the books into the least possible compass.

In London, the business of gilding the leaves of books is a separate employment, and it is done before the boards of the book are covered with the leather.

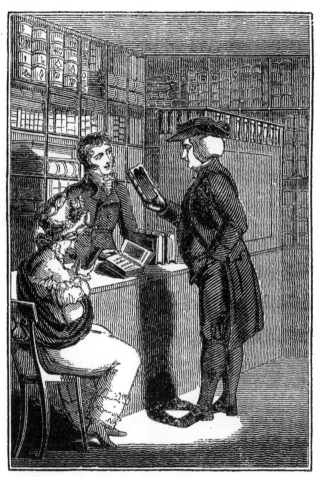

The Bookseller.

———

BEFORE the invention of printing, and of the manufacture of paper from linen, books were so scarce and dear, as to be without the reach of all but persons of considerable opulence. Though the materials of which they were made had been as cheap and as plentiful as paper is at present, the labour of multiplying copies in manuscript, would always have kept their number's comparatively scanty, and their price high.

Hence in all the nations of antiquity, learning was almost exclusively confined to the people of rank, and the lower orders were only rescued from total ignorance, by the reflected light of their superiors, and raised above the rudeness of barbarism, by that partial improvement which men of cultivation and refinement necessarily impart, in a greater or less degree, to all within the sphere of their influence. The Papyrus, a kind of broad-leaved rush, being the cheapest material for the reception of writing, was of course in most general use. When this could no longer be procured, in consequence of the conquest of Egypt by the Saracens, *parchment* was then substituted, but it was so difficult to be procured, that it was customary to erase the writing of an ancient manuscript to make room for some other composition. In this manner many of the best works of antiquity were lost for ever. Books were for many ages so scarce; that to present a book to a religious house, was thought so valuable a donation as to merit eternal salvation, and it was offered on the altar with great ceremony.

The making of paper, such as we now see it, is dated by the generality of writers at the eleventh or twelfth century ; but the honour of the discovery is claimed by different and distant nations. The first book which was printed on paper manufactured in England, came out without a date about 1495 or 1496, about fifty years after the invention of printing, although for a long while afterwards it was principally brought from abroad.

The art of printing necessarily produced the Bookseller. Indeed, we believe that the earlier printers were also Booksellers, as are some of the Printers of the present day ; but the lapse of years, and a variety of other circumstances, have generated many trades and subdivisions of trades, to our forefathers wholly unknown. Even the trade of a Bookseller is considerably subdivided, at least in London.

The Bookseller of the present day is a person of considerable importance in the republic of letters, more especially if he combines those particular branches of the trade denominated *Proprietor* and *Publisher :* for it is to such men our men of genius take their productions for sale : and the success of works of genius very frequently depends upon their spirit, probity, and patronage. It is also to such men that the reading public generally are indebted for almost every important work of a voluminous kind. Those bulky and valuable volumes, the various Encyclopædias, would never have made their appearance had not a Bookseller, or a combination of Booksellers, entered upon the speculation by employing men of science and learning in the various departments of those works, and embarking large capitals in the undertaking. The sums of money employed in such concerns as these are immense, and the regularity and dispatch with which some of these extensive bookselling concerns are conducted,

exceed the conception of those persons wholly unacquainted with the affair.

Paternoster Row has been, for a long period, no-
torious as the place in which some of these large
establishments are carried on, and where a great
number of Bookseller's shops and warehouses
abound. The Stationers' Company have a Hall not
far distant from it, where a copy of every book must,
by a late Act of Parliament, be deposited when
published, in order to secure to the proprietor or
author of it the sole profits arising from its publication and sale. A copy must also be deposited in
the British Museum, the two Universities, and some
other public establishments, amounting to eleven in
number.

In London, and some other large bookselling establishments in the kingdom, books in the wholesale
way are sold in quires: lists of such sales are constantly handed about amongst the large dealers in
books.

Some Booksellers in London confine their trade
to particular departments. There are Law Booksellers, Medical Booksellers, Foreign Booksellers,
Religious Booksellers, Booksellers of Education and
Children's books; others deal in old books only,
and some principally in rare and scarce books: the
rarity being in numerous instances the criterion of
value. A rare copy of the *Decameron* of Boccacio
was sold a few years ago, for upwards of *two thousand pounds*, when the book might have been bought
in London at the same time, recently printed, for a
few shillings! The form of a book, the style of the
printing, and the name of the printer, add materially
to the value of these conceits. The books called
black-letter books are also much esteemed.

The sale of some books of fancy and genius, in
the present age, if not in price, has exceeded in
number, the books of any former period. We may
mention those of Lord Byron, Sir Walter Scott,

and Mr. Thomas Moore, as instances of the extraordinary and rare good fortune of these gentlemen.
Whilst other works, perhaps of equal, although of
course of very different merit, have sunk almost
dead-born from the press.

The sale of periodical publications is in Great
Britain of considerable importance: it consists of
Magazines, Reviews, and a variety of other productions published for the most part monthly. Other
works are frequently divided into numbers and published weekly, in order to make the price, when they
are bulky, come easy to the purchasers. By these
means an infinity of books, and a vast body of information, have been diffused throughout the community, and which have made the trade of a Bookseller
one of the greatest interest and importance to mankind.

It is by the diffusion of knowledge by books that
all species of tyranny and oppression can be most
effectually resisted; it is by the diffusion of books,
that mankind become acquainted with their moral
and religious duties; and it is also by books that
men generally become distinguished for their intelligence, probity, and worth; for where the diffusion
of knowledge by books has not taken place, there
we most commonly find the relative and social duties
at a very low ebb.

Newspapers are another species of books very
valuable in their kind; but as they are not often
sold by Booksellers, we content ourselves with
merely making mention of them.

The plate represents the inside of a retail Bookseller's shop. No explanation whatever can be
necessary.

The Brazier.

———

THE Brazier makes kettles, pans, candlesticks, and other kitchen utensils, of brass, which is not a simple metal, but compounded of copper and zinc in certain proportions : if the proportion of copper be greater, the compound is pinch-beck. Copper alloyed with tin, makes bronze, bell-metal, &c.

Brass is capable of being wrought with very great facility, and is applied to a variety of purposes of the arts. It is of a beautiful yellow colour, more approaching to that of gold, and not so apt to tarnish or rust as copper. It is more ductile than either that metal or iron ; and hence peculiarly fitted to be made into wire. As brass is, in general, used for mathematical and astronomical instruments, where the greatest precision is required, its expansion has been very accurately determined.

This compound metal was known at a very early period. It was first discovered from the circumstance of copper ore and zinc earth, or calamine, sometimes called *cadmia* by the ancients, being found in one mine, and yielding, when melted, not pure copper, but a metal of a yellow colour ; and, from its resemblance to gold, the mines which contained this ore were held in the highest estimation. This earth, which must have been calamine, is mentioned both by Aristotle, Strabo, and Pliny. Its use has been handed down through every century, and is still retained in the manufacture of brass. This discovery was no sooner effected, than the ancient

c 5

method of procuring this metal was abandoned.
Pure copper was first extracted from the ore, and
then converted into brass, by the addition of calamine; but as the art of making brass with *lapis
calaminaris,* was not well understood by the ancients, but cost them much trouble, it was esteemed
next to silver, and was reckoned little inferior to
that metal, as we learn from Procopius.

In modern times, considerable improvements have
been made in the manufacture of this metal, and
some secresy is observed by those who have the
reputation of the finest article.

The use of brass seems to have been very preva-
lent amongst the ancients. Most of the arms and
instruments found in Herculaneum, Pompeia, &c.
whether culinary, mechanical, or agricultural, were
made of brass. It may be observed, however, that
most of the genuine relics of this kind, approach
nearer to bronze, than to our modern brass, and
appear to be composed of various mixtures of brass
with tin and other metals.

In the shops we often find that the same people
deal in brass, copper, and tin-ware; and not unfrequently the furnishing ironmonger sells almost every
article made in brass and copper, particularly in large
country-towns. In such cases the brazier neither
makes nor is supposed to make all the different articles in his shop; it is sufficient for his own purpose,
as well as for the advantage of his customers, that
he should be so much of a working brazier, as to
be a competent judge of the workmanship of all the
goods in which he deals. If he is a master in a
large way, he employs a great number of hands in
the different branches of his trade, and his profits
are of course in proportion to the magnitude of his
capital.

Some of the articles manufactured by the working
brazier are beat out with the hammer, and united
in their several parts by solder; others are cast:

those which are cast belong to the business of the *founder*, except the polishing and finishing, which require the art of the brazier.

The working brazier has need of strength, and if he would excel in his business, he should possess ingenuity to finish the work with taste.

The founder is employed in casting a thousand different articles in brass; for which purpose he has models of the work designed: to these he fits the mould in which he casts his metal. He rarely designs any thing himself, and his chief skill lies in melting the brass, and running it into the mould evenly. There are various kinds of founders; some who cast for braziers only, others who cast the different smaller articles for coachmakers, sadlers, &c. and some cast the brass cannon, to carry on the dreadful art of war.

The founder requires a strong constitution, to undergo the heat of immense furnaces: he may earn thirty shillings per week: but it frequently happens that he spends a large portion of it in porter.

Copper is dug out of the earth, or found united in many springs, containing sulphuric acid. The richest copper mines in the known world are in the Isle of Anglesea. The mountain from which the ore is dug is called Parys. This ore is a sulphate of copper, and in order to reduce it into the metallic state, it is heaped up in large masses against a wall, a fire is kindled under the heap, and it burns for many days, slowly, but strongly: holes are made in the wall, which lead to a kind of room, where the sulpher which escapes from the ore is collected, and with which the common roll-brimstone of the shops is made. There have been dug from the Parys mine, thirty thousand tons of ore in a year.

There are two springs at Sterngrundt, in Upper Hungary, so richly impregnated with copper and sulphuric acid, that iron thrown into these is dissolved by the acid, and the copper falls to the bot-

tom in its metallic form. Near these springs pits
are dug, and filled with water : old iron is then
thrown into them, which, in about a fortnight or
three weeks, is taken out, and the copper scraped
off. By this process a hundred pounds of iron will
produce from eighty to ninety pounds of copper.
The same method is adopted at some springs in the
county of Wicklow, in Ireland, and here twenty
pounds of iron will yield sixteen of copper, which
fetches a high price.

The coppersmith makes furnaces, boilers, and all
manner of large vessels for brewers, distillers, and
others. His work is very laborious, and the business is the most noisy of all mechanical employments. The wages of the journeyman are equal to
the powers of body required in the operation.

Copper is used in a variety of the arts : but vessels made of it for culinary purposes are highly prejudicial : for acid and fatty substances, when left
in them any time, combine with the copper, and form
verdigris, which is an absolute poison, and when
taken in the smallest quantities is very prejudicial
to the constitution.

To prevent these pernicious effects most copper
vessels are well tinned on their insides. This operation is thus effected : the surface is well cleaned
by rubbing it with sal-ammoniac, or an acid ; the
tin, or a composition of tin and lead, is then melted
in the vessel, and rubbed well about it with old rags
doubled up.

The plate which accompanies this article, represents the brazier working at his anvil : he has need
of a forge as well as the smith, and like him his
shop must be furnished with a strong bench, vices,
hammers, pincers, and files of various kinds.

The Brewer.

THE BREWER.

BREWING is the art of making porter, beer, or ale. This art is undoubtedly a branch of chemistry, and depends on fixed and invariable principles. These principles are now beginning to be better understood than they formerly were : and although no complete and unerring theory has yet been obtained, sufficient is now known to enable us to give directions for brewing with ease, certainty, and promptitude, and in the small space to which we are necessarily limited, we hope that we shall exhibit a compendium at once useful and correct.

Brewing is an art of the remotest antiquity; in no country has it been carried to a greater perfection than in our own. The inventor of it is not known, but the use of beer was common with the most ancient nations. History informs us that this liquor passed from Egypt into all the other nations of the world, and that it was first known under the name of *Pelusian drink*, from the name of Pelusium, a city near the mouth of the Nile, where they made the best beer. From the time of Strabo this drink was common in the provinces of the north, in Flanders, and in England. It was used even by the Greeks, according to the relation of Aristotle and Theophrastus, although they had excellent wines; and from the time of Polybius the Spaniards also made use of it.

Beer is a vinous liquor, which is made from the sugar obtained by infusion from many sorts of fari-

naceous grain, but barley is most commonly preferred. It is, however, quite evident that any vegetable matter which contains sugar, or from which
sugar by any process can be made or developed, is
proper for the production of such liquor. The
flavor depending of course in every instance, upon
the aroma, the extractive matter of the vegetable,
and a portion of essential oil, either in the vegetable
itself, or in the matters added to the liquor during
the process of making it, or afterwards; the hop,
for instance, is one of those additions: the flavor
which hops give to malt liquors is too well known to
be described.

Different counties of England are celebrated for
their peculiar ales, and London porter is famous in
almost all parts of the civilized world. Different as
these several sorts of liquor are, they are nevertheless, for the most part, composed of the same materials variously prepared.

Malt liquor, in general, is composed of water,
malt, hops, and a little yeast; and the great art is
to find out the proper proportions of each ingredient, to what degree of heat the water must be
raised before it is poured on the malt, and how best
to work it afterwards.

There are two kinds of malt, distinguished by the
colour; these are called *brown* and *pale* malt, and
they depend upon the degree of heat that is used
in drying. The malt which is dried by a very gentle heat differs in its colour but little from the barley,
but if exposed to a higher temperature, it acquires
a deeper hue, till at length it becomes of a dark
brown.

When the malt is made, it must be coarsely ground
in a mill: it is then fit for the brewer, in whose hands
the process of making beer is completed.

The first part of the operation is called *mashing*,
which is performed in a large circular vessel, such
as that represented in the upper part of the plate.

This vessel has a false bottom, pierced with small holes, fixed about six or eight inches above the real bottom. There are two side openings in the interval between the bottoms; by the one water is conveyed into the vessel, and by the other it is drawn off. When the malt is put on the false bottom of the *mash-tun*, the water being at a proper heat, is admitted, by means of the side pipe, from the copper, which is contained within the brickwork represented in the upper part of the plate. The water first fills the space between the false and real bottom, then forcing its way through the small holes in the false bottom, it soaks the malt, and when all the water is let in the process of *mashing* begins. The object of this part of the operation is to effect a perfect mixture of the malt with the water, so that the sweet part of the grain may be extracted by the fluid: for this purpose the mass is kept constantly stirred by means of iron rakes, or long wooden poles, as is represented by one of the men in the upper part of the plate; the other man is in the act of mending the fire under the copper.

In large breweries, such as that which belonged to the late Mr. Whitbread in Chiswell-street, the process of mashing cannot be performed by human labour; it is therefore effected by machinery that is kept moving by means of the steam-engine. As soon as the mashing is completed, the tun is covered in to prevent the escape of heat, and in this state it is suffered to remain till all the sweetness of the malt is extracted; then the spigot is withdrawn, and the clear wort allowed to run off, into a lower or boiling copper. The heat of the water used in mashing should be about 180° of Fahrenheit's thermometer. Before the goodness of the malt is exhausted it is usual to pour upon it two or three waters, but the wort which is drawn off the first is much the strongest. The proportion of malt to the water depends on the strength of the liquor wanted.

It is said that good small beer may be brewed at the
rate of thirty gallons to a bushel of malt, and excellent ale may be made in the proportion of one bushel
of malt to five or six gallons of water; indeed, if
this proportion be used, *strong beer* ought to be the
result of the operation, as will be seen when we
describe private brewing below.

The wort, when run into the lower copper, is to
be boiled with a certain quantity of hops; the stronger
the wort, the more hops are required; the common
proportion in private families is a pound of hops to
a bushel of malt, for weaker liquors; but the stronger
do not require hops in the same proportion. When
the hops are mixed with the wort in the copper, the
liquor is made to boil; and it must be kept boiling
as fast as possible, till, upon taking out a little of
the liquor, it is found to be full of small flakes,
something like curdled soap.

The boiling copper is, in small concerns, unco-
vered, but in large breweries it is fitted with a
steam-tight cover, from the centre of which passes
a cylindrical pipe, that terminates in several
branches in the upper or mashing-copper; thus the
steam produced by boiling, instead of being wasted,
is let into cold water of the upper copper, by which
it is made almost hot enough for mashing without
any additional expense of fuel; the steam carries
also with it the flavor of the hops, which, when
the operation is carried on differently, is lost in the
air.

When the liquor is sufficiently boiled, it is drawn
out into a number of shallow tubs called coolers, in
which it remains till it is cool enough to be submitted to fermentation. Liquor made from pale
malt, and intended for immediate use, need not be
cooler than 75° or 80°, and can of course be made
in almost every part of the summer; but that which
is for keeping should not be hotter than 65° or 70°,
when it is put together for fermentation.

From the coolers the liquor is transferred into the fermenting or working-tun, in which it is well mixed with yeast, in the proportion of one gallon of yeast to four barrels of beer. This part of the process takes from 18 to 48 hours, according to the state of the weather.

The last part of the operation is that of transferring the liquor from the working-tun to the barrels, where the fermentation is completed. For a few days there will be a copious discharge of yeast from the bung-hole. During which the barrels must from time to time be carefully filled up with fresh liquor. After this discharge is finished, the barrels are bunged up, and the beer is fit for use in the course of a week or two, if the proportion of malt to the water be small, but the stronger the liquor the longer time it takes to become fit for being drank. Strong beer made with a proportion of six gallons of water to one bushel of malt, and in the quantity of sixty gallons, will usually take, in the temperature of England, one year to become an agreeable liquor. In general the larger the quantity of liquor in one vessel, the longer time it takes to become mature : and it is of material importance that all vessels containing malt liquor, when bunged down, after its having finished the active fermentation, should be full.

Common report says, that in addition to malt and hops, a variety of other ingredients are used, and none of them of the most wholesome nature.

The lower part of the plate represents the brewhouse yard, with the casks ready to be taken away by the carman.

To see the several operations of this business, the reader is recommended to obtain permission to go over the immense works in Chiswell-street, and be very attentive to the several parts of the business; to examine the structure of the steam-engine, and to observe how much of the laborious part of the work is performed by this stupendous machine. He will see how the mashing is performed; how the malt is drawn up into the granary; how the vessels are filled with beer; with what ease they are re-filled after having worked over; and a multitude of other curious contrivances, of which, without an actual inspection, he cannot form the most distant conception.

So much for the brewing of malt liquor on a large scale. We shall now give our readers a method very generally pursued by families for brewing their own ale, which practice is getting general from a conviction of the very great unwholesomeness of ale, &c. from some of the public breweries.

In brewing, the first thing necessary is to take care that the cask, into which the liquor is to be put, is sweet and wholesome. The casks in most common request in London, are barrels containing 36 gallons. To make such a cask of good malt liquor the following proportions may be taken: malt three bushels, hops two pounds; having measured the quantity of water which your cask will hold, by a pail or bucket, you must put that quantity into your furnace and make it boil; as soon as it boils, dip off half of it into a tub or vat raised upon a bench, about a foot and a half from the ground, and which has a hole in its side near the bottom, into which is introduced a spigot and faucet, and over the end of which, in the vat, is fixed a bundle of small clean sticks, or other convenient apparatus, to prevent the malt from running out; let the water remain quiet in the vat till it has cooled to about the temperature of 175° or 180° of Fahrenheit's ther-mometer; or, in the absence of this instrument, till your face can be seen pretty distinctly in the water; —then mix the malt with the water, gradually stir-ring it with a mashing-stick, which is usually made for the purpose, and too well known to be described. Reserve a few handsfull of the dry malt to strew over the surface after it is mixed, in order to prevent the escape of the heat; and cover the vat besides with cloths, more effectually to keep the mixture hot; let it remain for three hours—then let the liquid run out by the spigot and faucet; and, as soon as it has done so, pour on the same quantity of water, cooled in a tub to the same degree of heat as before, and let it remain half an hour, or somewhat longer; let the liquor run off a second time; and as you will now be enabled to judge how much more fluid will be necessary to fill your cask, add as much more water, cooled as before, as will be sufficient for your purpose, letting the last portion stand a short time in the vat; always remembering that it is most advisable to have, for a barrel of 36 gallons, at least 10 or 15 gallons of wort more than sufficient to fill your cask, to allow for waste and evaporation; and keeping in mind also, that the more water is used, the more effectually will the sugar be washed out of the malt, and of course the stronger must your liquor become. When your liquors are all run off, mix them together, and put them into the furnace, making it to boil as soon as possible. It will be quite necessary that you should know how many gallons your furnace will contain, in order to judge of the evaporation; for the overplus of quantity must be reduced by boiling to the quantity of gallons which you want. When your wort is reduced, by boiling, to nearly the measure which you intend it to be, *and not before*, put in your two pounds of hops, and let them boil in the wort a *quarter* of an hour, or *twenty* minutes, and it would be most advisable, during the time of their boiling, that the furnace should be covered down.—Remove the fire from the furnace and strain off your wort into proper coolers; and when it is sufficiently cool, as before mentioned, mix one quart of good yeast with a few gallons of the wort first, and afterwards put the whole together into a vat to remain to ferment for a few days; or put it at once into your cask and let it ferment there : which last method is the most effectual to preserve all the strength of the liquor.

This ale will be fit for drinking in about two or at most three months, depending of course upon the season of the year in which it is made ; but *October* is a proverbial month for brewing, and from the equability of its temperature, it is undoubtedly the best.—The months of March and April are the next best. If, instead of three bushels of malt, six be added to the same quantity of water, and four pounds of hops, an excellent strong beer will be the result : ten gallons of good small beer might be afterwards made from the not wholly exhausted malt.

The Bricklayer.

THE BRICKLAYER.

BRICKLAYING is the art of cementing bricks, by lime or some other cement, so as to form one body; hence its use and importance in building walls, houses, &c. In London this business includes tiling, walling, chimney work, and paving with bricks and tiles. Tilers and bricklayers were incorporated, 10th of Elizabeth, under the name of master and wardens of the Society of Freemen of the mystery and art of Tilers and Bricklayers. In the country, plasterers' work is always joined to the business of a Bricklayer, and not unfrequently, stone-masons' work also.

Bricklaying is of great antiquity, for we read of it very early in the Mosaic history.

Structures of brick, as we now see them, are by no means of so old a date as may probably be supposed. Bricks, indeed, were much used by the Romans, though of a different size and shape to those of our own time. Instances of them may be particularly seen in the walls of Old Verulam, in the Castle at Colchester, and in different parts of the Abbey church at St. Alban's, which was built in the Saxon times, out of the ruins of the Roman city.

Bricks appear to have been again introduced in one or two instances as early as the reign of Richard the Second, though few buildings of consequence were erected with them before the reign of Henry the Sixth. Some of the oldest and best specimens now remaining, may be found in the remains of

Hurstmonceaux castle, in Sussex, and the gate of the Rye-house in Hertfordshire, both built very early in the reign of Henry the Sixth; the Lollards' tower, at Lambeth Palace, built in 1454; Dandelion gateway, of the time of Henry the Seventh; and the old part of Hampton-Court, built in 1514 by Cardinal Wolsey.

The materials made use of by Bricklayers are bricks, tiles, mortar, laths, nails, and tile-pins.

Their tools are a brick-trowel to take up and spread the mortar; a brick-axe, to cut the bricks to the proper shape and size; a saw is also occasionally wanted, and a stone to rub the bricks smooth when great exactness is required. A square is always wanted to lay the bed or foundation of any wall or building; a bevel, with which the under-side of the bricks are cut to a required angle; a piece of timber, called a *banker:* this is about six feet long, and laid on two other piers of timber, three feet high from the floor on which they stand, and on this they cut the bricks. Line-pins and a line, are used to lay the courses or rows of bricks by: a plumb-rule, by which they carry their work upright. A level is wanted to conduct the building exactly horizontal; a small square to set off right angles; a ten feet rod to take dimensions, and a jointer, or long flat lath, about three inches wide, which is held by two men while another draws the long joints; a rammer, to render the foundation firm, by beating or ramming; a crowe, pick-axe, and shovel, with which they dig through and clear away any obstacles that may oppose their progress.

Bricklayers are supplied with bricks and mortar, by a man they call a *labourer,* who is also employed in making the mortar from lime. The labourer brings the mortar and the bricks in a machine called a hod, which he carries on his shoulder. Before he puts the mortar into the hod, he throws over every

8

part of the inner surface, fine dry sand, to prevent it from sticking to the wood.

A Bricklayer and his labourer will lay in a single day about a thousand bricks, in what is called whole and solid work, when the wall is either a brick and a half or two bricks thick; and since a cubic yard contains 460 bricks, he will lay above two cubic yards in a day.

The wages of a journeyman Bricklayer are from four shillings to five shillings and sixpence a day; the wages of a labourer, from half-a-crown to three shillings and sixpence a day.

In the plate the Bricklayer is building a house: in his left hand is a brick, and in his right the trowel: the trowel is made of fine steel; and of so much importance is this instrument in the arts of life, that the inventor of a new hammer, by which trowels are better and more expeditiously made, has lately received forty guineas as a reward for his ingenuity, from the *Society of Arts, Manufactures, &c.* in the Adelphi. The superior merit of trowels made by this hammer consists in their great elasticity, by which they always instantly return to their original shape, although ever so much bent out of it. The Bricklayer is standing on a scaffold: this consists of upright poles, to which two or more horizontal ones are tied at one end, having the other fixed in the wall; and on these flat boards are laid: at his right foot lies his mortar, and on his left are his bricks; but these cannot be seen in the plate. On the ground the labourer is seen making his mortar: near this the ladder is placed, by which he and the Bricklayer ascend the scaffold; his hod rests against the end of the new building, and near the space left for the lower window.

Paving-tiles are a long flat kind of brick used for laying the floors of Dairies, Cheese-houses, &c. Their size is about nine inches long, $4\frac{1}{2}$ broad, and $1\frac{1}{2}$ thick; but some are made nine inches square.

The different sorts of tiles for covering houses, are pantiles, which are 13 inches long, 8 inches broad, and about half an inch thick; their transverse section somewhat resembles the letter ∽, being two portions of cyclindric surfaces on both sides;—plain tiles, which are about 9 inches long, and about 5 inches broad.—In different parts of the country, slate is used instead of tiles. In and about London, either Welch or Westmoreland slate is used.—In the formation of the pan-tile and the plain-tile a knob is made to project from the under surface of the upper end, which serves to hang it on the lath. Laths for tiling are about three-fourths of an inch thick, and $1\frac{1}{4}$ inch broad, and are most commonly made of deal. The other sorts of tiles are, hip tiles, and ridge or crest tiles.

Bricklayers compute new work, such as the walls of houses, &c. by the rod of $16\frac{1}{2}$ feet, and the price charged includes the putting up and use of scaffolding; but the clearing out and carrying away the rubbish, is an extra charge. In digging and steening wells, the work is charged at a certain price per foot, and the price is higher for each foot according as the depth is greater.

The emptying and carrying away soil that is to be removed for making foundations of vaults is charged by the ton : eighteen cubic feet of soil is reckoned to weigh a ton.

For the method of making mortar, see the article Stone-mason.

The Brick Maker.

THE BRICK-MAKER.

BRICK-MAKING is the art of forming and manufacturing Bricks.

The earliest mention of Bricks is to be found in the historical books of the Old Testament, where we find that Noah's three sons, together with their wives and children, departed from the eastward and travelled into the land of Shinar. " And they said one to another, go to, let us make brick, and burn them thoroughly; and they had Brick for stone, and slime had they for mortar." Whether these Bricks were really exposed to the action of fire, as the passage seems to imply, or merely dried in the sun, is a point by no means settled; but according to the testimony of Herodotus, who was upon the spot, the Bricks which composed the tower of Babylon were baked in furnaces. That unburnt Bricks were also employed in the earliest buildings appears certain, from the testimony of some of the oldest historians, and from proofs still existing.

Unburnt Bricks were used in Egypt; the making of them was one of the tasks imposed on the Israelites during their servitude in that country; but the oldest edifices which at present remain there are principally of stone. At what time burnt Bricks were first introduced, or in what country, cannot be determined; the Greeks were certainly acquainted with the art of burning Bricks, as appears from Vitruvius, who instances several buildings in which this material was used, and both sun-dried and burnt.

D

The business of a Brick-maker is carried on in
the open fields, and its mode of operation may be
seen in the neighbourhood of most large towns.
The art, in almost all its branches, is regulated by different acts of parliament: and Bricks may be made
of pure clay, or clay mixed in certain proportions
with sand or ashes.

The clay is first moistened and tempered with
water, either by the feet, or by means of a machine
or mill worked with one or more horses.

When it is fit for moulding into bricks, several
persons are usually, in the neighbourhood of London,
employed upon the business of making a single
Brick; these are called gangs: they consist of one
or two men, a woman, and two children, to each of
which is assigned a different department in the occupation. A gang in full work will make many
thousaud Bricks in a day.

In the plate the man only is represented, in the
act of moulding the clay into the shape of a Brick :
he stands under a sort of thatched cover to keep off
the sun and the rain; on the board before him are
all his implements ; the mould into which the clay is
put, the clay itself, which is brought to him by
another person, a vessel with some water, and a
little heap of sand; and on his left hand lies the
ruler with which he takes off the superfluous clay
from the mould.

The inside of the box or mould is exactly the
shape and size of a Brick: the workman throws the
clay into this with some violence, having first scattered a little sand about the sides of it; and then
scraping off the superfluous clay, he turns up the
mould on one side, and placing a small board at the
bottom of the mould, shakes out the Brick and
places it down in order to be placed by another person on the barrow, which, when loaded with about
20 Bricks, is wheeled away, and the Bricks are packed
upon their edges by the assistance of the boards;

which, when drawn from them, leave sufficient space
for the air to circulate between them to dry them.
When the pile is made of the proper height, generally three, or at most four feet from the ground,
they are covered with long straw or tiles, so that
they may dry gradually without being exposed to the
direct rays of the sun, which would crack them;
heavy rains would also be injurious to them; these
are likewise kept off by straw or tiles. As soon as
they are sufficiently dry for the purpose, they are to
be burnt in a kiln. Here great art is required in
piling the Bricks, so that the fire may circulate
through every course and in all directions. Brees,
that is small cinders from sea-coal, is the fuel used
in burning Bricks, and when once well lighted, it
will keep burning several days, till the Bricks are
completely finished.

Bricks when finished are of different colours, according to the clay of which they are made, but they
must be all of one size; namely, nine inches long,
four inches and half broad, and two inches and a
half thick. A duty of 5s. 10d. is charged upon every
thousand of common Bricks; of course this business
affords a large revenue to government.

The most beautiful white Bricks in this country
are manufactured at Woolpit in Suffolk; these are
brought, by means of water-carriage, to all parts of
England, where great neatness in Brick-work is an
object.

Stourbridge clay and Windsor loam are esteemed
the best for making Bricks that are required to bear
a very intense heat. These are used for coating furnaces, and lining the ovens of glass-houses, where
they stand the utmost fury of the fire.

A gang of Brick-makers will earn a handsome
living: sometimes it happens that the whole gang
consists of branches of the same family, as the father
and mother, and four or five children of different
ages; these will earn from two to three guineas a

week; but they work many hours, and their labour is very hard.

In connection with the trade of Brick-making, we must notice the manufacture of tiles, which is a sort of thin Brick, made use of in the roofing of houses, and also, when something thicker, for the purposes of paving. Those for covering the roofs of houses are of different shapes, according to the uses for which they are intended; there are plain-tiles, ridge-tiles, gutter-tiles, pan-tiles, &c. they are all made according to certain guages; and the makers are subject to heavy penalties if their tiles exceed the dimensions fixed on by the several acts of parliament. The kilns in which tiles are burnt are large conical buildings: in these the tiles are piled from the bottom to the top before the fire is lighted. A very large manufactory of this sort is situated near Bagnigge Wells.

Dutch clinkers are imported into England for the purposes of paving; they are long narrow Bricks of a brimstone colour, very hard and well burnt, so as to be nearly vitrified.

Flemish or Dutch tiles, which are glazed and painted, were formerly much used for chimney jambs. Some thirty or forty years ago it was not uncommon to see a complete Scripture history, and other curious devices, in a parlour fire-place.

There is an article also called *Scouring-Bricks,* which is a mixture of clay and sea-sand, and slightly baked. These Bricks are, as far as we know, only made at or near the town of Bridgewater, in Somersetshire, from the clay obtained on the sides of the river Parret, which flows through the town. This peculiar mixture of clay and sea-sand is occasioned by the velocity with which the tide flows at this port. The trade in *Scouring-Bricks* has materially increased during the last twenty years: they are sent to London and various other parts of Great Britain.

Brush Maker.

THE BRUSH-MAKER.

THE nature of this man's business is very well displayed in the plate. He makes brushes, hair and carpet brooms, and mops of all sorts; he is generally the manufacturer of wooden coal-hods, and of measures for corn and coals, of all which articles there are representations in the engraving.

The operation of making a brush is one of the most simple that can be described, as there is scarcely a tool made use of in the business, which is not familiar to every workman.

The wooden part of brushes is generally of oak or elm, which is cut to its proper size by the instrument which the man in the figure is supposed to be using. The instrument is a large knife, fastened down to the block with a staple at one end, in such a manner, that it is moveable up and down; to the other end is a handle. The wood to be cut is held in the left hand, while the knife is worked with the right. The knife is always kept very sharp; and by its make and mode of using hard wood is very readily reduced to any shape and size. This wood, when cut into the proper sizes, is drilled with as many holes as is necessary, and into these the hair is put.

The hair made use of by brush-makers is hog's bristles, vast quantities of which are imported every year from Germany and Russia, when we are not at war with those powers. These are subject to a heavy duty.

Whalebone split very fine, so as to resemble bristles, has of late been much used as a substitute for hair, and will be generally found in most black-coloured brushes, mixed with the black hair. Some brush-manufacturers have also offered brushes made with whalebone entirely. They are of course cheaper, but not so durable.

In choosing brushes, observe if the hair is fast bound, and if it lies close together; if it is not well bound, and the hair appears to fly out, the brush will never work well; and if the hair is not fast bound, it will come out on the work, and disfigure it, as is discoverable from loose hairs lying about when the paint is laid on. Brushes in which the hair is fastened with a silver wire, are superior to those fastened with copper or iron wire, especially when they are to be used with water: brushes for the hat-maker are best fastened with card and wooden pegs, instead of wire and the usual cements, as they have to be frequently dipped in a boiling, though weak mixture of water and sulphuric acid.

There are brushes of various sorts, shapes, and sizes; but the structure of them all is the same, or nearly so. When the bristles are sorted, combed, and picked, a certain portion of them is taken and tied together in the middle with string, fine copper, or iron wire, and then doubled: in this double state they are fastened into the wooden stock with hot cement, made of melted glue, or pitch and rosin. The ends of the hair are now to be cut off, and the surface to be made even or uniform.

Common hearth-brushes and hair-brooms are made in a slighter way. As soon as the stock is brought to its proper shape, it is drilled, and the bushes inserted in the manner above mentioned.

In some brushes, as those represented hanging on the beam, at the left-hand corner of the plate, the wires are visible on the back; in others, the backs are smooth, there being thin slices of wood glued over the wires. The brush resting with its head against the wall, is called a scrubbing-brush : brushes of this kind are sometimes used to dry-rub oaken floors ; in that case, the backs are loaded with lead. In London, and its vicinity, where the high wages of female servants render them impertinent and slothful, it has become, by custom, a part of the manservant's business to use them, but in the country, where wages are lower, the female servants consider this sort of work theirs beyond dispute, and would ridicule a man for " doing women's work."

In this business, Mr. Thomassin, of Birmingham, has obtained a patent for a new method of making hearth-brushes, perhaps more ingenious than useful ; they are so constructed, as to conceal the hair in a metal case, by means of rack work.

Mops are made of woollen yarn, spun for the purpose. Besides these, there are other kinds of mops, manufactured of woollen rags, which are collected by poor women from the dust taken from the dunghills, &c.

The coal-hods are usually made of oak, with two wooden or iron handles on the sides ; they are not so neat as copper ones, or as those made of iron and varnished : but they are much cheaper, and will last much longer than iron hods.

Great nicety is required in making the corn measures, which stand behind the man ; they must contain a certain exact quantity. The standard for measuring corn, salt, coals, and other dry goods, is the Winchester gallon, and it must contain $272\frac{1}{4}$ cubic inches ; the bushel contains eight such gallons, or 2178 inches.

A journeyman in this business, will earn a guinea, or thirty shillings a week ; the profits to masters are pretty considerable where the returns are great.

Such are the divisions of labour in this country, that the same persons do not make the brushes and the long handles ; these last are made by turners, who are thus employed by the master brush-maker. In Kent-street, and several other places, there are broomstick manufactories. The making of birch-brooms is a distinct and profitable trade. The birch will grow in land which is hardly fit for any-thing else. Ground covered with moss, has been known. to produce birch-trees so well, that in a few years they have sold for ten pounds per acre, and the after produce has been considerably increased.

Besides broom makers, who are constant customers for the birch: hoop-benders are considerable purchasers of the same article. The largest trees are often bought by turners, and the wood is used for yokes and other instruments of husbandry. In the northern countries of Europe, birch-wood is used for wheels of carriages.

Button Maker.

THE BUTTON-MAKER.

Buttons are articles of dress serving to fasten clothes tight about the body. There are several kinds of buttons; some are made of gold and silver lace, others of mohair, silk, horse-hair, thread, metal, glass, &c.

The wrought buttons in silk, mohair, thread, &c. are chiefly made at Macclesfield, and form the staple commodity of the place. The use of them may be traced back nearly two hundred years; they were formerly curiously wrought with the needle, and made a great figure in full-trimmed suits. The form of buttons vary continually, as fashion prompts the wearer or the workmen.

Shirt buttons are made in considerable quantities at Axminster, in Devonshire. Metal buttons are principally made in Birmingham.

The plate represents a man who makes, or stamps metal buttons only. The process is very simple after the metal comes out of the founder's hands. The pieces of metal are either cast or cut to the proper size, and then sent to the button-maker, who has dies or stamps according to the pattern wanted. The machine by which they are stamped is well exhibited in the plate. The man stands in a place lower than the floor, by which he is nearer on a level with the place on which his die stands. By means of a single pulley he raises a weight, to the lower part of which is fixed another die; he lets the weight fall down on the metal, which effects his object. After this operation they are to be shanked, which is performed by means of solder; they are then polished by women. At Birmingham this manufacture is carried on upon a very large scale. The late John Taylor, Esq. was the inventor of gilt buttons, and in his house buttons have been manufactured to the amount of 800*l.* per week.

Besides those cast in a mould, there are great quantities of buttons made of thin plates. The plates are brought to a proper degree of thickness by the rolling-mill: they are then cut into round pieces of the size wanted. Each piece of metal thus cut is reduced to the form of a button by beating it in several spherical cavities, beginning with the flattest cavity, and proceeding to the more spherical till the plate has all the *relievo* required; and the more readily to manage so thin a plate, ten or a dozen of them are formed to the cavities at once. As soon as the inside is formed, an impression is given to the outside, by working it with an iron puncheon, in a kind of mould like minters' coins, engraven indentedly, and fastened to a block or bench. The cavity of the mould in which the impression is to be made is of a diameter and depth suitable to the sort of button to be struck in it; each kind requiring a particular mould.

The plate thus prepared makes the upper part or shell of the button. The lower part is formed of another plate, made after the same manner, but flatter, and without any impression. To this is soldered a little eye, made of wire, for the button to be fastened by.

The two plates are soldered together with a wooden mould covered with wax or rosin between, to render the button solid and firm: for the wax or other cement entering all the cavities formed by the *relievo* of the other side, sustains it, prevents its flattening, and preserves its design.

Glass buttons are composed of glass of various

colours. The glass is kept in fusion, and the button nipt out of it while in that state, by a pair of iron moulds, like those for casting shot, adapted to the intended form of the button, the shank having been inserted in the mould, so that it may become imbedded in the glass when cool.

In the year 1790, a patent was granted to Mr. Henry Clay of Birmingham, for a new method of manufacturing buttons of slate or slit stone.

By 36 Geo. 3. c. 60, any person putting false marks on gilt buttons, erasing any marks except such as express the real quality, or any other words except real gilt, or plated, forfeits the buttons and incurs a penalty of 5l. for any quantity not exceeding 12 dozen ; and if above, after the rate of 1l. for every 12 dozen. The penalty however does not extend to those who mark the words double and treble gilt, provided in the case of double-gilt buttons, gold shall be equally spread upon their upper surface exclusively of their edges, in the proportion of 10 grains to the surface of a circle 12 inches in diameter, and in that of treble gilt, the gold shall amount to 15 grains in the same proportion.

The art of button-making, in its various branches, is encouraged and protected by divers acts of parliament. It is unlawful to import foreign buttons ; and buttons made of, or covered with cloth, cannot be worn, without subjecting the wearer to very severe penalties, if any person choose to sue for the same.

THE CABINET-MAKER.

––––—◆—––––

THE business of a CABINET-MAKER, and that of an UPHOLSTERER are now so generally united together, that any observations on either of these branches may, with propriety, be comprehended under one general head.

As Cabinet-making may be considered a superior kind of joinery, so much of its principles and practice will be found under the article Carpenter, as to render it unnecessary to enter fully into the constructive art in the present article; we shall, therefore, confine ourselves to such particulars as are peculiar to this branch, and endeavour to point out, for the direction of the student, some of the qualifications necessary for his excelling in it.

The Cabinet-maker uses various kinds of wood for the formation or ornamenting of his goods, but his principal wood is *Mahogany*, a species of cedar, growing in the warmest parts of America. It is found in abundance in the islands of Cuba, Jamaica, and Domingo, as well as the Bahamas: the trees grow to a very large size, and a great height.

The first use to which mahogany was applied in England, was to make a box for holding candles. Dr. Gibbons, an eminent physician at the latter end of the seventeenth century, had a brother, a West-India captain, who brought over some planks of this wood as ballast. As the Doctor was then building a house in King-street, Covent-garden, his brother thought they might be of service to him; but the

The Cabinet Maker.

carpenters finding the wood too hard for their tools, they were laid aside as useless. Soon after, Mrs. Gibbons wanting a candle-box, the Doctor called on his Cabinet-maker (Wollaston, of Long-Acre) to make him one of some wood that lay in the garden. The candle-box was made, and approved; and the Doctor then insisted on having a bureau made of the same wood, which was accordingly done; and the fine colour, polish, &c. were so pleasing, that his friends were invited to come and see it, amongst whom was the Duchess of Buckingham. Her Grace begged some of the wood of Dr. Gibbons, and Wollaston made her a bureau also; on which the fame of the mahogany, and Mr. Wollaston, was raised, and things of this kind became general.

All the arts of life have, no doubt, been the result of a gradual and progressive improvement in civilization. In nothing is it exhibited more than in an Upholsterer's warehouse.

What a difference is there between the necessary articles of furniture to be found in a cottage, and the elegantly furnished house of a merchant or a peer! In the former, there is nothing but what is plain, useful, and almost essential to the convenience of life: in the latter, immense sums are sacrificed to magnificence and show. The cottager is contented with a deal table, an oaken chair, and a beechen bedstead, with other articles equally plain and unexpensive. The wealthy possess sumptuous beds, inlaid tables, silk or damask chairs and curtains, sofas, and carpets of great value; large looking-glasses, and brilliant lustres; together with a variety of carved work and gilding. The furniture of a cottage or a small farm-house, will cost but a few guineas; that of a single room, in the wealthy parts of the metropolis, will be valued at from five hundred to a thousand pounds.

The art of the Cabinet-maker differs from most other arts in many particulars. In the first place,

the articles made by him, are not only very numerous, but there are not, even from the same shop, two
articles of the same description, which do not vary
in their form and manufacture; and fashion is continually changing the forms of almost all Cabinet-
maker's articles, so that it must be obvious no rules
can be laid down, as to the formation of particular
articles of furniture; and, indeed, were it practica-
ble, it would be necessary that cabinet, like female
fashions, should be published monthly, : in fact, this
is, in some degree, done in a publication by Mr.
Ackerman.

The Cabinet-maker furnishes chairs, tables, chests
of drawers, desks, scrutoires, bureaus, sofas, book-
cases, and bedsteads, of all sorts of prices. But,
in almost all places, the business of the Cabinet-maker is united to that of the upholsterer; and the
furniture collected in one of their warehouses is
worth from ten to thirty thousand pounds. Such
warehouses may be seen in St. Paul's Church-yard,
Bond-street, and other parts of London.

As a first step, we should recommend to the student the practice of drawing from any good models,
but more particularly from subjects connected with
architecture, by which means he will gradually become more and more familiar with the beautiful combinations, so eminently conspicuous in the remains
of ancient Greece and Rome. An acquaintance
with perspective is no less useful than a knowledge
of drawing: for it is sometimes necessary, not only
to, delineate the particular articles of furniture, but
to shew the effect it is likely to produce, when placed
in the apartment for which it is designed.

As it is the fashion of the present day to resort
to a number of contrivances for making one piece of
furniture serve many purposes, " a bed by night,
and a chest of drawers by day," it becomes important, on this account, as well as on many others, that
the Cabinet-maker should be acquainted with the

principles of mechanics, which will materially assist him in the formation of his works ; and enable him to outstrip those persons who act from no principles, or whose ignorance and illiterateness prevent them from a comprehension of them.

All the remarks on the various tools, woods, &c. not belonging exclusively to this trade, will be found under the article *Carpenter;* but there is a process or two of which we shall say. a few words.

Veneering is a kind of marquetry, or inlaying, by which several thin slices, or leaves of fine wood, of different kinds, are applied, and fastened on a ground of some common wood. The wood intended for veneering, is first sawed out into slices or leaves, about a line (one-twelfth of an inch) thick ; and in order to saw them, the blocks, or planks, are placed upright in a kind of vice or sawing press; these slices are afterwards cut into slips, and fashioned divers ways according to the design proposed ; after the joints have been carefully adjusted, and the pieces brought down to their proper thickness, with several planes adapted for. the purpose, they are glued down on a block or ground of dry wood, with good strong English glue. After the pieces have been thus joined and glued, the work, if small, is put into a press; if large it is laid on a bench, covered with a board, and pressed down with poles, or pieces of wood, the upper ends of which reach to the ceiling of the room, and the lower ends on the board. When the glue is quite dry, the veneered work is taken out of the press, and finished with proper planes, scrapers, rasps, &c.

Marquetry differs from veneering in many particulars, and may be properly called painting in wood, as various imitations of nature are produced in this way. The art of inlaying is very ancient, and is supposed to have passed from east to west, among other branches of knowledge brought to the Romans from Asia: but it did not arrive at any tolerable perfection till the fifteenth century amongst the Italians: it seems, however, to have attained its greatest perfection in the seventeenth century in France. We have seen the representation of a tiger and other animals, done in this way, which might certainly be mistaken for an oil painting.

The Cabinet-maker, represented in the plate, is one who makes chairs, tables, looking-glass frames, book-cases, &c. His chief tools are saws, axes, planes, chisels, files, gimlets, turn-screws, hammers, and other implements, which are used in common by the Carpenter and Cabinet-maker. The workman, represented in the plate, is in the act of making a looking-glass frame; he is putting some glue on one of the side pieces, in order to fix it in the hole that is prepared to receive it.

The goodness and value of furniture depends on the fineness of the wood and other materials of which it is made, and on the neatness of the workmanship. A young man brought up to this business, should possess a good share of ingenuity, and some talents for drawing and designing, as we have before hinted, because much depends on fashion, and in pleasing the various tastes of the public.

The Calico Printer.

THE CALICO-PRINTER.

Calicos were first brought to England from India, in the year 1631, and derived their name from the province of Calicut, where they were chiefly made or exported. Calico is a sort of cloth resembling linen, but is made of cotton. It was first manufactured in this country about the year 1772, or 1773. Various attempts had been made, previous to this time, to manufacture cloth with cotton warp or web, but owing to a variety of imperfections, they all proved unsuccessful; but the improvements which rapidly followed the introduction of machine spinning, soon remedied the defect.

The manufacture of calicos was begun in Blackburn, in Lancashire, which has since become the great mart for calicos, and the chief source whence the printers of Lancashire, as well as those of London and Scotland, are supplied.

The art of Cloth-printing, or Calico-printing, in other words, of dying in certain colours particular spots of the cloth, while the ground shall be of a different colour or entirely white, affords, perhaps, the most direct and obvious illustration of the application of chemical principles.

The first hint towards this branch of business was had from the Indian chintzes. Calico-printing was introduced into London in the year 1676, and it has since been encouraged by various acts of parliament.

In the East Indies they paint all their calicos with the pencil, which they must do with great expedition, as the price there is very low; but here the following method is adopted: the pattern is first drawn on paper the whole breadth of the cloth intended to be printed ; the workman then divides the pattern into several parts according to its size, each part being about 8 inches broad by 12 inches long; each distinct part or pattern thus divided is cut out upon wooden blocks ; the cloth to be printed is extended upon a table, and the types being covered with the proper colours, are laid on after the manner represented in the plate, and the impression is left upon the cloth. The workman begins to lay on the types at one end of the piece, and so continues till the whole is finished ; great care must be taken that the patterns join with accuracy, and that there is no interstice or vacancy left.

Cutting the pattern in wood being the most curious part of the process, we shall describe that particularly. The cutters in wood begin with preparing a plank or block of the proper size: beech, pear-tree, and box, are used for this purpose ; but the box-tree is the most fit for the business, as being the closest and least liable to be worm-eaten. As soon as the wood is cut into the proper size, and made very smooth, it is fit to receive the drawing or design. Sometimes ink is used ; and, to prevent its running, it is rubbed over with a mixture of white lead and water, and after it is dry it is rubbed off and polished.

On this the design is drawn ; and those who cannot draw themselves make use of designs furnished by others whose profession is to draw patterns. The drawing marks out so much of the block as is to be spaced or left standing. The rest they cut off, and take away very curiously with the point of exceedingly sharp knives, or little chisels or gravers, according to the bigness or delicacy of the work; for they stand in need of no other instruments.

Block-engraving differs from that on copper in this, that, in the former the impression comes from the prominent parts or strokes left uncut, whereas in the latter it comes from channels cut in the metal.

The manner of printing with wooden prints is easy and expeditious, if there be only two colours; —as green and blue; or black and a white ground, then the block requires only to be dipped in the printing-ink and impressed on the cloth. If more colours are used, then they are to be laid on with a brush or brushes, and the impressions to be made as before with the hand.

When the whole piece is printed, the cloth is washed and bleached, to take away any accidental stains it may have acquired in the operation; it is then dried, calendered, and laid up in folds fit for the shop.

The application of engraving on copper has given birth to a new and important branch of Calico-printing. It first introduced those machines, whose subsequent improvement has so much contributed to the perfection of the art, and which surpasses the ordinary mode of block-printing, not only in neatness, accuracy, and precision, but still more in the economy and art with which the labour is performed.

These machines are of two kinds :—the flat press, and the rolling or cylinder press.

The flat press, in its original form, was merely a modification, considerably enlarged, of the press for ornamental prints or engravings; to which was added a contrivance for joining with accuracy the numerous and successive impressions necessary to cover a piece of cloth. It was confined at first to one colour, but later improvements have extended it to two or even three. The single-colour presses are, however, principally in use.

In order to the proper reception of the different colours on the calico, it is necessary that it should be prepared by a previous process with what is usually called a *mordant;* that which is principally used is the ascetate of argil. It is prepared by dissolving 3lbs. of alum, and 1lb. of ascetate of lead, in 8lbs. of warm water. An exchange of the principles of these salts takes place; the sulphuric acid of the alum combines with the lead, and the compound thus formed being insoluble in water, is precipitated: the ascetic acid remains united with the argil of the alum in solution; there are added at the same time two ounces of the potash of commerce, and two ounces of chalk; the principal use of which appears to be to neutralize the excess of acid that might cut on the colouring matter and alter its shade. The calico is steeped in this liquor, and afterwards rinced and dried: it is then proper for the reception of the colours.

Calico-printing is reckoned a very good business both for the master and his journeyman: the master, however, requires a large capital, a situation plentifully supplied with good and clear water, and extensive ground for bleaching and drying the cloths. He employs three sorts of hands; the pattern-drawer, the cutters of the types, who are also the operators in printing, and a number of labourers to assist in washing. The pattern-drawer is paid according to the variety and value of the designs; and the printer, who is able also to cut with ability and taste, can, in the summer-months, earn four or five guineas a week or more.

A youth designed for this business ought to have a genius for drawing, a good eye, and a delicate hand. The business is not laborious, and the chief care is in the choice of a master who will do justice to his apprentice. Most Calico-printers have some peculiar secrets in the preparation of their colours, which they ought to be bound to reveal to those whom they undertake to teach the art, since on the knowledge of this depends principally the success of the lad.

THE CARPENTER.

The art of the *Carpenter* is employed in framing and joining pieces of timber, and fitting them up in houses and other buildings, as well as in numerous other employments of a similar kind.

It was in the use of wood in the building of his dwelling, that man first began to exercise his ingenuity: and it is evident that he would soon endeavour to find out tools for working it; but the first were, of course, of a very rude construction. In the cabinets of the curious are still to be found some formed of hard stones. The most part of the savage nations of America, and of the Islands of the Pacific Ocean, were not acquainted with any other when Europeans first arrived amongst them.

Joinery is, also, the art of working in wood, or of fitting various pieces of timber together, for the convenience or ornament of certain parts of edifices, and is called, by the French *menuiserie,* " small-work."

Both these arts are subservient to architecture, being employed in raising, roofing, flooring, and ornamenting buildings of all kinds. The rules in Carpentry are much the same as those of Joinery; the only difference is, that Carpentry includes the larger and rougher kinds of work, and that part which is most material to the construction and stability of an edifice; while Joinery comprehends the interior finishing, and ornamental wood-work; but

The Carpenter.

most of those who are brought up to the trade, are both Carpenters and Joiners.

There are two kinds of Carpenters, the House-Carpenter and Ship-Carpenter. The wood which they principally make use of, is deal, oak, elm, and mahogany.

Deal is the wood of the fir-tree, which is chiefly brought from Sweden, Norway, and other northern European countries. The most common species of fir-trees, are the *silver-leafed* and the *pitch, Norway,* or *spruce-fir.* The first of these grows in many parts of Germany, from whence turpentine is sent to England. The Norway fir produces the *white* deal, commonly used by Carpenters; from this pitch is also drawn; whence it takes its second name of the *pitch* fir. There is also the *red* deal, which is also very much used where great durability is wanting, not having been deprived of its turpentine as the white deal has.

Oak and elm are too well known in this country to need any description, as they both grow in abundance in various parts of England. English oak is proverbial for its strength and durability; it is chiefly used for ship-building, of which we shall speak hereafter.

Mahogany has been mentioned before, under the article Cabinet-maker, to which we refer.

There has latterly been planted in many parts of Great Britain, a species of pine called *Larch-fir,* a deciduous tree, which grows very fast, and which promises, in time, to supersede, in part at least, the very great importations of fir timber from abroad.

The Carpenter stands in need of a great variety of tools, such as saws, planes, chisels, hammers, hatchets, axes, awls, gimblets, &c. Common workmen are obliged to find their own tools, a set of which is worth from ten to twenty pounds, or even more. But for different kinds of mouldings, for beads, and fancy work, the master Carpenter supplies his men with the necessary implements.

The practices in the art of Carpentry and Joinery are called planing, sawing, mortising, scribing, moulding, gluing, &c.

The Carpenter, in the plate, is represented in the act of planing the edge of a board that is held to the side of the bench, by means of a screw, which is always attached to it. On his bench are a hammer, pincers, mallet, and two chisels; a box, also, containing the Turkey stone, with which he sharpens his tools: the shavings taken off from his plane, are scattered on his bench and on the ground. At the right-hand corner, stands some course boards, and his bag, in which he carries his tools: on the other side is the saw, upon the four-legged stool, which he uses for various purposes. Behind him is a new door, some other boards, a saw hanging against the wall, and a basket, in which he puts his smaller tools.

He is represented preparing boards to lay upon the roof of a new house in the back-ground. The rafters are already in their places: the boards are to be laid next, in order to receive the slates.

The art of *sawing*, and the different kinds of saws made use of, will be described when we come to speak of the Sawyer.

A *mortise* is a kind of joint in which a square hole of a certain depth is made, in the thickness of a piece of wood, in order to receive another piece, called a tenon.

Scribing is a term made use of when one side of a piece of stuff is to be fitted to the side of some other piece, which is not regular, or not having straight-lined edges or surface. To make the two join close together, all the way, the Carpenter *scribes* it; that is, he lays the piece of stuff to be scribed close to the other piece he intends to *scribe* to, and opens his compasses to the greatest distance the two pieces any where stand from each other; then, bearing one of the legs against the side to be scribed to, with the other leg he draws a line on the stuff to be scribed. Thus he gets a line on the irregular piece, parallel to the edge of the regular one; and if, by the saw or other instrument, the wood be cut exactly to the line, when the two pieces are put together they will make a neat joint.

Planing consists in taking off, as occasion may require, all the rough parts from the surface and edges of wood, boards, &c. A plane consists of a piece of box-wood, or beech-wood, very smooth at the bottom, serving as a stock or shaft; in the middle of which is an aperture for a plate of iron, with a steel edge, or a very sharp chisel to pass. This edge is easily adjusted by a stroke or two of the hammer at one of the ends of the stock, on the iron itself, or the wedge, which is contrived to keep the plane-iron in its place. Planes have different names, according to their forms, sizes, and uses; as the *jack-plane*, which is about eighteen inches long, and is intended for the roughest kind of work.

The *long-plane* is two feet in length; it smooths the work after the rough stuff is taken off; it is one of this kind which the Carpenter in the plate is represented as using, and it is well adapted for smoothing and making straight the edges of boards that are to be joined.

The *smoothing-plane*, or hand-plane, is only six or eight inches long, and is used on almost all occasions.

The *rabbit-plane* cuts the upper edge of a board straight or square down into the stuff, so that the edge of another board cut in the same manner, may join with it on the square.

Besides these, there are *plowing-planes, moulding-planes, hollow-planes, snipe's-bill planes,* and a variety

E

of others, used more particularly by the Joiner in finishing his work.

Glue is a very important article in the Carpenter's and Joiner's, as well as the Cabinet-maker's trade. It is made of the skins of animals, as oxen, sheep, &c. and the older the animal, the better is the glue. Whole skins are never used for this purpose, but only the shavings and parings made by tanners, curriers, fell-mongers, &c. These are boiled to the consistence of jelly, and poured into flat moulds to cool; it is then cut into square pieces, and hung up to dry.

A Ship-carpenter is an officer at sea, whose business consists in having things in readiness for keeping the vessel in which he is stationed in repair; and attending to the stopping of leaks, to caulking, careening, and the like; which terms we shall explain under the article Shipwright. He is to watch the timber of the vessel to see that it does not rot; and in time of battle he is to have every thing prepared for repairing and stopping the breaches, made by the enemy's cannon.

A journeyman Carpenter, when he works by time, receives from three shillings and sixpence, to four shillings and sixpence a day.

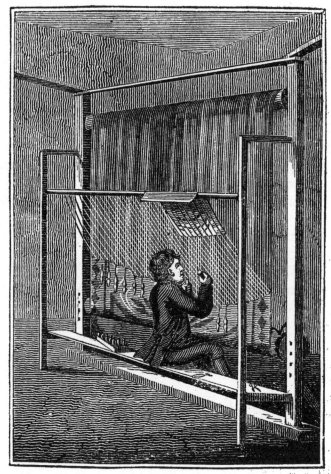

Carpet Weaver.

THE CARPET-WEAVER.

———

CARPET, in the manufacture of cloth, is a species of woollen-stuff, made of variegated colours, and used for covering the floors of rooms.

The manufacture of Carpets we may reasonably conclude originated in Asia, from whence most of our knowledge of the manufacture of cloths of almost every description appears to have been derived; and to this day the finest and most expensive of the ornamental kinds are distinguished by the name of Turkey carpets. They are now, and have long been, manufactured both in France and Italy; and those used in Great Britain of internal manufacture, are equal both in fabric and design to any imported. In England they are generally called Wilton Carpets, from the county which is the chief seat of that and the other finer branches of the woollen manufacture. Some manufactories are, and have long been established in Scotland, of which Stirling and Kilmarnoch are the chief seats, but they are generally confined to the coarser and low-priced kind.

Carpeting possesses this peculiar property different from almost every other kind of cloth, that it contains two distinct webs woven at the same time, and firmly joined together by the operation: hence arises the common effect that on the two sides of a carpet, the form of the pattern is the same, but all the colours are reversed.

The Carpet-loom is very well represented in the

E 2

plate: it is placed perpendicularly, and consists principally of four pieces, two long planks or cheeks of wood, and two thick rollers or beams.

The planks are set upright, and the rollers across, the one at top, and the other at bottom, about a foot or more distant from the ground. They are suspended on the planks, and may be turned with bars. In each roller is a groove from one end to the other, in which the ends of the warp are so fastened that all the threads of it are kept perpendicular.

The warp is divided, both before and behind, into parcels of ten threads, through the whole width of the piece. The Weaver works on the foreside. The design, or pattern, is traced in its proper colours on cartons, a kind of pasteboard, tied about the workman, who looks at it every moment, because every stitch is marked upon it, which it is his business to imitate. By these means he always knows what colours and shades he is to use, and how many stitches of the same colour. To accomplish this, he is assisted by squares, into which the whole design is divided : each square is sub-divided into ten vertical lines, corresponding with the parcels of ten threads of the warp: and besides, each square is ruled with ten horizontal lines, crossing the vertical lines at right angles. The workman having placed his spindles of thread near him, begins to work on the first horizontal line of one of the squares.

The lines marked on the carton are not traced on the warp, because an iron wire, which is longer than the width of a parcel of ten threads, supplies the place of a cross line. This wire is managed by a crook at one end, at the workman's right hand; towards the other end it is flatted into a sort of knife, with a back and edge, and grows wider to the point. The Weaver fixes his iron wire horizontally on the warp, by twisting some turns of a suitable thread of the woof round it, which passes forward and backward behind a fore-thread of the warp, and then behind the opposite thread, drawing them in their turn by their leishes. Afterwards he brings the woof-thread round the wire in order to begin again to thrust into the warp. He continues in this manner to cover the iron rod or wire, and to fill up a line to the tenth thread of the warp. He is at liberty either to stop here, or to go on with the same cross line in the next division, according as he passes the thread of the woof round the iron wire and into the warp, the threads of which he causes to cross one another at every instant; when he comes to the end of the line, he takes care to strike in, or close again all the stitches with an iron reed, the teeth of which freely enter between the empty threads of the warp, and which is heavy enough to strike in the woof he has used. This row of stitches is again closed and levelled, and in the same manner the Weaver proceeds; then with his left hand he lays a strong pair of shears along the finished line, cuts off the loose hairs, and thus forms a row of tufts perfectly even, which, together with those before and after it, form the shag. Thus the workman follows stitch for stitch, and colour for colour, the plan of his pattern, which he is attempting to imitate; he paints magnificently without having the least notion of painting or drawing.

The manufacture of carpets after the manner of Chaillot, was introduced into London in the year 1750, by two workmen, who left the manufactory in disgust, and came here to procure employment. They were first encouraged by Mr. Moore, who succeeded in establishing this important and useful manufacture; and who, in the year 1757, obtained a premium from the Society of Arts, for the best Carpet in imitation of the Turkey Carpets. We have Carpet manufactories, beside those before mentioned, at Axminster, Kidderminster, Leeds, and many other places.

Axminster Carpets are manufactured of any size;

they are woven in one entire piece, and several persons are employed at the same time in working the coloured patterns.

Another sort of carpet in use is made of narrow slips of list sewed together; these of course are very inferior to those just described, but they employ many women and children. A considerable trade in list carpets is carried on at the Orphan working school in the City Road, an institution that does honour to the liberality and public spirit of the Dissenters in and near the metropolis.

This is a good business for the masters and journeymen; and now Carpets are become of such general use, a great number of people are employed in their manufacture.

they are woven in one entire piece, and several persons are employed at the same time in working the coloured patterns.

The Chemist.

THE CHEMIST.

CHEMISTRY is the science which treats of those events or changes in natural bodies, by which new bodies are composed, or compound ones divided: its principal object is to ascertain the principles or elements of which bodies are composed, and the laws by which the simple atoms of matter unite together, and form compounds.

Neither the origin nor primitive meaning of the word Chemistry is accurately known. That it was used by the Greeks, soon after the commencement of the Christian æra, is certain; and many reasons coincide to render it probable, that it was of Egyptian origin. It is certain that the Chemistry of the ancients was the name of an art of some kind or another. Suidas, a Greek writer, mentions this particularly in his Lexicon.

The honour of laying the foundation of the present science of Chemistry belongs to John Joachim Becher, who was born at Spires, in Germany, in 1645, where he became professor of medicine, and afterwards was appointed first physician, to the elector of Mentz and Bavaria; but he ended his days in England. His writings testify with what success he applied himself to the study of this important branch of natural philosophy. To name the illustrious men who laboured in this science during the eighteenth century, would require a volume. Priestley, Scheele, Macquer, Black, Cavendish, and Lavoisier, are amongst the most eminent,

some of whom have only within a few years past
paid the debt of nature. Of living Chemists, Sir
Humphry Davy, and Mr. Brande, the present professor of Chemistry at the Royal Institution, are
eminently conspicuous.

Formerly the preparations of drugs were divided
into two classes, termed *chemical* and *galenical;* idle
distinctions, which have nearly disappeared before
the light which modern Chemistry has spread
abroad. A more correct and just classification has
obtained both in the science itself, and in the terms
and names of the several substances, in consequence
of the assiduity with which chemical investigation
has been followed in many of the nations of Europe.
The hidden qualities, or supposed qualities of matter, are now no longer taken for granted; all must
be weighed in the balance of experiment, and submitted to the severe test of philosophical truth : it
is utterly impossible to say where our experiments
may end. *Water,* for a long time supposed to be
a simple body, is now known to be a compound
one; the great powers which have been latterly acquired by a modified operation of electricity, called
the *Galvanic* apparatus, have unfolded to us results
and changes as extraordinary as unexpected, and
which lead us not less to wonder at the infinite variety of the powers abounding in nature, than at
the ingenuity and perseverance of man; we may
well conclude, therefore, that much yet remains to
be explored : a deep mine for the future active genius of research.

It is scarcely possible to name a thing in the natural world, to which Chemistry does not either
directly or indirectly, apply. Heat, light, air, electricity, the phenomena of the seasons, the different climates, the sea, mountains, volcanoes, mines,
have all an intimate connexion with this the first
of all sciences. The boiling of a potato, the roasting of a piece of beef, the baking of a pie, or of a

loaf of bread, are equally objects of the science of Chemistry. But, in a more confined sense, the Chemist is employed in the composition and decomposition of medicines designed for the cure or alleviation of disease: and in the manufacture of a variety of articles used in the arts.

The Chemist of trade might be defined the maker of medicines; the Druggist, the seller of them. In London, and many other places, a Chemist and Druggist are frequently combined in the same person, and in other instances, the trade of a Chemist is divided into a variety of branches. Some prepare compositions of mercury; others refine saltpetre; some distil essential oils; and others, as the Apothecaries' Company, prepare the greatest part of the compositions themselves: some prepare the sulphuric acid, the nitric acid, the muriatic acid, and a few neutral salts only, in a very large way; whilst others distil oil of turpentine, make pitch, lamp-black, &c.

The whole world is ransacked for the supply of the Chemist's elaboratory, and the Druggist's shop.

The Elaboratory is a room provided with proper conveniences for carrying on all the operations which the Chemist might choose, or have occasion for: it is generally constructed with an open chimney, in such a way, that if any unexpected explosion should take place, the ignited materials might find a ready escape. It is furnished also with suitable benches, mortars, a sand heat, a variety of glass vessels, consisting of retorts, matrasses, funnels, &c. &c. and a copper alembic, or still, for the purpose of procuring a variety of distilled waters, oils, &c. and a circular furnace for the purpose of boiling, melting, and other processes, requiring the immediate contact of fire. But, indeed, from the great variety of operations in Chemistry, we scarcely find two elaboratories alike, either in their structure, or in the different vessels which they contain.

E 5

The light, however, in them all, is most desirable when thrown down from above; and, of course, an elaboratory ought not to have any room, loft, or building over it.

The Chemist and Druggist usually makes some of his articles, even if he be only a retailer: he also sells numerous quack medicines, and frequently makes many of these when the patents have expired, or if the nostrums be known: but this is a branch of his trade by no means so reputable as could be wished, although it generally brings in a good profit, and in stamps, produces a considerable revenue to government. To sell these an annual licence must be taken out from the Stamp-Office, and a stamp of a certain value, in proportion to the value of the article sold, must be affixed to every individual phial, box, pot, or other package or inclosure.

The Chemist and Druggist generally, also, dispenses Physicians' prescriptions, and by a late Act of Parliament, he is privileged so to do, without being obliged to undergo an examination at Apothecaries' Hall.

We wish that it was in our power to speak of this trade as one in which the composition of medicines was uniformly correct, and according to the directions of the *London Pharmacopœia;* but we are sorry to say, that tales are told, which give us great reason to fear, that many unworthy persons have obtruded themselves into this respectable body; and that too much of system pervades the trade generally, for it to be quite free from that sophistication which, in medicine, is, above all things, so much to be deprecated.

Except this drawback, the preparation and sale of medicines is a very respectable line of business, and one in which, with a tolerable share of judgment, great fortunes have been made. We believe, however, that the impressions of its profitableness have directed more competitors into it than can now find room; the profits are, in consequence, a good deal lessened, and, perhaps, its respectability impaired.

The Drug-trade, as well as the Chemist's, in the large way, is a good deal sub-divided; there are Drug merchants: those who import Drugs from abroad, and sell them to wholesale Druggists, who sell them again to the retailer. Some of these merchants import and sell only particular articles.

A lad who is designed for this trade will certainly best succeed in it if he is previously acquainted with the rudiments of Latin at least; and has some knowledge of Botany, and the Materia Medica. It is a trade of all others the most intimately connected with science. A premium of one hundred guineas is sometimes given with an apprentice. The stock in trade of a retail Chemist and Druggist may amount to a few hundred pounds. The stock of a Chemist and Druggist, in the wholesale trade, sometimes to many thousands.

The plate represents the interior of a Chemist's elaboratory. On the left is an alembic made of copper, with the worm-tub by its side. On the right is a sand heat, with digesting bottles, retorts, receivers, &c. &c. In the middle is the furnace, where all the common operations are performed. The light is thrown from above, that being the best way in which the progress of the processes can be seen.

THE COACH-MAKER.

⸻

THE Coach-Maker makes coaches, chaises of all kinds, and other vehicles of the more elegant kind for travelling.

The use of coaches has been carried by many writers much higher than is authorized by facts. Vehicles, approaching them in form, though under a variety of designations, have certainly been used at different times in different countries. Coaches, however, were not known in Europe till the beginning of the sixteenth century, when they were used only by women of the first rank, it being considered disgraceful for men to ride in them. At that period, in Germany, when the electors and princes did not wish to be present at the meetings of the states, they excused themselves by informing the emperor that their health would not permit them to ride on horseback.

The oldest carriages used by the ladies in England, were known under the now-forgotten name of *whirlicotes*.

We are expressly informed by Stow, that in 1555, Walter Ripon made a coach for the Earl of Rutland, "*which was the first that was ever used in England.*" In his larger Chronicle, however, he states, that coaches were brought more generally into fashion by one William Boonen, a Dutchman, in 1564, who was coachman to the Queen. It was not till the beginning of the seventeenth century, that a coach-box was added to the body. In 1605,

Coach Maker.

coaches began to be in general use among the nobility and gentry in London. *Hackney-coaches* began to ply in London streets in 1625, when twenty only was the number allowed; in ten years, their numbers multiplied so much that their increase was restrained by order of Council. In 1637, fifty coaches were allowed to be licensed by the Master of the horse. In 1652 they were increased to 200. In 1661 to 500. In 1694 to 700. Afterwards, to 800. In 1771 to 1000: and since to 1100.

Stage-Coaches were not in general use till the beginning of the eighteenth century. *Post-Chaises* were introduced by Mr. Tull, son of the well-known writer on husbandry.

The celebrated Duke of Buckingham was the first person who rode in a coach with six horses. To ridicule this new pomp the Earl of Northumberland put eight horses to his carriage.

The fashions with regard to the form and ornament of coaches and other carriages for pleasure, are perpetually changing. The chief kinds now in use are the close coach and chariot; the landau, which can lower its roof and part of its sides, like the head of a phaëton; the barouche, or open summer carriage; the chariot intended only for two or three persons; the landaulet, or chariot, whose head folds back; the phaëton and caravan, which have only a head and no windows, with a leathern apron arising from the foot-board to the waist: the post-chaise is a sort of chariot without a box. There is also the berlin, which, and the landau, take their names from the places at which they were first made. Coaches are also distinguished according to the uses for which they are designed: thus we have travelling-coaches, stage-coaches, hackney-coaches, &c. these all run on four wheels. Of the two-wheeled vehicles there is the curricle, drawn by two horses; the gig, chaise, or whiskey, having one horse only. When a gig has two horses, one precéding the other in harness, the machine and its horses together are denominated a *Tandem*, a Latin word, signifying at length.

, Coaches consist of two principal parts, the *body* and the *carriage*. The body is that part which is intended for the passengers; the carriage is that which sustains the body, and to which the wheels that give motion to the whole machine are fastened.

The body of the coach is built chiefly with ash, on account of its great toughness, and its not being liable to snap by jerking; but the pannels are generally made of mahogany; the upper parts are covered with well-dressed and highly-varnished leather. The inside of a coach is lined with woollen cloth, and stuffed with horse hair. Coaches, however, made in a very high style, are lined with silk, sometimes with velvet; and not unfrequently with exceedingly fine and beautiful leather.

The carriage consists, principally, of two pair of wheels, with axle-trees and a perch.

, The perch is that long pole which is fastened to the middle of the hind axle-tree, and passes between the fore axle and its bolster, being secured by the pole-pin, so as to move about it, and connecting the fore and hind wheels together. It is plain that in turning a carriage of this construction, the larger the wheel the sooner it will strike against the perch : on account of the axle being under the perch ; and to accommodate some other contrivances in the lower part of the carriage, the forewheels are usually made smaller than the hind ones.

Coaches on the most elegant construction are made in London, whence they are exported to the Continent, to the East-Indies, and America : indeed, they are made more elegant for the East-Indies than those used in this country.

Modern European coaches were unknown in

China, till Lord Macartney's embassy to that empire. With his Lordship two of Hatchett's most
splendid carriages were sent as presents to the Emperor. These puzzled the Chinese more than any
of the other presents. Nothing of the kind had
ever been seen at Pekin; and the disputes among
themselves as to the part intended for the seat of
the Emperor were whimsical enough. The ham-
mer-cloth that covered the box of the winter-car-
riage had a smart edging, and was ornamented with
festoons of roses. Its splendid appearance and
elevated situation, determined it at once, in the
opinion of the majority, to be the Emperor's seat;
but a difficulty arose how to appropriate the inside
of the carriage. They examined the windows, the
blinds, and the screens; and at last, concluded that
it could be for nobody but his ladies. An old
eunuch sought particularly for information: and
when he learned that the fine elevated box was to
be the seat of the man who managed the horses,
and that the Emperor's place was within, he asked,
with a sneer, if it could be supposed that the Emperor would suffer any man to sit higher than himself, and to turn his back towards him? He wished
the coach-box to be removed and placed behind
the body of the carriage.

The business of a Coach-Maker is divided into
several branches; the wages are in proportion to
the nicety of the work; thus the body-makers in
general have from two to three pounds per week:
the carriage-makers, between one and two pounds:
the trimmers about two guineas: the painters from
twenty to thirty shillings: the body painters about
forty shillings: the herald painters from three to
four pounds: the smiths about thirty shillings.

Hackney-coaches and coachmen are subject to
strict regulations; they are stationed at certain
stands in the streets of London, and other large
cities; for the convenience of passengers, and are

hired at fixed rates. The coachmen are liable to be punished for any offences, such as insults to their passengers, or for over charges.

Coach-Makers are now obliged to take out an annual license, and to render an account of the number of carriages they sell, and to whom sold.

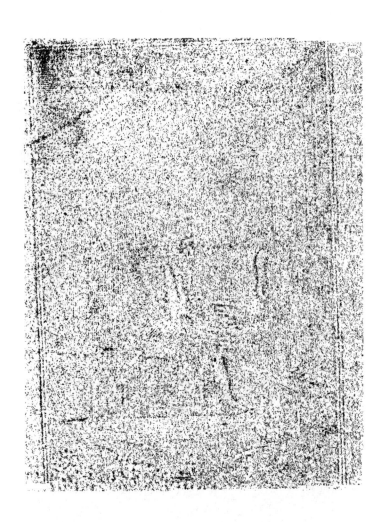

The Comb Maker.

THE COMB-MAKER.

THE comb is a well-known instrument, made of horn, ivory, tortoise-shell, box, or holly-wood, and is used for separating, adjusting, cleansing, and ornamenting the hair. The commoner sorts of combs are generally made of the horns of bullocks', or of elephants' and sea-horses' teeth ; some are made of tortoise-shell, and others of box, holly, and other hard woods.

The savages of the islands in the Pacific Ocean, make combs of a kind of wood which are shaped like a fan, and which prove that the use of the comb must have been very early introduced amongst mankind.

Bullocks' horns are thus prepared in order to manufacture combs: the tips are first sawn off; they are then held in the flame of a wood fire ; this is called roasting, by which they become nearly as soft as leather. While in that state, they are split open on one side, and pressed in a machine between two iron plates : they are then plunged into a trough of water, from which they come out hard and flat.

After the horn is cut to the intended size, three or four pieces are laid upon a pair of tongs over a fire of joiners' shavings to soften them ; they are turned many times, and when sufficiently soft are put into a vice, and screwed tight; to complete the flattening, they are suffered to remain a short time until they become perfectly flat and hard again ; they are then given to a man who shaves, planes, or scrapes off the rough parts, with a knife having two handles, similar to those used by coopers, which he works from him across the grain of the horn from one end of the intended comb to the other; when both sides are perfectly smooth it is delivered to the person who cuts the teeth; he fastens it by that part meant for the back, into an instrument for holding it, called a " clam," by wedges; the clam has a long handle, which the workman places under him as he sits : by this mean he steadies the object of his work, as both hands are to be employed in the operation. The cutting of the teeth is commenced by a double saw, each blade of which is like the small one with which joiners and cabinet-makers cut their fine work ; with this he forms the teeth, but as this instrument leaves the work square and rough in the inside edge of each tooth, it is followed by another, about the size and shape of a case knife, having teeth like a file on each flat side ; after this, two others of the same shape, but each finer cut than the other, follow ; one stroke on each side of the comb is then given by a rasping tool, in which, also, a little attention is used, to give the ends of the teeth a small bevel or angle ; this tool is used to take off any roughness that may remain on the sides of the teeth; it is now delivered to another operator who polishes it with rotten stone and oil, applying them with a piece of buff leather ; after which the article is ready for sale.

The process used for making ivory combs is nearly the same as that already described, except that the ivory is first sawed into thin slices. The best ivory comes from the Islands of Ceylon and Achen, in the East Indies; this has the property of never turning yellow; of course the ivory from these places is much dearer than that brought from other parts.

Having described the usual method of making combs, it is right to inform the reader, that about ten years ago, Mr. Bundy, of Camden-Town, obtained a patent for cutting combs by means of machinery. It will be thought a very singular circumstance, that before this period no method was practised in this country for cutting the teeth of combs, but that in which a pair of saws, rudely fastened in a wooden back, was directed by the human hand, with these implements, however, it is that the very delicate, superfine ivory combs, containing from fifty to sixty teeth in an inch, are manufactured.

By Mr. Bundy's machine the business of comb-making is greatly expedited; the teeth of two combs may be cut in about three minutes. The combs are afterwards pointed, by applying them to an arbor or axis, clothed with cutters, having chamfered edges and teeth.

Tortoise-shell combs are very much used: and there are methods of staining horn so as to imitate tortoise-shell, of which the following is one: the horn to be dyed must first be pressed into a flat form, and then spread over with a paste made of two parts of quick lime and one of litharge, brought into a proper consistence with soap-ley. This paste must be put over all the parts of the horn, except such as are proper to be left transparent to give it a nearer resemblance to tortoise-shell. The horn must remain in this state till the paste is quite dry, when it is to be brushed off. It requires taste and judgment to dispose the paste in such a manner as to form a variety of transparent parts, of different magnitudes and figures to look like nature. Some parts should also be semi-transparent; which may be made by mixing whiting with a part of the paste to weaken its operation in particular places; by this means, spots of reddish brown will be produced, so as greatly to increase the beauty of the work. Horn thus dyed is manufactured into combs, and these are frequently sold for real tortoise-shell.

Another method of imitating tortoise-shell in horn, is to take of nitrous acid two ounces, of fine silver

one drachm: let the silver be dissolved, and having
spotted or marked your horn with wax, strike the
solution over it; let it dry of itself, and the horn will
be in those places which are free from wax, of a
brown or black colour.

A green dye may be given to ivory by steeping it
in nitrous acid, tinged with copper or verdigris; or
in two parts of verdigris and one of sal ammoniac,
ground well together with strong white wine vinegar
poured on them; and by converting the nitrous acid
into the oxygenated muriatic acid *(aqua regia);* i. e.
by dissolving a fourth part of its weight of sal ammoniac in it, ivory may be stained of a fine purple
colour.

Ivory, bone, horn, and other substances adapted
to the manufacture of combs, may be stained yellow,
by boiling them in a solution of one pound of alum
in two quarts of water, and afterwards boiling them
in a decoction of turmeric root. Ivory, &c. may be
stained blue by first staining it green, and then dipping it in a solution of pearl-ashes made strong and
boiling hot. It may be done also by boiling in a
tincture of indigo prepared by the dyers, and afterwards in a solution made with three ounces of cream
of tartar dissolved in a quart of water. Combs are
not only made for the purpose of cleaning hair but for
ornament; they are sometimes set with brilliant stones,
pearls, and even diamonds; some again, are studded
with cut steel; these are of different shapes, and are
used to fasten up the hair when ladies dress without
caps. Of course, combs may be had of all prices,
from the value of a few pence to almost any sum.

Journeymen Comb-makers will earn a guinea or
thirty shillings a week.

Horn from which combs are generally made, when
very thin becomes transparent, and has been used
instead of glass for windows. When heated it may
be bent to any shape, and wrought into trinkets of
all forms. Tortoise-shell, upon being analysed, is

found to consist of very thin membranes laid over each other, and is in its nature very like the nails that defend the human toes and fingers.

The Comb-maker represented in the plate, is cutting the teeth of a comb: on his left hand is a bench with combs already finished; on the ground are the horns from which he manufactures them; and in the right hand corner is a heap of shavings.

THE CONFECTIONER.

A CONFECTIONER is one who makes sweetmeats, preserves of various kinds, jellies, jams, gingerbread, &c. and is generally combined with the Pastry-cook, who makes tarts, cheese-cakes, pies, &c.

Confects, or `confits, is a denomination given to fruits, flowers, herbs, roots, and juices, when boiled and prepared with sugar or honey to keep them, or to render them more agreeable to the taste.

The ancients only confected with honey; at present sugar is more frequently used. Confits, half sugared, are those only covered with a little sugar, to leave more of the natural taste of the fruit.

The making of gingerbread, we are told, is an art of the highest antiquity, and that its use has come to us from Asia. We read, in fact, that a bread sweetened with honey was made at Rhodes, of such an agreeable taste, that it could be eaten with pleasure after the most sumptuous feasts. The Greeks called this bread *melilates:* thence it came into Europe, and descending to our own times, has obtained the name of gingerbread.

Confects are reduced to eight kinds, viz. liquid confects, marmalades, jellies, pastes, dry confects, conserves, candies, and sugar-plums, sometimes called comfits.

Liquid confects are those whose fruits, either whole, in pieces, in seeds, or in clusters, are confected in a fluid, transparent syrup, which takes its colour and name from that of the fruit boiled in it.

5

The Confectioner.

A good deal of art is necessary in preparing these well; if they be too little sugared, they will ferment and spoil, and if too much, they will candy. The most esteemed of the liquid confects, are plums, especially those called mirabels, barberries, quinces, apricots, cherries, orange-flowers, little green citrons from Madeira, green cassia from the Levant, myrobalans, ginger, cloves, &c.

Marmalades are a kind of pastes, almost liquid, made of the pulp of fruits or flowers that have some consistence; such as apricots, apples, pears, plums, quinces, oranges, and ginger. Marmalade of ginger is brought from the Indies by way of Holland. It is esteemed good to revive the natural heat in aged persons.

Jellies are juices of several fruits, wherein sugar has been dissolved, and the whole, by boiling, reduced into a pretty thick consistence, so as, upon cooling, to resemble a thin transparent glue or size. Jellies are made of various kinds of fruits, especially gooseberries, currants, apples, and quinces: there are other jellies, made of flesh, fish, hartshorn, &c. but they are not kept long, being very subject to corrupt.

Pastes are a kind of marmalades, thickened to that degree, by a proper boiling, as to assume any form when put into little moulds, and dried in an oven. The most in use are gooseberries, quinces, apples, plums, pears, and orange-flowers; those of pistachoes are the most esteemed; those of ginger are brought from the Indies.

Dry confects are those whose fruits, after having been boiled in the syrup, are taken out again, drained, and put to dry in an oven. These are made of so many kinds of fruit, that it would be troublesome to mention them all: the most considerable are citron, lemon, and orange-peel; plums, pears, cherries, and apricots.

Conserves are a kind of dry confects, made with

sugar-pastes of flowers or fruits, &c. The most usual amongst them, are those of roses, mallows, rosemary, of hips, of orange-peel, orange-flowers, violets, jessamine, pistachoes, citrons, and sloes.

· Candies are, ordinarily, entire fruits, candied over with sugar having been boiled in the syrup, which, renders them like little rocks crystallized, of various figures and colours, according to the fruits enclosed in them. The best candies are brought from Italy.

' Sugar-plums, or comfits, are a kind of little dry confects, made of small fruits or seeds, little pieces of bark, as cinnamon or cassia, or odoriferous and aromatic roots, &c. incrusted, and covered over with a very hard sugar, ordinarily white, but sometimes of other colours. Of these there are various kinds, distinguished by various names; some are made of raspberries, others of barberries, melon seeds, pistachoes, filberts, almonds, cinnamon, cassia, orange-peel, coriander, aniseed, carraways, &c.

Ice-cream is, also, an article to be found in the Confectioner's shop; who generally lays in, during the winter, a competent supply of ice, preserved in a proper receptacle, to furnish his customers with this agreeable treat in the summer months.

' The Confectioners of London are famous for the elegance and size of their Twelfth-Day cakes: for some days previously to this period, their shops are decorated with a great variety of them, made of different shapes, and with various devices upon them : some weigh many hundred pounds.

There are various forms and preparations of gingerbread: we shall content ourselves with giving the following recipe, which is well recommended.

' Into a pound of almonds, blanched and pounded, grate a penny white loaf; sift and beat them together; to the mixture add an ounce of ginger scraped fine, and of liquorice and aniseed, in powder, of each a quarter of an ounce ; pour in two or three spoonfuls of rose water, and make the whole into a paste with half a pound of sugar: mould and roll it; print it, and dry it in a stove. Some make gingerbread of treacle, citron, lemon, and orange-peel, with candied ginger, coriander, and carraway seeds, mixed up with as much flour as will make it into a paste.

The plate represents the Confectioner's shop, with jellies, sugar-plums, jams, &c.

THE COOPER.

A COOPER manufactures casks, tubs, pails, and various other articles in domestic concerns, as well as vessels for carrying and transporting all kinds of liquids, and many dry wares.

The art of the Cooper is very ancient, and appears to have soon arrived to the degree of perfection in which it now is. The operations in this trade are referred to two thousand years ago by the Roman writers on rural economy. Notwithstanding which, it is still unknown in some countries; for in those where wood is scarce, they carry wine in skins daubed over with a mixture of pitch and tar. The custom of keeping wine in earthen vessels is still in use in some of the southern parts of Europe. Pliny gives to· the Piedmontese the merit of having first made use of casks: in his time they were daubed with pitch.

The art of coopering has enabled man to possess and retain the richest viands and liquors of foreign climes. It promotes and facilitates the export and import of the produce of distant countries, which have enriched the merchant, supplied the wants and luxuries of the people, enriched the revenues, and given spirit to navigation. It is impossible, in reflecting on this trade, not to feel that it occupies a much greater space in our existence than it at first appears to do.

The Cooper principally employs oak in the manufacture of his different articles, a great part of which

The Cooper.

comes from America: but he also uses, occasionally, other woods, as deal and beech. The oak is usually imported, cut up into narrow pieces, called staves; for tubs, pails, &c. the bottoms of which are less than the tops, the staves are wider at the top than they are at the bottom. After the staves are dressed, and ready to be arranged, the Cooper, without attempting any great nicety in sloping or beveling them, so that the *whole* surface of the edge may touch in every point, brings them into contact only at the inner surface, and then, by driving the hoops tight, he can make a closer joint than could be done by sloping the staves from the outer to the inner side. These staves are kept together by means of hoops, which are made of hazel and ash; but some articles require iron hoops. To make them hold water, or other liquids, the Cooper sometimes places between each staves from top to bottom, split flags, which swell with moisture, and effectually prevent the vessel from leaking: but this is more commonly done in repairing old casks: if the new work be properly conducted there is no necessity for the use of flags.

The trade in London is divided into several branches, and the persons carrying it on, as well as the journeymen, confine themselves to the different branches respectively.

They are designated first by *Butt-Coopers,* whose employ consists in making all kinds of casks for breweries, and the puncheons and hogsheads for distilleries.

The *Dry-Cooper* finds his employment in manufacturing hogsheads and other casks for the containing of every kind of dry produce; the leading feature of the consumption in his line is hogsheads for sugar.

The employ of the *White-Cooper* comes home to every house-keeper: he makes all domestic utensils, such as are used in private brewing, washing, dairies, &c.

The *Wine-Cooper* is a person employed in drawing off, bottling, and packing wine, spirits, or malt liquor. In London many persons follow this business only; it is common for persons of the first consequence to employ the Wine-Cooper to take charge of their wines.

The Cooper derives large profit, and great part of his employment, from the West-India trade. The puncheons and hogsheads are used in the voyage out to the Islands for packing coarse goods, as coarse woolen cloaths, coarse hats, &c. whence those vessels return filled with rum and sugar.

The tools required by the Cooper are numerous, some of which are peculiar to his art; but most of them are common both to him and the Carpenter.

In the plate we see the Cooper busily employed in putting together a hogshead. In his left hand he holds a flat piece of wood, which he lays on the edge of the hoop while he strikes it with the hammer in his right hand. To make the hoops stick, he takes the precaution to chalk the staves before he begins this part of the operation. The tops and bottoms he puts together by means of wooden pegs.

Around the wall of the shop, and on the floor, we see the iron and wooden hoops, and various tools, such as saws, axes, spoke-shaves, stocks, and bits, adzes, augers, &c. &c. The structure and uses of the saw and the axe are too well-known to stand in need of description.

Spoke-shaves are of different kinds; they are intended for uses similar to those for which the Carpenter adapts his planes: two of them are represented in the plate; one hangs by a handle not far from the right hand of the Cooper, and the other lies on the large block of wood, which is useful for various purposes.

The *stock and bit* make but one instrument; it hangs over the left shoulder of the Cooper. The *stock* is the handle, and the *bit* is a sort of piercer, that fits into the bottom of the stock: bits of various sorts are adapted to the same stock, of course the bit is always moveable, and may be instantly re-placed to one of a different bore.

An *adze* is a cutting tool of the axe kind, having its blade made very thin and arching: it is used chiefly for taking off thin chips, and for cutting the hollow sides of boards, &c.

Augers are used for boring large holes: they are a kind of large gimblet, consisting of a wooden handle and an iron blade, which is terminated with a steel bit. One of these instruments hangs between the saw, and stock and bit, but above them; and two different kinds are near the right hand of the Cooper.

A *drawing-knife* is also a tool of the utmost im-portance in this trade; it is sometimes straight and sometimes bent, in order to give the staves that cir-cular form which they are designed to have in a cask, or other round vessel: this tool, and the spoke-shave, with the Cooper almost supersede the neces-sity of the plane.

There is one other little tool peculiar to the Cooper, called a *drift,* which he uses for the purpose of striking on, to drive down the hoops. It is made of iron, for driving down iron hoops, and of some hard wood for wooden hoops: without this little tool the operation of straining the hoops could not be per-formed.

The trade of the Cooper was formerly among the cries of London; " any work for the Cooper?" is now heard, though rarely, in some parts of the country. A travelling Cooper carries with him a few hoops of different sizes, some of iron, rivets, and wooden pegs; his hammer, adze, drift, and stock and bit. With these few instruments he can repair all washing and brewing utensils, besides the churns and wooden vessels made use of in dairies. An in-genious workman will, in his peregrinations, readily

F 3

perform various jobs which belong to the carpenter, in villages which are too small to support a person of that trade.

A journeyman Cooper will earn from three to five shillings per day.

Every custom-house and excise-office has an officer called *the King's-Cooper;* and every large ship has a Cooper on board, whose business is to look after all the casks intended for liquids.

The Copper-Plate Printer.

THE COPPER-PLATE PRINTER.

THE COPPER-PLATE PRINTER is a person who transfers portraits, landscapes, and a variety of other pictures and writing, from engravings on copper to paper, by a very ingenious process, of which we are now to speak.

This art is said to have been as ancient as the year 1450, and to owe its origin to Finguerra, a Florentine goldsmith, who accidentally pouring some melted brimstone on an engraved plate, found the exact impression of the engraving left in the cold brimstone, marked with black taken out of the strokes by the liquid sulphur: upon this he attempted to do the same on silver plates with wet paper, by rolling it smoothly with a roller; and this succeeded. But this art was not used in England till the reign of King James I. when it was brought from Antwerp by Speed.

The principal things requisite in this business, are the ink, and a press, called a rolling-press.

The ink used for Copper-plate printing is a composition made of stones of peaches and apricots, the bones of sheep, and ivory, all well burnt; and, as the best which is used in this business comes from Frankfort on the Main, it is known by the name of Frankfort-black. It comes over in cakes, and being mixed with nut-oil, that has been well boiled, it is ground by the printer on a marble, after the same manner as painters do their colours: a palette knife is of course used in this part of the business.

F 4

The rolling-press may be distinguished into two parts, the *body* and the *carriage;* the body consists of two cheeks or upright posts, joined at top and bottom by cross pieces, and placed perpendicularly on a wooden stand or foot, which sustains the whole press. From this foot rise four other perpendicular pieces, joined also by cross ones: this may be considered as the carriage, because it serves to sustain a smooth even plank, upon which the engraved plate is placed.

Into the cheeks are inserted two wooden cylinders, the ends of which being much smaller than the bodies, are called *trunnions,* and turn in the cheeks between two pieces of wood, in form of half-moons, lined with polished iron to prevent friction.

The spaces left vacant by the trunnion are filled with paste-board or paper, that they may be raised or lowered at discretion; so as only to leave the space between them necessary for the carriage of the plank, loaded with the plate, paper, and cloths, which consist of swan-skin and a piece of broadcloth.

To one of the trunnions of the upper roller is fastened a cross, consisting of two levers, the arms of which give a motion to the upper roller, and that again to the under one, so that the plank is drawn by this means backwards and forwards.

The press and the ink being prepared, the printer takes a small quantity of this ink on a rubber made of linen rags, with which he smears the whole face of the plate as it lies on a grate over a small fire made of old coal, (the grate, linen rubber, &c. are represented in the left hand side of the engraving, which accompanies this description.)

The plate being sufficiently inked, the printer takes it to a part of the bench called the jigger, and wipes it first with a rag, then with the hand, over which he has rubbed a piece of whiting. The great art consists in wiping the plate perfectly clean, without taking the ink out of the engraving. The plate thus prepared, is laid on the plank of the press; over the plate is spread the paper, which has been previously moistened; and the arms of the cross are now to be pulled, and by that means the plate, with its furniture, is carried between the rollers, over which are the swan-skin and broad-cloth : these pinching very strongly, yet equally, in every part, force the moistened paper into the strokes of the engraving, whence it brings away the ink.

Some works require to be passed through the press twice, and once is sufficient for others, according as the graving is more or less deep, or as the print is required to be of a lighter or darker shade.

After the prints are taken off, the plate is rubbed over with olive oil to prevent its rusting, and set by against a new impression. If the strokes get filled within, and hardened in the course of working, the plates are boiled in strong ley before the oil is applied.

It is said that earl Stanhope has introduced such improvements in the art of engraving, as will enable the artist to take off, from a well-engraved plate, at least ten thousand impressions.

Thus the paintings of the greatest masters are multiplied to a boundless extent; and the lovers of the polite arts, in every part of the globe, are enabled to enjoy those advantages from which their situations seem to have deprived them.

A journeyman Copper-plate printer, will earn forty shillings a week. And from a strongly engraved plate, three or four thousand good impressions may be taken; and even then the plate may be repaired, and fitted up for other editions.

THE CORK-CUTTER.

The Cork-cutter cuts the bark which is stripped from the cork-tree, into a variety of small round cylindrical pieces, for the purpose of stopping casks, bottles, phials, &c.

The Cork-tree is a species of oak, and this, as well as the uses to which its bark is put, was known to the Greeks and Romans: by the former of whom it was called *phellos*, and by the latter *suber*. By the Romans, we learn from Pliny, it was even employed to stop vessels of every kind; but its application to this use seems not to have been very common, till the invention of glass bottles, of which professor Beckmann finds no mention before the fifteenth century.

The Cork-tree grows thirty or forty feet high, having a thick, rough, and fungous bark: its leaves are green above, and white underneath; its fruit is an acorn, which is produced in great abundance. The bark is taken off by making an incision from the top to the bottom, and likewise one at each extremity round the tree, and perpendicular to the first. The old bark being thus detached, the tree still lives, not being in the smallest degree injured; and in six or seven years a succeeding bark is again fit for use.

The Cork-tree is found in great abundance in France, Spain, and Italy: from these countries we receive the bark.

The bark, when stripped from the tree, is piled

The Cork Cutter.

up in a pit or pond, and loaded with heavy stones to flatten it; it is then taken to be dried, when it is fit for sale.

Corks are divided into bungs for stopping casks, wine-corks for bottles, and phial-corks for stopping phials, &c.

The Cork-cutter's business requires but little ingenuity; the knives used in the operation have a peculiar construction, and they must be exceedingly sharp. The knife is almost the only instrument wanted in the trade. The principal demand for corks, is for the purpose of stopping bottles; these are cut by men and women, who receive a certain price *per gross* for their labour. Cork-cutters sell, also, corks by the gross. It is one of the blackest and dirtiest of trades, and not very profitable either for the master or the journeyman.

Cork is, likewise, used by young people in learning the art of swimming; such are those represented in the plate as hanging from the ceiling.

The cork waistcoat is composed of four pieces of cork; two for the breast, and two for the back, each nearly as long as the waistcoat without flaps. The cork is covered and adapted to fit the body. It is open before, and may be fastened either with strings, or buckles and straps. The waistcoat weighs about twelve ounces, and may be made at the expence of a few shillings. This article of dress would be very useful to all persons who travel much by water, or who are in the habit of bathing in the open sea. Cork is also used for the inner soles of shoes.

A cork spencer has lately been invented, to save persons from drowning in cases of shipwreck. It consists of a belt, containing refuse pieces of cork, inclosed in any kind of covering, and fastened round the body with tapes.

In Spain cork is burnt to make that light kind of black, called Spanish-black, which is very much used by painters. The Egyptians make their cof-

F 6

fins of cork; and these, when lined with a certain resinous composition, preserve the dead a great length of time. In Spain, they even line the walls of their houses with cork, which not only renders the apartments warm, but corrects the moisture of the air.

Cork, when burnt and reduced to powder, is often taken internally as an astringent ; and it has been said that cups made of cork are useful for hectic persons to drink their common beverage from.

Fossil cork is the name given to a kind of stone, which is the lightest of all stones ; it is a species of amianthus, consisting of flexible fibres loosely inter-woven, and resembling the vegetable cork ; it is fusible in the fire, and forms black glass.

The Currier.

THE CURRIER.

———

THE business of the Currier is to prepare hides which have been under the hands of the tanner, for the use of shoe-makers, coach-makers, saddlers, book-binders, &c.

The Currier derives his name from *Coriarius*, a worker in leather; and for the antiquity of the trade, although not the modern art of currying, the reader may be referred to the seventeenth book of Homer's Iliad, line four hundred and fifty.

The use of skins is very ancient, the first garments in the world having been made of them. *Moroccos* are made of the skins of a kind of goats. Parchment is made of sheep-skins. The true chamois leather is made of the skin of an animal of the same name, though it is frequently counterfeited with common goats' and sheeps' skins.

The Curriers have been an incorporated company ever since the beginning of the reign of James the First: during the reign of Queen Elizabeth, history records an account of a fierce contention between the Curriers and Shoe-makers, respecting the dressing of leather, and the price to be paid them for their work; and also respecting the places in which leather should be sold. At length it was stipulated, in the year 1590, among other articles, that the Curriers should have the dressing of all the leather brought into Leadenhall and Southwark markets, and within three miles of London.

Currying is the last preparation of leather, and puts it into a condition to be made up into shoes, saddles, harness, &c.; it is performed in two ways, either upon the *flesh* or the *grain.*

In dressing leather for shoes, on the *flesh*, the first operation is soaking the leather in water till it be thoroughly wet; then the flesh side is shaved on a board, called a *beam-board;* that is, a piece of *lignum-vitæ*, about two feet long, two inches thick, and six inches wide, placed on a wooden block fixed on the ground, to which the Currier stands at his work, with a knife which has two edges; the blade is rectangular, about twelve inches long, and from four to six inches wide, and varying in size and weight according to the work to be performed; one end has a straight, the other a cross handle, in the plane of the knife. It is brought to a wire edge by rubbing on a stone of a coarse grit, which is afterwards taken off, and a finer edge produced by a finer and softer stone. The cross handle of the knife is then firmly fixed between the workman's knees, and while in a kneeling posture, he turns the edges to an angle with their former position, by means of a polished steel, similar in shape to a butcher's steel. They are kept in order chiefly by a smaller steel, which the man holds constantly between his fingers, and passes along the knives, the point within, and the side without the groove, formed by the turned edge, as occasion requires; and as often as the edges are worn they are renewed in the same way.

Beam-boards are imported sawed into the size and shape in which the Curriers use them. The name of Cox of Gloucester, is known throughout Europe as the principal maker of Curriers' knives. Lane of Cirencester, is also an approved maker; a patent has lately been obtained by Mr. Bingley, of Birmingham, for an improvement in the manufacture of their knives; but they have not been sufficiently tried to enable us to decide on the merits of the improvement: from what we have seen, they are, however, certainly well worth the master's attention.

Having thus prepared the knife, the wet skin is thrown over the beam with the flesh side outwards, and the man keeps it in its position, by the pressure of his knees as he leans over the beam. The knife is then applied horizontally to the leather, and by repeated strokes downwards it is reduced to the substance required.

After the leather is properly shaved, it is thrown into water again, and scoured upon a board or stone appropriated to the use. Scouring is performed by rubbing the grain or hair side with a piece of pumice-stone, or some other stone of a good grit, by which means a white sort of substance is forced out of the leather, called the bloom, produced in the operation of tanning. The hide is then conveyed to the shade, or drying-place, when the oily substances are applied, which are put on both sides of the leather, but in a greater and thicker quantity on the flesh than on the hair side. Thus far is the process of currying in its wet state, and thus far it is called *getting out*.

When the skin is quite dry, it undergoes other operations for the purpose of softening the leather. Whitening or paring succeeds, which is performed with a fine edge on the knife already described. It is then *boarded up*, or grained again, by applying the graining board first to the grain, and then to the flesh side.

It is now fit for waxing, which is performed by rubbing it with a brush dipped in a composition of oil and lamp-black, on the flesh side, till it be thoroughly black, it is then *sized*, called black-sizing, with a brush or sponge, dried and tallowed. After undergoing some other operations, this sort of leather, called waxed leather, is curried.

For leather curried on the hair side, termed black on the *grain*, the first operation is the same as that already described, till it is scoured. Then the black, which is a solution of copperas in bark liquor, is applied to it while wet: this is first put upon the grain, after it has been rubbed over with a brush dipped in urine; and when it is dry, it is *seasoned*, that is, rubbed over with a brush dipped in copperas water on the grain, till it be perfectly black: after this the grain is raised with a fine graining-board, and the leather is oiled with a mixture of oil and tallow, when it is finished, and fit for the shoe-maker.

Hides are sometimes *curried* for the use of saddlers and collar-makers, but the principal operations are much the same as those which have been already described. Hides for the roofs of coaches are shaved nearly as thin as those for shoes, and blacked on the grain.

A fact worthy of remark is, that oil is imbibed more uniformly and effectually by wet than by dry leather, and this most probably arises from the gradual evaporation of the water, which gives place to the introduction of the oil, by capillary attraction; whereas the air, if interspersed in the pores, would resist it.

In the plate we see the Currier engaged in his business: on his right hand and on his left are hides which have undergone part of the operation; and behind him, pinned to the wall, are two skins, finished except the drying.

In many places the business of a Currier connects with it that of the leather-dresser and leather-cutter, who supplies the shoe-makers and others with all their leather, black, red, blue, green, &c.

Leadenhall-Market, in London, is one of the principal marts for leather: and shoe-makers and leather-cutters in the country, who command the capital, buy the greater part of their goods, particularly their sole or butt leather, there.

The Indian women, in Carolina and Virginia, dress buck and doe-skin with a considerable degree of skill; and so quick, that a single woman will completely dress eight or ten skins a day.

Curriers exercise their trade under a license from the Board of Excise, which they take out annually, and they are obliged to specify in the entry every room in which leather is deposited, as well as the vats and tubs in which it is soaked. Their premises are of course subject to the inspection of Excise-Officers, and any hide not having the tanners' duty-mark is liable to seizure.

No Currier can use the trade of a butcher, tanner, &c. nor shall he curry skins insufficiently tanned, nor gash hides or leather on pain of forfeiting for every hide or skin 6s. 8d. Curriers not currying the leather sufficiently shall forfeit the ware or the value, &c. 1 Jac. c. 22. If Curriers do not curry leather sent to them within sixteen days, between michaelmas and lady-day, and in eight days at other times, they are liable to a forfeiture of 5l. 12 Geo. II. c. 25.

THE CUTLER.

———

The manufacture of edged tools is one of the first arts amongst men in every state of society.

Though the art of the Cutler, in a general sense, comprises all those articles denominated edge-tools, it is more particularly confined to the manufacture of knives, forks, scissars, pen-knives, razors, and swords.

Damascus was anciently famed for its razors and swords. The latter are said to possess the advantages of flexibility, elasticity, and hardness.

Knives and swords have been in use amongst mankind from the earliest periods, but forks and bayonets are comparatively of modern invention.

Forks have not been invented much more than two hundred years: in early times they were not known, even at the entertainments of a sovereign; but the guest who sat nearest to a joint held one part with his fingers while he carved the other with his knife. They appear to have had their origin in Italy, and to have been introduced into this country either in the latter end of Queen Elizabeth's reign, or in the beginning of the reign of James the First; but they were not very common till after the restoration.

The first bayonets were daggers, which, after the soldiers had exhausted their ammunition, they fitted to the bore of their muskets. They were introduced into France about the year 1673; and among the English grenadiers in the short reign of

The Cutler.

James the Second. Many are yet to be seen in the small armoury in the Tower. The use of them, fastened to the muzzle of the firelock, was also a French improvement, first adopted about 1690, and which was universally followed by the rest of Europe a few years afterwards.

Those articles of cutlery which do not require a fine polish, and are of low price, are made from blistered steel. Those articles which require the edge to possess great tenacity, and at the same time superior hardness is not required, are made from sheer steel. The finer kinds of cutlery are made from steel which has been in a state of fusion, and which is termed cast-steel, no other kinds being susceptible of a fine polish. Table-knives are mostly made of sheer-steel, the tong and shoulder being of iron, the blade being attached by giving them a welding heat. The knives after forging are hardened by heating them red-hot, and plunging them into water; they are afterwards heated over the fire till they become blue, and then ground. The handles of table knives are made of ivory, horn, bone, stag-horn, and wood, into which the blades are cemented with rosin and pulverized brick. Forks are made altogether by the aid of the stamp and appropriate dies. The prongs only are hardened and tempered. Razors are made of cast-steel; the edge of a razor requiring the combined advantages of great hardness and tenacity.

The chief art in this business consists in softening hardened steel, by the application of a heat not greater than that which was employed in hardening it; for this purpose it is gradually heated, more or less according to the temper required, and cooled again either gradually or rapidly, this making no difference; after which the steel is found to be softened or tempered exactly in proportion to the heat which it has undergone; while the steel is tempering its surface displays a succession of colours, supposed to arise from a commencing oxidation, in, proportion as it becomes more and more heated, which the workmen in this metal have ingeniously taken advantage of, as serving to denominate the degree of temper required for different articles.

The first perceptible colour is a light straw-colour, and this being produced by a small degree of heat, indicates the highest or hardest temper; to this succeeds a full yellow, then a brown, afterwards a reddish blue, then a light blue, and lastly a, full deep blue, passing into black; which being the, other extremity of the series, denotes the lowest degree of temper, and a hardness only a little superior to what the piece of steel would have acquired if, when heated for the purpose of being hardened, it had been allowed to cool gradually, instead of being plunged into a cold liquid.

The old method of tempering, which is practised even yet by many manufacturers, is to lay the articles on a clear coal-fire or on a hot bar, till they exhibit the requisite colours; but small articles which are to be reduced to a blue temper are commonly blazed; that is, they are first dipped in oil or melted grease, and then held over the fire till the oil becomes inflamed and thus evaporated.

The following table shews the temperature at which the various colours make their appearance.

430° to 450° the several tints of straw-colour fit for razors, and such instruments as have a keen edge and a stout back.

470° a full yellow, and proper for scalpels, penknives, and other fine-edged instruments.

490° the brown yellow, and a proper temper for scissars and small shears.

500° the first tinge of purple, the proper temper for pocket and pruning-knives.

530° indicates purple, the temper for table and carving knives.

550° to 560° the different shades for blue, a temper fit for watch-springs, swords, and wherever great elasticity is required.

600° corresponds with black, and the lowest degree of temper. *Aikin's Dictionary.*

The principal places in this country for the manufacture of cutlery wares are Birmingham, Sheffield, Walsall, Wolverhampton, and London; at those towns goods of all kinds in steel are made much cheaper than in any other part of the world. In London, the same goods bear a much higher price than those manufactured in the country, although perhaps the latter may be as good in quality, yet they are not so neatly finished. Surgeons' instruments are, however, beyond question best of metropolitan manufacture.

It is said that it is not a very uncommon practice for London Cutlers to affix their own names and marks on goods wrought in Birmingham, Sheffield, &c. by which names they can obtain for them more readily the price of town-made goods.

The man represented in the back part of the plate is supposed to be forging some instrument, while the other in the front is grinding a knife on the stone, which is turned round by the labourer at the wheel. On the ground are supposed to lie a pair of irons for skates, and two sword-blades. The manufacture of skates is a part of the Cutler's business in severe winters; and in some of the principal shops swords are also mounted; but this does not properly belong to the Cutler's profession. The sword-blades almost all come from abroad, where they are forged by large hammers moved by watermills. In this manner the celebrated sword-blades of Solingen are made. Here the Cutler is only concerned in mounting the blades, and in making the scabbards, the expense of which may be carried to any extent. It is no uncommon thing for a sword highly finished to be worth from a hundred and fifty to three hundred guineas.

As shaving to many people is a very painful operation, Cutlers, in different countries, have long exerted all their skill to remove the inconvenience, but without that sort of success which may always be relied on. To whatever price we go for razors, we cannot depend upon their goodness; and it often happens that in a case of razors purchased at Sheffield at a shilling a piece, we may find as many good ones as in a case bought in London at ten times the price.

Ivory, with which some handles of knives are made, may be turned like wood, and it may by a chemical process be softened, worked into a particular form, and hardened again. There are methods also of colouring or staining ivory, so that we have red and green ivory as well as white: some of these methods may be seen in the article Combmaker.

The surgical instrument-maker is another species of Cutler: he makes use of the best steel, and is supposed to be more careful in finishing his instruments with a neater polish than common Cutlers.

It has been recommended by a professional gentleman to dip all surgical instruments in oil previously to using, except the lancet intended for inoculation.

A journeyman Cutler will with ease earn two guineas a week: those employed in the finer sorts of work much more. In all large shops one man is employed a certain number of days in each week in grinding old work; and this part of the business pays the master well.

THE DISTILLER.

DISTILLATION is the act of dropping or falling in drops, and is more particularly applied to a process in which water or other liquids are placed over fire in suitable vessels, and certain parts are separated from other parts of the same liquid by the agency of heat: it is in every sense of the term a chemical process.

Distillation is of considerable antiquity: of all the vessels destined to this use the alembic is the simplest and the most ancient. Both Dioscorides and Pliny mention the ambix, which is described by the latter of these writers: it is probable that it was in his time a mere plain still, without any beak or gutter. The Alchemists having adopted this instrument, prefixed the Arabian article *al* to its name, and made considerable alteration in its form: the characteristic difference between an alembic and a still seems to be in the construction of the head or capital, which in the alembic is contrived not merely to collect, but to condense the vapour; whereas the corresponding part of a still serves merely to collect the vapour which is transmitted in an elastic state through the beak and condensed in the worm. Most of the French brandies, we are informed, are prepared by the alembic, properly so called, whereas all British spirits are drawn over from a still.

The English still is of a very simple construction; it is usually made of copper, and consists of a body somewhat cylindrical, and contracted at the top, called the neck, so as to admit conveniently the head or moveable upper part, which is contracted also from its bellied rotundity above, into it a few inches; by which means, with proper luting, the head and body become one vessel. At the top of the head is soldered a curved tube, gradually lessening as it descends in the shape of a swan's neck, the beak of which tube is inserted a few inches into another tube called a *worm*, from its spiral convolutions: this juncture is also in distillation closely luted. The worm is made of pewter, and is fixed in a frame in a vessel called a worm-tub; it goes gradually descending about six times round; the upper end projecting a few inches out of the upper part of the side of the worm-tub next the still, and the lower end projecting also a few inches out of the side of the lower part of the worm-tub at a suitable distance from the still, where can be placed a proper vessel to receive the distilled product. The worm-tub is of course filled with water, to condense and cool the liquor as it comes over.

The still is usually, unless very small, furnished with a cock at its bottom, to draw off the remaining fluid after the distillation is effected; and is set with bricks in the same way as the common furnace for boiling liquids usually is.

We shall include Distillation and Rectification in one article, although in this country, particularly in the metropolis and its neighbouring villages, they make two distinct trades.

The great object of the Distiller ought to be to procure a perfectly flavourless spirit, which is not an easy task. The materials for distillation that have in this country been used in large quantities, are malt, molasses, and sugar. All these abound with an oily matter, which rising with the spirit, communicates a disagreeable flavour, from which it is with the utmost difficulty freed.

Previously to the operation of distilling, those of brewing and fermentation are necessary. Methods have been suggested, and, we believe, carried into practice, for reducing the brewing and fermentation to one operation, which are said to improve the spirit in quality, and greatly to augment its quantity. The following is the process: take ten pounds of malt, reduced to fine meal, and three pounds of common wheat-meal: add to these two gallons of water, and stir them well together; then add five gallons of water boiling-hot, and stir the whole well together. Let it stand two hours, and then stir it again; and when grown cold add to it two ounces of solid yeast, and set it by, loosely covered, in rather a warm place, to ferment. This is called the Dutch method of preparing what is called the wash for malt spirit. In London and its neighbourhood, the method is to draw and mash for spirits, as is done for beer in the article brewing, except, that instead of boiling the wort, it is pumped into coolers, and afterwards drawn into backs to be then fermented: of course no hops are used. Thus, in the opinion of some persons conversant with the subject, twice as much labour as is necessary is bestowed, and a large quantity of spirit is lost by leaving the gross bottoms out of the still for fear of burning.

All simple spirits may be considered in their different states of low-wines, proof-spirits, and alcohol, or rectified spirits. The first contain only one-sixth of spirit to five-sixths of water. Proof-spirits contain about one half, or rather more, of totally inflammable spirits; and alcohol, if very pure, consists wholly of spirit without any admixture or adulteration.

Malt low-wines, which is the first state after distillation from the *wash,* prepared in the usual way,

G

are exceedingly nauseous, owing to the gross oil of the malt which abounds in it. When these are distilled gently, and by a slow fire, into proof-spirits, they leave a considerable quantity of this fœtid oil behind in the still, with the phlegm; the liquor loses its milky colour, and is clear and bright. When the proof-spirit, from malt, is distilled over again, to be brought to the state of alcohol, or rectified spirits, the utmost attention must be paid to the fire, or some of the oil will be forced over, and injure the whole process. The use of the *balneum mariæ*, instead of the common still, though a much more tedious process, would effectually prevent this mischief, and give a purer spirit in one rectification, than can be procured by many, by the common methods. The *balneum mariæ*, is a copper cylinder, with a bottom made to be inserted into the still, and to descend within a few inches of its bottom, so that the materials to be distilled can be placed within it, and yet have no communication with the other part of the still, which is filled two-thirds, or thereabouts, with water: the head of the still is made to fit the bath, the same as it does the still itself: by these means a more regular and equable heat is applied to the liquor to be distilled, and which cannot be easily raised much above the boiling point, or 212° of Fahrenheit's thermometer.

Malt spirit, and indeed spirits from other substances, must be brought into the state of alcohol, before they are adapted to internal uses; after which they are said to be more fit for the purpose than even French brandy; but this admits of considerable doubt: French Brandy containing an essential oil, or some resinous matter, which English spirits have not, that is peculiarly grateful to the stomach.

A quarter of malt will generally afford, depending upon its goodness and the season of the year, from eight to fourteen gallons of alcohol.

The Malt Distiller always gives his spirit a single rectification, *per se*, to purify it a little; in this state, though certainly not adapted to internal use, it is frequently, and at once, distilled into gin, or other ordinary compounds, for the common people; who, in this country, injure their health, and eventually destroy their constitutions, by the free use of them. The Dutch never give it any further rectification than this: they distil the *wash* into low wines, and then at once into full-proof spirit, from which they manufacture their celebrated Holland's geneva, or gin.

The spirit loses in these processes the vinous character which it had when it came out of the hands of the Malt Distiller: the alkaline salts, used by the rectifier, uniting with the oleous and aqueous parts of the liquor, it is necessary to add an extraneous substance, to give it a flavour, and this is frequently done by sweet spirits of nitre; the common method of applying this, is by mixing it to the taste with rectified spirits. This is said to give the flavour of French brandy to our English spirits; but we think it a poor imitation, and that it is readily detected, by even indifferent judges of that liquor: other flavours are given to spirits, by putting articles into the still, so that the flavours may come over with the distilled liquor. Compound Distillers mix with malt spirits, juniper berries, angelica root, aniseeds, turpentine, &c. and distill the whole over again, the produce of which is gin, spirit of aniseed, &c.

Rum is distilled from sugar in the West Indies; and having a great quantity of the essential oil of the sugar dissolved in it, it obtains by these means its characteristic taste and smell. The brandy made in France, particularly in Cogniac, Bourdeaux, and Rochelle, bears the highest price: it is, in its pure state, colourless, and obtains, perhaps, its yellow tint by extracting the colouring matter from the casks in which it is kept, or more probably it is coloured specifically by the French themselves, or by the first importers.

The Malt distillers feed and fatten innumerable quantities of pigs upon the grains left after brewing: but the pork and lard obtained from these pigs have a flabby softness about them, very different from pork fed in the usual way in the country; and, of course, do not fetch so high a price.

Spirits from sugar and molasses, are made by distilling them in water, and fermenting them in the same way as the wort from malt.

Perhaps there is no trade in the British dominions, the drug-trade excepted, which affords such facilities for fraud and adulteration; and not one in which larger fortunes have been made, we hope to the satisfaction of the minds of those now enjoying them. A Malt Distiller requires a large capital, and much room to carry on his various operations.

Distilleries are under the close inspection and superintendence of the Board of Excise, and the proprietors of them are obliged to take out an annual license.

The Dyer

THE DYER.

The art of the Dyer consists in tinging cloth, stuffs, or other substances, with a permanent colour, which penetrates its substance. Dyeing differs from bleaching, which is not the giving of a new colour, but brightening an old one. It differs, also, from painting, printing, or stamping, because the colours in these only reach the surface. The nature of the Dyer's business is very well represented in the opposite plate.

The origin of the art of dyeing is involved in the same kind of obscurity which pervades the history of all those arts connected with the common wants and necessaries of life. Accident, probably, furnished a multitude of instances of observation, which enabled the rudest people to imitate the colours of birds and beasts. The bruising of a fruit, a flower, a leaf, is one of the most natural and obvious occurrences to which we should look for the first notion of applying vegetable juices to dyeing, and a knowledge of the tingent properties of various herbs was thus early acquired. The art of dyeing, probably, made considerable progress antecedent to the period in which regular history begins. Moses speaks of stuffs dyed blue, and purple, and scarlet, and of sheep-skins dyed red.

That the people of this country were acquainted with the art of dyeing wool, yarn, and cloth, of different colours, at a very early period, will need no proof here. The art of dyeing the scarlet

G 3

colour, however, by a small insect of the kermes or cochineal kind, appears to have been discovered A.D. 1000.

By an act of parliament, passed in 1581, for abolishing certain deceitful stuff used in dyeing cloth, we find logwood, or blackwood, of late years brought into this " realm," expressly prohibited; " the colours thereof being false and deceitful to the queen's subjects at home, and discreditable beyond sea to our merchants and dyers." Its use was again prohibited in 1597' as well as in the reign of James. But in 1661, the different laws, prohibiting its use were repealed, it being found that " the ingenious industry of these times hath taught the Dyers of England the art of fixing the colours made of logwood, *alias* blackwood, so as that, by experience, they are found as lasting and serviceable as the colours made with any other sort of dyeingwood."

The mystery of the art of dyeing consists chiefly in chemical processes; and it comprises a vast collection of chemical experiments.

The substances principally subjected to this art, are wool, hair, silk, cotton, hemp, and flax. Of these, the animal productions, namely, wool, hair, and silk, take the dye more readily than the vegetable substances, cotton, hemp, and flax, because they seem to have a stronger attraction for the colouring particles of the various dyes employed.

Wool is naturally of a greasy nature, and requires to be scoured before it is submitted to the process of dyeing.

Silk, previously to dyeing, must be washed with soap and warm water, and then in a cold solution of alum and water.

Cotton and *linen* require bleaching and scouring in alkaline ley. After this, they must be steeped in a strong solution of alum and water, then washed in clear water, and afterwards rinsed in a decoction of galls, or some other astringent, as hot as the work-man can bear.

The first step of dyeing is the application of what is termed a *mordant:* that is, something must be employed to make the substances take the dye : for by merely immersing them in the dyeing liquor, they will seldom take or retain a deep dye.

., Different mordants are used for preparing the same goods, and for preparing goods for different colouring drugs. Alum is the most extensively useful, being always employed for linens and cottons. For the dyeing of silk and wool, metallic solutions are more frequently used as mordants, because they have a stronger attraction for animal than vegetable substances.

In dyeing, there are but three simple colours, the *red, yellow,* and *blue;* all other colours are compounded of these. Different shades or tints of the same colour are produced by using different drugs, or by varying the quantity of colouring particles.

Cochineal, kermes, and gum-lac, amongst the animal productions; and madder, archil, carthamus, and Brazil-wood, amongst the vegetable, are the chief substances employed as *red* dyes.

All the substances employed for dyeing *yellow* colours are vegetable productions; and the principal *blue* dyes are from indigo, woad, logwood, and Prussian blue.

Compound colours are produced sometimes, by mixing the simple colours in the dyeing liquor, and sometimes by dyeing the stuff first in a bath of one simple colour, then in another.

The principal substances employed to give a *black* colour, are *galls,* which contain the astringent principle, or tannin, and an acid, called the gallic acid, and the red oxide of iron. The black colour is produced by the combination of the astringent principle, with the oxide of iron in conjunction with the acid, and fixed on the stuff.

Logwood is not to be considered as affording a black dye, but it is much employed to give a lustre to black colours.

Of the substances employed in dyeing *brown*, walnut-peels and sumach are the principal.

Scarlet dyeing in general, is a distinct and separate branch of trade; the materials being of that delicate kind, as easily to be injured by any accidental admixture of other colours, and part of the apparatus being somewhat different from common dyeing.

A dye-house, which should be set down as near as possible to a stream of water, should be spacious and well lighted. It should be floored with plaster, and proper means should be adopted to carry off water, or spent baths, by channels or gutters, so that every operation may be conducted with the utmost attention to cleanliness. The size and position of the caldrons are to be regulated by the nature and extent of the operations for which they are designed. Excepting for scarlet and other delicate colours, in which tin is used as a mordant, the caldrons should be of brass or copper. Brass being less apt than copper to be acted on by chemical agents, and to communicate spots to the stuffs, is fitter for the purpose of a dyeing vessel. It is of the greatest consequence that the coppers or caldrons be well cleaned for every operation; and that vessels of a large size should be furnished at the bottom with a pipe and a stop-cock for the greater convenience of emptying them. There must be a hole in the wall, or chimney, above each copper, to admit poles for the purpose of draining the stuffs which are immersed, so that the liquor may fall back into the vessel, and no part may be lost.

Dyes for silk, where a boiling heat is not necessary, are prepared in troughs or backs, which are long copper or wooden vessels. The colours which are used for silks are extremely delicate; they must, therefore, be dried quickly, and not be long exposed to the action of the air, that there may be no risk of change: for this purpose it is necessary to have a drying-room heated with a stove.

Notwithstanding the discoveries of modern chemistry in the art of dyeing, and the permanency with which colours are now affixed to cloths, there yet remain many secrets in this branch of the arts known but to a few persons; and who in consequence have much emolument to themselves: and it will sometimes happen that with the utmost skill and ingenuity, and the application of chemical principles too, that the unlettered plodder shall in the arts excel the most acute practical philosopher of the age.

In London there are dyers of all sorts; some dye only wool, others silk; some confine themselves to particular colours, such as scarlet and blue. The scarlet dyeing is said to be the most ingenious and the most profitable. The business of a Dyer is laborious and chilly; the workmen are constantly dabbling in water, hot and cold. Silk-dyers have the least laborious business: journeymen will earn thirty shillings a week.

THE ENGRAVER.

——◆——

ENGRAVING on copper, wood, stone, &c. is employed in representing different subjects, as portraits, historical pieces, landscapes, &c. either after paintings, or after designs made for the purpose. It is performed either with the *graver,* the *dry point,* or with *aquafortis.*

The art of engraving in England has gradually arisen to its present advanced state from the rude mechanical practice of our British ancestors. That it was practised in this island from a very early period, may be seen by the remains of the instruments of war, and other antiquities which have been found in the Celtic and Saxon *tumuli :* these frequently bear the marks of the graver, or some tool very similar to it ; and the numerous coins of antiquity must satisfy every inquirer of the early British existence of this species of engraving ; an art which is thought to have been introduced from Rome.

Engraving has been performed in different countries and at different periods of time on various substances, chiefly on metals, wood, and the oriental precious stones called gems ; but with instruments which have varied but little since their first invention. Engraving on copper for the purpose of producing impressions on paper may almost be said to be an art of modern invention ; for though the ancients ornamented their armour, metal vases, &c. by this means, they

5

The Engraver.

never appear to have thought of printing from the incisions or lines cut with the graver; nor was it thought of till about the middle of the fifteenth century. This art is ascribed to a goldsmith at Florence, who having placed a sheet of oiled paper under a plate of silver that was engraved, and on which by accident he had laid a heavy weight, was surprised to find a complete impression of the plate on the paper.

Engravings on copper may be divided into several species as engraving in aquatinta; in the chalk manner; with aquafortis in mezzotinto; and the original art of engraving in lines. We shall begin with the latter.

The tools necessary for engraving in lines are gravers, a scraper, burnisher, an oil-stone, a sand-bag, an oil-rubber, and some good charcoal.

The gravers are instruments of tempered steel fitted into a wooden handle. They are either square or in the lozenge form; the first is used in cutting very broad strokes, and the other for fainter and more delicate lines.

The scraper is a three-edged tool for scraping off the burr or roughness raised by the graver.

Burnishers are for rubbing down lies that may be cut too deep, or for taking out scratches or defects in the copper; they are made of hard steel well rounded and polished.

The oil-stone is for sharpening the gravers, and the oil-rubber and charcoal for polishing the plate when necessary.

The sand-bag or cushion is for laying the plate upon for the convenience of turning it round in any direction: this is principally used by engravers of writing.

Having the copper, tools, and drawing ready, the first thing is to lay the design on the plate: for this purpose the plate is to be covered over with a thin

skin of virgin wax; and the drawing or picture is
to be copied on paper with a black-lead pencil, or
any matter that is free from gum : this paper is to
be laid upon the plate with its penciled side upon
the wax, and pressed all over so completely that
when the paper is withdrawn the impression may
remain upon the waxed plate; then with a sharp
pointed tool trace the design through the wax on to
the copper. The plate is now to be warmed and
the wax cleaned off; after which the engraving is to
be finished by means of the gravers.

The dry-point or needle, so called, because not
used till the ground is taken off the plate, is principally employed in the extremely light parts of water,
sky, drapery, &c.

Etching is a method of engraving on copper, in
which the lines or strokes instead of being cut with
a tool or graver are bit in with aquafortis or nitrous
acid, which is thus performed : the copper-plate is
first warmed, and then thinly covered with varnish ;
it is then to be blackened over with the smoke of a
wax candle.

The *ground* being now *laid* and suffered to cool,
the next operation is to transfer the design to the
plate. For this purpose the drawing must be traced
on oiled paper with pen and ink, having some ox's
gall mixed with it. Another piece of white paper
must be rubbed with flake-white, and laid on the
varnished copper, with the white side next the
plate: upon this is to be put the traced oil paper,
and fastened with a piece of bordering wax to the
copper.

When this is done all the lines in the tracing
must be gone over with a blunt etching-needle; by
which means the lines will be transferred to the
ground when the papers are taken away.

The plate is now prepared for drawing through
the lines which have been marked upon the ground.

For this etching, points or needles are employed, leaning hard or lightly, according to the degree of strength required in the lines.

A margin or border of wax is now to be formed all round the plate, to hold the aquafortis when it is poured on; where it is to be left till the operation is completed. The biting-in of the plate, as it is so called, is the most uncertain part of the process, and nothing but experience can enable a person to know when the plate is sufficiently bit.

When the acid has been long enough to bite the lines that are to be faintest, the aquafortis is poured off, the plate washed and dried, and those lines that are to be made no deeper must be stopped with turpentine varnish, mixed with a little lamp-black, and laid on with a camel's-hair pencil; and when thoroughly dry the aquafortis may be poured on again to bite the other lines that are required to be deeper.

When the biting is finished, the bordering-wax and ground are to be taken off, the plate cleaned, and an impression taken upon paper by a Copper-plate Printer; which impression is called a *proof.*

In almost all engravings on copper that are executed in the stroke manner, etching and graving are combined; the plate being generally begun by etching, and finished with the graver. Landscapes, architecture, and machinery, are subjects that receive most assistance from the art of etching : it is not so applicable to portraits and historical designs.

Mezzotinto is an art of a late date : it is recommended by the ease with which it is executed, especially by those who understand drawing. Mezzotinto prints are those which have no strokes of the graver, but whose lights and shades are blended

together, and appear like a drawing of Indian-ink.
They are different from aquatinta : but as both resemble Indian-ink their difference is not easily
described.

Engraving on wood is a process exactly the re-
verse of engraving on copper. In the latter the
strokes to be printed are sunk or cut into the copper, and a rolling press is used for printing it;
but in engraving on wood all the wood is cut away
except the lines to be printed, which are left standing up like types, and the mode of printing is the
same as that used in letter-press. The wood for
this purpose is box-wood, which is planed quite
smooth. The design is then drawn upon the wood
itself with black-lead, and all the wood is cut away
with gravers and other proper tools, except the
lines that are drawn; or sometimes the design is
drawn upon paper, and pasted on the wood, which
is cut as before. This art is of considerable difficulty ; and there are comparatively few who practise it. But of late years the art of cutting designs
upon wood has arrived at a vast degree of perfection, especially under the celebrated Bewicks
of Newcastle, who have carried their execution
in this respect to a pitch of elegance, rivalling, and
in some instances almost surpassing, copper-plate
engraving; which before their time was believed
to be utterly unattainable. There are at the present time some Engravers on wood in the metropolis, whose workmanship is exquisite. The
best light to work at this kind of engraving is
that passed from a lamp through a glass globe
filled with water, which, by its concentrating
power, throws a suitable light on the Engraver's
cushion.

The screen that is suspended in the plate before the window is to keep off the glare of light,
which would be mischievous to the Engraver's

business. The screen consists of four laths joined at their ends, and covered on both sides with silver paper.

Engraving is one of the fine arts, and some of its professors, as well now as in the last century, have obtained great celebrity in consequence of their productions.

THE GARDENER.

———

AGRICULTURE is the first and noblest of all arts.
It is this which manifests the pre-eminence of man,
and which most distinguishes him from all other
animals. In hunting and fishing man has innumerable rivals. Many quadrupeds and birds excel in
these two arts, but man alone cultivates the earth,
and sows to gather the harvest.

This art is scarcely known to savage nations:
for till man becomes settled into fixed commu-
nities, it is neither his interest nor his inclination
to derive advantages from the culture of the soil:
he would of course learn from the inferior animals
to gather some of nature's produce, but his more
ready means of support would be the chase; which
is at this day the method adopted for the most
part by the savages of America to supply their
wants.

Gardening must have been of course for a long
time in a very rude and imperfect state. Even in
England, many of the conveniences and luxuries
supplied by the modern garden are comparatively of
recent introduction; ingenuity and research are
continually adding to the stock. Rewards from
agricultural and other societies are now constantly
held out to stimulate us to overcome the deficiences
yet abounding in the produce of the earth, which
operate to the perfection of this invaluable art, and
to the advantage and support of mankind.

The Romans are said to have first brought *Cher-*

The Gardener.

ries to this country, which were afterwards lost, and are supposed to have been brought in again from Flanders, by Richard Harris, fruiterer to Henry the Eighth.

The *Perdrigon Plum* was introduced by Lord Cromwell, in the reign of Henry the Seventh. *Apricots* were brought from Italy, by Wolf, the King's Gardener, in 1524. The *Pale Gooseberry* came from Flanders about the same time when *Figs* were also introduced. The first *Mulberry-trees* are said to be those which still remain at *Sion-house.*

Melons, Cucumbers, and some other of the more expensive productions of the kitchen-garden, are said to have been very common in the time of Edward the Third. *Oranges* do not seem to have been grown in England before the reign of Queen Elizabeth.

It was in 1590 that the first two *Lime-trees* were brought to England. The *Pine-apple* was introduced about the time of Charles the Second. The *Tea-tree* was brought over from China, about sixty years ago. *Artichokes* were first grown in the time of Henry the Eighth. Sir Anthony Ashley, in the reign of Queen Elizabeth, first planted *Cabbages* in England, which were brought from Holland: and *Potatoes* were introduced from America by Sir Walter Raleigh, about 1580.

Of *Flowers,* those which are not of our own indigenous growth have been improved by culture. The *Tube-rose* was brought to Europe from the East Indies, about 1594, where it grows wild in Java and Ceylon. The *Auricula,* which grows wild among the long moss covered with snow on the confines of Switzerland and Steyermark, was first cultivated with care by the Flemings.

The *Crown Imperial* was brought from Persia to Constantinople in the sixteenth century, and thence to Vienna; whence it was dispersed all over Europe. The *Persian Lily* was brought from Susa to Constantinople. African and French *Marigolds*, with the *Bella-donna Lily*, were brought from South America. The first account we have of *Rue*, in England, is in 1562. *Lavender* appears to have been cultivated in Europe but a short period before 1568. The *Christmas-rose* and the *Iris*, both natives of Italy, were unknown to the gardens of this country till 1596. The *Guernsey Lily* was first cultivated in Europe in the beginning of the seventeenth century.

The Gardener, who may be called a refined agriculturist, is one who is engaged in the management and cultivation of fruit-trees, shrubs, flowers, plants, and vegetables of all kinds.

Gardens are distinguished into *Flower*, *Fruit*, and *Kitchen-gardens*. The first are for pleasure and ornament, and are therefore placed in the most conspicuous situation; the two latter are for service, and are made in more obscure and retired places. They were formerly distinct, but they are now generally united, because they both require a good soil and exposure, and are generally placed out of view of the house.

The principal operations of the Gardener are planting, and transplanting, engrafting, inoculating, pruning, sowing, &c. most of these are so well understood, that we shall only speak on the subject of *engrafting*, which is the art of inserting the shoot of one tree into the stock of another, in order to obtain fruit of a specific character and known quality.

The implements necessary for this business are a grafting-knife, a quantity of strings for bandages, (Russia matting is very commonly used for this purpose,) to tie the stocks and grafts firmly together; and some well-wrought clay to put over the tying, to secure them from the air and the wet.

When the grafts or shoots, which are generally to be preferred of the last year's growth, are quite ready, fix upon a smooth part of the stock, and then pare off the rind with a little bit of the wood in a sloping direction about an inch in length; then, having the shoots cut into lengths with four or five eyes on each, prepare one to fit the stock exactly, then cut a slit or tongue about half an inch in length upwards in the shoot, and another the same length downwards in the stock to receive it; and in that manner fix the graft in the stock, taking care that the sap and rind of both may join as exactly as possible in every part. Having thus fixed the graft, let it be immediately tied with a string of some material, bringing it several times round the graft and stock, taking care to preserve the graft in its proper position; and let the bandage be neatly tied, and the place be covered with some grafting-clay, in such a manner that neither the air, the rays of the sun, nor the wet can enter. This is called whip-grafting, and is only one of several ways, in which engrafting is performed by Europeans.

The Chinese, in place of raising fruit-trees from seeds or from grafts, as is the custom in Europe, have adopted the following method of increasing them.

They select a tree of that species which they wish to propagate, and fix upon such a branch as will least hurt or disfigure the tree by its removal.

Round this branch, and as near as they can conveniently to its junction with the trunk, they wind a rope made of straw, besmeared with cow dung, until a ball is formed, five or six times the diameter of the branch. This is intended as a bed into which the young roots may shoot. Having performed this part of the operation, they immediately under the ball divide the bark down to the wood, for nearly two-thirds of the circumference of the branch. A cocoa-nut shell, or small pot, is then hung over the ball with a hole in its bottom, so small that water put therein will only fall in drops; by this the rope is constantly kept moist, a circumstance necessary to the easy admission of the young roots, and to the supply of nourishment to the branch from this new channel.

During three succeeding weeks nothing further is required, except supplying the vessels with water. At the expiration of that period one-third of the remaining bark is cut, and the former incision is carried considerably deeper into the wood, as by this time it is expected that some new roots have struck into the rope, and are giving their assistance in support of the branch.

After a similar period the same operation is repeated, and in about two months from the commencement of the process, the roots may generally be seen intersecting each other on the surface of the ball, which is a sign that they are sufficiently advanced to admit the separation of the branch from the tree. This is best done by sawing it off at the incision, care being taken that the rope, which by this time is nearly rotten, is not shaken off by the motion. The branch is then planted as a young tree.

To succeed in Europe in this operation, as vegetation is slower, a longer period would probably be necessary; one month additional will be however sufficient. The advantages arising from this method, are, that the trees so produced will arrive much sooner to bearing fruit than by the common method.

The cultivation of flowers is a very pleasing employment; by a proper attention many flowers are brought from a mean and simple appearance to a large, brilliant, and beautiful one. There are many Florists' gardens in the neighbourhood of the metropolis, which, in the summer, afford a high gratification to those persons who have any relish for the smells and colours which nature, aided by art, so profusely scatters abroad.

There are several kind of Gardeners; some gain a living by looking after other people's gardens; for which they receive a certain sum per annum, according to the size of the garden. Others live in gentlemen's houses, and, like domestics in general, receive wages for their labour, from twenty to a hundred pounds per annum, according to their merit, or what may be expected of them. Some Gardeners go out to day-work, whose wages are from three to five shillings a day.

Besides these we have Market-Gardeners, that is, persons who raise vegetables and fruit, which they expose to sale in markets and other places. Gardens for the raising of vegetables for sale were first cultivated about Sandwich in Kent. The example was soon followed near the metropolis; and, perhaps, there is not a finer sight any where than Covent-Garden market, about six or seven o'clock in a morning of a Saturday, during the early part of the summer.

Within a few miles of the metropolis there are supposed to be about five thousand acres of land constantly cultivated for the supply of the London markets with garden vegetables, exclusive of about eight hundred acres cropped with fruit of various kinds, and about seventeen hundred acres cultivated for potatoes.

In the parish of Fulham the cultivation of gardens for the market is carried on to a greater extent than in any other part of the kingdom. The parishes of St. Paul's Deptford, Chiswick, Battersea, and Mortlake, are celebrated for their asparagus. Deptford is also famous for the culture of onions for seed, of which, on an average, there are about twenty acres annually.

The Gardener represented in the plate is in the Flower-garden, in the act of digging with his spade: the watering-pot, rake, &c. stand before him; on his right hand is a bed of tulips; and beyond them, on a stand, several pots of auriculas; on his left hand is the aloe, which blossoms once only in a cen-tury. In the smaller pots are some young plants of the same kind, not yet transplanted into separate boxes or tubs made for the purpose.

Glass Blower.

THE GLASS-BLOWER.

———

GLASS is a transparent, solid, brittle substance, formed by the combination of flint or silex, with alkaline salts and metallic oxydes. It is applicable to innumerable purposes of ornament and comfort, as well as of scientific investigation and research.

The invention of glass is very ancient: the books of *Moses* and of *Job* make mention of it. *Aristophanes, Aristotle,* and *Pliny,* speak of it in their works. *Aristotle,* who flourished three centuries and a half before the Christian æra, proposes two problems concerning glass: one is, why we see through it, the other, why it will not bend. *Theophrastus,* who flourished about three hundred years before Christ, describes glass as having been made of the sand of the river *Belus:* and the sphere of *Archimedes* is a remarkable instance of the perfection to which the art of glass-making had been brought at that early period, namely, two hundred and nine years before Christ. For the sake of our young readers, we may remind them that Virgil, in his fifth Eneid, compares the clearness of the water of the Facine lake to glass: and Horace, in his third book of the Odes, mentions glass in such terms as shew that its transparency was brought to great perfection. In the time of *Strabo* the manufacture of glass was well understood, and had become a considerable article of trade. *Seneca* seems not only to have been well acquainted with glass, but also understood its magnifying powers when formed into a convex shape. *Pliny* relates the manner of the discovery of glass: it was, he says, first made from sand found in the river *Belus;* a Phœnician merchant-ship, laden with mineral alkali (now understood to be some preparation of soda), being driven on the coast, and the crew going ashore for provisions, and dressing their victuals on the sand, made use of some lumps of alkali to support their kettles. Hence a vitrification of the sand beneath the fire was produced, which afforded a hint to the manufacturer.

The earliest positive authority relating to the use of *glass* in windows, is said to be in a passage of *Lactantius,* one of the Fathers of the Christian Church, in the third century.

Bede mentions, that artificers skilled in making glass were brought over to England in the year 674; glass windows did not begin to be used before 1180: for a long time they were very scarce, and considered as a kind of luxury, and as marks of great magnificence.

Painted glass is supposed to have been introduced in the reign of John, although we have no known specimens earlier than the time of Henry the Third.

The regular glass manufacture was begun in England, in 1557.

As it would be impossible, in the small limits to which we are confined, to enter at large into the composition of glass, we shall merely state, that *flint-glass* is made by melting, in a very strong fire, one hundred and twenty pounds of white sand, fifty pounds of red lead, forty pounds of the purest pearl-ash, twenty pounds of nitre (nitrate of potash), and five ounces of magnesia. Crown, or window-glass, contains no lead; it consists of soda and fine sand. Bottle-glass is the coarsest of all, and is composed of kelp and common sand, or sand and the refuse of the soap-boiler. Of these the most fusible is the flint-glass, and the least fusible the bottle-glass.

The furnace in which the glass is melted is round, and has several apertures, in one of which the fuel is introduced; the others serve to lade out the melted metal.

When the ingredients are perfectly fused, and have acquired the necessary degree of heat, part of the melted matter is taken out at the end of a hollow tube about two feet and a half long, which is dipped into it, and turned about till a sufficient quantity is taken up; the workman then rolls it gently upon a piece of iron to unite it more intimately. He then, as it is represented in the plate, blows through the tube till the melted mass at the extremity swells into a bubble; after which he again rolls it on a smooth surface to polish it, and repeats the blowing till the glass is brought as near the size and form of the vessel required as he thinks necessary.

There are three principal kinds of glasses distinguished by the form or manner of working them, viz. round glass, as bottles, drinking-glasses, &c. table or window-glass; of this also there are several kinds, and plate-glass.

If a bottle is to be formed, the melted glass at the end of the tube is put into a mould of the exact size and shape of its body, and the neck is formed on the outside by drawing out the ductile glass.

If it be a vessel with a *wide orifice* the glass in its melted state is opened and widened with an iron tool; after which, being again heated, it is whirled about by a circular motion, till it is extended to the size required. If a handle, foot, or any thing else of the kind be required, these are made separately, and stuck on in the melted state.

Window-glass is formed in a similar manner, except that the liquid mass is blown into large globes, and detached from the first iron tube by the assistance of a second person, who fixes his iron tube at the opposite side of the globe; and the man who originally blew it then separates his tube from it; the mouth of the globe is gradually widened till it ultimately becomes, in the hand of the workman, a circular planisphere. The best window-glass was, till within these few years, made at Radcliffe : but this manufactory is now abandoned, and the crown, as well as the green and black-bottle glass, is brought principally to London from Newcastle-upon-Tyne.

Plate-glass for looking-glasses, and some superior windows, is made by suffering the mass in a state of complete fusion to flow upon a table covered with copper, with iron ledges to confine the melted matter, and as it cools a metalic roller is passed over it to reduce it to an uniform thickness.

Glass is sometimes coloured by mixing it while in a fluid state with various metallic oxydes. It is coloured blue by the oxyde of cobalt; red by the oxyde of gold; green by the oxyde of copper or iron; yellow by the oxyde of silver or antimony; and violet by the oxyde of magnesia.

Although glass when cold is brittle, it is one of the most ductile bodies known in its melted state; if a thread of melted glass be drawn out and fastened to a reel the whole of the glass may be wound off; and by cutting the threads of a certain length there is obtained a sort of feather glass. A thread of glass may be drawn or spun so fine as to be scarcely visible to the naked eye. Glass is very elastic and sonorous; fluoric acid dissolves it; it is by this acid that engravings are made upon glass; and the alkalis act upon it when in a melted state.

Articles made of glass require to be gradually cooled in an oven; this operation, called annealing, is necessary to prevent them from breaking by change of temperature, wiping, &c.

Plate-glass comes from the manufactory in a very rough state; it is scarcely transparent. It is then, ground with sand, and polished with emery and putty, formed of lead and tin, calcined together. This last substance is the principal thing used in forming white enamels and glazings for earthenware.

Glass-makers usually work in the cold months, owing to the great heat of their furnaces: their wages are large in proportion to the disadvantages attending their labours.

Glass-grinders and polishers work by the piece, and may get a good living, considering that little more ingenuity is required than that which is necessary for common labourers.

THE GOLD-BEATER.

—◆—

THE GOLD-BEATER is a workman who by continually beating gold or silver upon marble with a hammer, in thin skins, reduces these metals into very thin leaves proper for gilding or silvering copper, iron, steel, wood, and a variety of other materials.

This art is very ancient. Although the Romans did not carry it so far as we now do, it is very certain that immediately after the destruction of Carthage, and during the censorship of *Lucius Mummius* they began to gild the interior of their houses in Rome. The wainscots of the capitol were the first done, and luxury afterwards became so great, that private persons had both the walls and ceilings of their apartments ornamented with this precious metal.

Pliny assures us that they made from one ounce of gold five or six leaves four fingers square; but that a much greater number could be made having regard to their thickness. That the thickest were called *prænestines*, from a statue of Fortune at *Præneste*, which was gilt with thick leaves, and that those which were thinner were called *questoriales*.

Gold in itself, and when very pure, is soft, easily cut or graved, and so tough that when at length made to break by repeated bendings backwards and forwards, the fracture on each of the pieces appears drawn out like a wedge.

The fineness to which a body of gold may be

The Gold Beater.

reduced is almost incredible. Mr. Boyle found that upwards of fifty square inches of gold weighed but a single grain; and as a cubic inch of gold contains four thousand nine hundred and two grains, the thickness of the gold-leaf was less than the two hundred and forty thousandth part of an inch.

Gold to be made into leaf is first melted in a crucible with some borax; it is then poured into an iron mould, from which it is taken and made red hot and forged into a long plate, which is farther extended by being passed repeatedly between polished rollers till it becomes as thin as paper. It is now cut into pieces of equal size and weight, which are forged and well annealed to correct the stiffness which the metal has contracted in hammering and flatting.

In farther extending these pieces into fine leaves it is necessary to interpose some smooth body between them and the hammer for softening the blow, and defending them from the rudeness of its immediate action; as also to place between every two of the pieces some proper intermedium, which, while it prevents them from uniting together or injuring one another, may suffer them freely to extend. For this Gold-Beaters use three kinds of membranes: for the outside cover common parchment made of sheep-skin; for interlaying with the gold the closest vellum made of calf-skin; and afterwards finer skins made of a thin substance stript off from the gut, slit open and curiously prepared for the purpose; hence the name of *Gold-beater's skin.* The preparation of these membranes is a distinct business, practised only by a few persons in the kingdom.

The beating of the gold is performed on a smooth block of marble, weighing from two to six hundred weight; fitted into the middle of a wooden frame, so that the surface of the marble may form one plane. Three of the sides are furnished with a high ledge; and the front, which is open, has a leathern flap fastened to it, which the Gold-beater takes before him as an apron for preserving the fragments of gold which fall off.

Three hammers are employed; all of them with two round and somewhat convex faces, though the workman seldom uses more than one of the faces. The first hammer weighs fifteen or sixteen pounds, and is called the *catch* hammer; the second is called the *shodering* hammer, and weighs twelve pounds; the third is the *finishing* hammer, and weighs about ten pounds.

One hundred and fifty pieces of gold are interlaid with leaves of vellum three or four inches square, one vellum leaf being placed between every two of the pieces, and about twenty more of the vellum leaves on the outsides; over these is drawn a parchment case open at both ends; and over this another in a contrary direction. So that the assemblage of gold and vellum leaves is kept tight and close on all sides. The whole is beaten with the heaviest hammer, and every now and then turned upside down till the gold is stretched to the extent of the vellum. The pieces taken out from between the vellum-leaves are cut into four with a steel knife: the six hundred divisions are next interlaid in the same manner with pieces of ox-gut skins, five inches square. The beating is to be again repeated till the golden plates have acquired the extent of the skins, when they are a second time to be divided into four. The instrument used for this division is a piece of cane cut to an edge, the leaves being now so slight that the moisture of the air or the breath condensing on a metallic knife would occasion them to stick to it.

After a third beating in a similar way the leaves are taken up by the end of a cane instrument, and, being blown flat on a leathern cushion, are cut to a size one by one with a square frame of cane, made of a proper sharpness; they are then fitted into books of twenty-five leaves each, the paper of which is well smoothed, and rubbèd with red bole to prevent their sticking to it.

The process of Gold-beating is very much influenced by the weather; both damp and frost are injurious to the operation.

Gold-leaf ought to be prepared from the finest gold, as an admixture of other metals, though in too small a proportion sensibly to affect the colour of the leaf would dispose it to lose a part of its beauty in the air. Besides the greater hardness of alloyed gold occasions as much or even more to be lost in time and labour than can be gained by adulterating the metal.

Gold-leaf is applied in the art of gilding to the surface of bodies, and it is done in two ways. Wood, leather, paper, and other like substances, are gilt by fastening on leaves of gold by some cement; but metals are gilt by a chemical application of gold to the surface. This last is called water-gilding. Silver-leaf is, however, often applied to the plating of metals without the intervention of chemical agents, if we except pumice-stone and heat.

THE GUN-MAKER.

The business of the Gun-maker is the manufacturing of fire-arms of the smaller sorts, as muskets, fowling-pieces, pistols, &c.

The exact time when gun-powder and fire-arms were first employed in war by the British nation is difficult to be discovered. If Robert Bruce may be credited, Edward the Third used cannon in his first campaign against the Scots, in 1327. The French undoubtedly used them in 1338, as well as Edward at the battle of Cressy in 1346.

But fire-arms of a portable construction were not, however, invented till the beginning of the sixteenth century. In 1521, the musket, mounted on a stock, was used at the siege of Parma; and probably was soon after adopted in England. Its form was clumsy, and its weight inconvenient; while the bow in the hands of an English archer retained the credit of having, within a determinate range, a steadier aim and greater execution.

The pistol had its origin from Pistoya, a town of Tuscany, and was introduced into England about the middle of the sixteenth century. Many of the shields said to have been the spoils of the Armada in 1588, have pistols in the centre with little gratings for the aim. They were sometimes introduced at the butt-end of the pike, as well as in the time of Edward at the Sixth, at the lower end of the battle-axe.

In the reign of James the First we find muskets

and calivres among the principal weapons of the infantry, as well as pistols and carabines of the cavalry. The great alteration when matchlocks were no longer used took place about the third or fourth year of William the Third.

The progress of fire-arms in France was not dissimilar to that in England. It was not till after the accession of Francis the First, in 1515, that any considerable change was effected. Between that time and the death of Henry the Third, in 1589, pikes, the ancient weapon of the French infantry, gave place to the arquebuss; while in the cavalry lances were gradually and reluctantly exchanged for the pistol. At that period, the Spaniards were far superior to the French in the art of war. The infantry of Philip the Second, by whom the use of fire-arms was very early adopted, spread terror over Europe.

For the introduction of the bayonet we refer to the article Cutler.

The principal part of the musket, fowling-piece, pistol, &c. is the barrel, which, however, is not made by those who call themselves Gun-smiths, but by persons who forge them in a large way, and who have forges and premises adapted to the business; the forges used by Gun-smiths being on a much smaller scale than those required for the manufacture of the barrels.

Among Gun-smiths great attention is paid to the division of labour: one man or set of men is employed in what is termed the boring, though in truth the barrels are formed at first with a bore throughout, but not with that accuracy which is required for these kind of instruments; other persons are employed to file and polish the outside of the barrel; to some is allotted the business of making and fixing the breech, the touch-hole, &c. others forge the locks in a rough way, and others are employed to file, polish, and put together the several parts of which the locks are composed.

The barrel ought to possess the following properties : *lightness,* that it may be as portable as possible, and *strength* to bear the effect of a full charge without bursting : it ought to be constructed so as not to recoil with violence, and it ought to be of sufficient length to carry the bullet to as great a distance as the force of the powder employed is capable of doing.

To form a gun-barrel in the manner generally practised for those denominated common, the workmen begin by heating and hammering out a bar of iron into the form of a flat ruler, thinner at the end intended for the muzzle, and thicker at that for the breech; the length, breadth, and thickness of the whole plate being of course regulated by the intended length, diameter, and weight of the barrel. This oblong plate of metal is then by repeated hammering turned round a cylindrical rod of tempered iron, called a mandril, whose diameter is considerably less than the intended bore of the barrel. The edges of the plate are made to overlap each other about half an inch, and are welded together by heating the tube in lengths of two or three inches at a time, and hammering it with very brisk but moderate strokes upon an anvil which has a number of semicircular furrows upon it, adapted to the various sizes of barrels. The heat required for welding is the bright white heat which precedes fusion, and at which the particles of the iron unite so intimately with one another, that when properly managed no trace is left of their former separation. These heatings and hammerings are repeated until the whole barrel has undergone the same operation, and all its parts are rendered as perfectly continuous as if it had been bored out of a solid piece. For better work the barrel is forged in separate pieces of eight or nine inches in length, and then welded together lengthways as well as in the lapping over. The other mode being the easiest and quickest done is the most usual.

The barrel is now either finished in the common manner, or made to undergo the operation of twisting, which is a process commonly employed on those barrels which are intended to be of a superior quality and price. This operation consists in heating the barrel in portions of a few inches at a time to a high degree of red heat, when one end of it is screwed into a vice, and into the other is introduced a square piece of iron with a handle like an auger, and by means of these the fibres of the heated portion are twisted in a spiral direction, which is thought to resist the efforts of the powder much better than a longitudinal one.

Pistol-barrels, which are to go in pairs, are forged in one piece, and are cut asunder at the muzzles after they have been bored; by which there is not only a saving of iron and labour, but a certainty of the calibre being the same in both.

The next operation consists in boring; this is done in the following manner : two beams of strong wood, as oak, each of about six inches in diameter, and six or seven feet long, are placed horizontally and parallel to each other, having their extremities mortised upon a strong upright piece about three feet high, and firmly fixed. A space of from two to four inches is left between the horizontal pieces, in which a piece of wood is made to slide, by having at each end a tenon let into a groove, which runs on the inside of each beam throughout its whole length. Through this sliding piece a pin, or bolt of iron, is driven or screwed in a perpendicular direction, having at its upper end, a round hole, large enough to admit the breech of the barrel, which is secured on it by means of a piece of iron, that serves as a wedge and a vertical screw passing

through the upper part of the hole. A chain is
fastened to a staple on one side of the sliding piece,
which runs between the two horizontal beams, and
passing over a pulley at one end of the machine
has a weight hooked to it. An upright piece of
timber is fixed above this pulley, between the end
of the beams, having its upper end perforated by
the axis of an iron crank furnished with a square
socket; the other axis being supported by the wall
on a strong post, and loaded with a heavy wheel of
cast iron to give it force. The axes of the crank
are in a line with the hole in the bolt already described. The borer being then fixed into the socket
of the crank has its other end, previously well oiled,
introduced into the barrel, whose breech part is
made fast in the hole of the bolt; the chain is then
carried over the pulley and the weight hooked on;
the crank being then turned with the hand, the
barrel advances as the borer cuts its way, till it has
passed through the whole length.

The *boring bit* is a rod of iron somewhat longer
than the barrel, one end being made to fit the
socket of the crank, and the other being furnished
with a cylindrical plug of tempered steel about an
inch and a half in length, and having its surface
cut in the manner of a perpetual screw. A number of bits, each a little larger than the preceding
one, are afterwards passed successively through the
barrel in the same way, until it has acquired the intended calibre.

The last operation is that of colouring the barrel,
previously to which it is polished with fine emery
and oil, until it presents to the eye throughout its
whole length a perfectly smooth and even surface.
The practice of blueing is now discontinued, and
browning is adopted in its stead. To do this, the
barrel is rubbed over with nitric or sulphuric acid,
diluted with water, and laid by until a coat of rust is
formed upon it, more or less according to the colour

wanted; a little oil is then applied, and the surface being rubbed dry, it is polished by means of a hard-brush and bees-wax.

The proving of barrels differs in different countries. The English Tower proof, and that of the Whitechapel company, incorporated by charter for proving arms, are made with a ball of the proper calibre, and a charge of powder equal in weight to this ball: the proof is the same for every size and species of barrel, and not repeated.

Rifling consists in forming upon the inside of barrels a number of furrows, either in a straight or spiral direction; into these the ball is moulded, and any rolling motion along the sides of the barrel in its passage out is thereby prevented. This process is supposed to direct the ball more effectually to the object against which it is intended to operate. Barrels of this construction have been long in use upon the Continent, but were little known, and still less employed in England till within these fifty years.

On the upper surface of the barrel, at right angles with its axis, is fixed a piece of flat thin iron, about six inches from the breech, and on the centre of its top a small square notch is filed; this is called the back-sight. The front-sight is nothing more than the small iron knot which is fixed on all fowling-pieces about half an inch from the muzzle. When the aim is taken, the eye is raised over the back-sight till the front-sight appears through the notch, which is then brought upon the object.

Great care is taken in the manufacture and finishing of the gun-lock: it consists of divers parts, such as the cock which holds the flint, the priming-pan to hold a small quantity of powder, which is connected by the touch-hole with that in the barrel; the hammer which covers the priming, and against the upper part of which the flint strikes; the trigger used to bring the flint and hammer in contact; and certain springs, as the main-spring, the rear-spring,

&c. which are concealed in the stock, and which are adapted either to hold the cock on the half-cock, whole-cock, or to extricate it at the moment of firing the piece.

Improvements upon gun-locks to prevent their going off accidentally, have latterly been made; and Mr. Manton, of Dorset-street, has obtained a patent for one upon improved principles: but we doubt whether any effectual improvement could be adopted, consistent with the simplicity required in this destructive weapon.

The lock is let into the gun-stock, which is uniformly manufactured from the wood of the walnut-tree, of which the Gun-smith always keeps a large stock, and well seasoned. The gun-stocks are usually made by workmen at their own homes, because one man will fashion gun-stocks sufficient for the wants of several Gun-smiths.

Before any of the pieces described are appropriated for service, it is necessary, as we have already observed, that each barrel should undergo a particular trial of its soundness, to be made by or before a person authorized for the purpose, called the Proof-master.

Gun-flints are made in large quantities, both in France and England, from the nodules of flint found in various places, particularly in chalk districts. The whole operation of making a gun-flint is performed in less than one minute. A good workman is able to manufacture a thousand good chips, or scales, in a day, if the flint nodules be of a good quality: and in the same manner he can fashion five hundred gun-flints in a day; so that in the space of three days he is able to cleave and finish a thousand gun-flints without farther assistance. The gun-flints are sorted out according to their perfection. They are classed into extra and common flints; flints for pistols, muskets, and fowling-pieces.

The Hair Dresser.

THE HAIR-DRESSER.

THE HAIR-DRESSER cuts and dresses ladies' and gentlemen's hair; he also makes wigs and braids, and in most cases the business includes the art of shaving.

The fashion of wearing wigs and false hair is not peculiar to modern times; it was common to the Greeks and Romans. The peruke of the Emperor Commodus, is described as having been powdered with scrapings of gold, which were made to adhere to the hair by means of glutinous perfumes.

Perukes, in their present form, were introduced into Paris in the year 1629, whence they have spread by degrees through the rest of Europe. At first it was reputed a scandal for young people to wear wigs, because the loss of their hair, at that age, was attributed to a disease which was of itself disgraceful.

The custom of wearing the beard in its natural state, of giving it a certain form, or of shaving it off entirely, has varied a good deal: these customs have been among some nations, formerly, subjects of war and of revolt.

The inconvenience of wearing the beard, no doubt, caused many people to shave themselves. Plutarch informs us that Alexander ordered the Macedonians to be shaved, that their enemies might not lay hold of them by the beard.

According to Varro, it was Menas, on his return from Sicily, who first brought to Rome a certain

number of Barbers. These Barbers did not exercise their trade in shops, but shaved at the corners
of the streets, or wherever they might happen to be.
Julian the Apostate drove the Barbers from his
court, but Scipio Africanus introduced the fashion
of shaving every day. We are told that the young
men of Rome, when their beards were first cut off,
made visits with great ceremony. The beard was
inclosed in a box of gold or silver, and consecrated
to some Divinity, chiefly to Jupiter Capitolinus. In
short, the ancients in wearing or in cutting off the
beard, do not appear to have been less capricious
than the moderns have been in the manner of wearing their hair.

Wigs and other ornamental decorations made of
hair are now become so common, that there are few
ladies, notwithstanding they possess the most beautiful hair, who will not wear a manufactured article
in preference to their own hair, under the impression
that they can improve nature, and add to their
charms. Hence, we sometimes see a fair skin and
light eyes decorated with black hair; and a dark
complexion with black sparkling eyes, set off with
flaxen locks. Such is the fashion at the commencement of the nineteenth century; it is, however, but
justice to say, that to this mistaken attempt at
beauty there are many exceptions.

The Hair-Dresser who is represented in the plate
engaged in his profession, requires a pair of scissars,
combs, a pair of curling-irons, some powder and
pomatum, as well as razors, and a strap and hone;
all things too well known to stand in need of description.

The principal requisites in a Hair-Dresser, are a
light hand, an aptness in catching the changing
fashions of the times, and a taste to improve upon
them.

Perukes or wigs are less in fashion among gentlemen than they were formerly, but, perhaps, they

were never more common among the fair sex than at present, and if we may judge from the splendid appearance of many shops in which ladies' wigs, braids, and curls are manufactured, no business is more flourishing or more profitable.

Hair makes a very considerable article in commerce. The merit of good hair consists in its being well fed, and neither too coarse nor too slender ; the largeness rendering it less susceptible of the artificial curl, and the smallness making its curl of too short duration.

There is no certain price for hair, but it is sold from five shillings to five pounds per ounce, according to its colour.

Hair which does not curl naturally is brought to it by boiling and by baking in the following manner : after having sorted the hair, it is rolled up, and afterwards fastened upon little cylindrical instruments, either of wood or earthenware, called pipes; in which state it is put into a vessel over the fire and boiled about two hours ; it is then taken out and dried, and sent to be baked in an oven.

Hair thus prepared is woven on strong thread which is sewed on a cawl, fitted to the head for a peruke.

Formerly peruke-makers made no difference between the ends of the hair, but curled and wove them by either indifferently ; but it is now known that hair to curl well must be woven by the end which grows next to the head.

Perukes much worn may, with attention, be made to look very smart, so long as they are kept from the wet.

The operation of shaving, which is another part of the Hair-Dresser's business, stands in need of no description; the great art depends on a light hand and a good razor.

Mr. Nicholson, in an early volume of his Chemical Journal, has favoured us with a scientific account of this business, to which we refer with peculiar pleasure, as it shews that nothing ought to be beneath the attention of a man of science.

The business was of much more importance than it now is, previously to the year 1795. In that year an annual tax of one guinea was laid upon all persons who should in future wear hair powder: this very much injured the trade; the following year, and also the year 1799, were seasons of uncommon scarcity with regard to wheat, from which hair-powder is manufactured : these circumstances produced a revolution in the trade ; the wearing of hair-powder was nearly abandoned, and still continues out of fashion.

Journeymen Hair-Dressers earn from fifteen shillings to a guinea per week ; but those who work on wig-making and working of hair, will, if very expert, earn much more than this.

Hat Maker.

THE HATTER.

Some kind of covering for the head, either for defence or ornament, appears to have been generally worn in all ages and countries where the inhabitants have made any progress in the arts of civilized life. Herodotus, indeed, states that the Egyptians were accustomed to appear bare-headed, but this assertion must be considered subject to limitation, probably comprising only some of the poorer classes, as from other documents it appears they were no strangers to this article of dress; and it is well known that a crown was the sign of royal authority.

The form, substance, and colour of head-dresses have been exceedingly various, according to the different circumstances or humours of the wearer. The Persians wore turbans, and other nations inhabiting the Indian Peninsula wore a kind of covering for the head, which, like the thatch of a lowly cottage, seemed calculated to divest the building of all proportion. The imperial turban is said to have been composed of almost a whole bale of muslin, variously twisted and formed: the ministerial turban was smaller, but of superior height. From the Persians the Jews borrowed those large turbans which adorned their elders, doctors, and scribes. The mitre of the priests was their own. Several of their tribes adopted the caps which the Romans were accustomed to give to their slaves on their being given their liberty: hence, in numerous instances, the cap has been a symbol of liberty.

The ancient helmets were a substitute for hats, made of steel, brass, and sometimes more costly metals. In our own country, Stowe informs us that the English used to ride, and go winter and summer in knit caps and cloth hoods; and the best sort in silk thrummed hats.

Head-dresses, from their variety, simplicity, and mutability, had hitherto been an object of little regard in a manufacturing or commercial point of view. The introduction of felt hats has occasioned a uniformity and extent to this article of dress, unknown to former ages, and has proved of considerable importance to the manufacturer and the tradesman. Curiosity is naturally excited to become acquainted with the particulars respecting their invention, but the the operation of individual interest in this, as in numerous other instances connected with the arts, seems to have buried it in obscurity, and little information on the subject can now be obtained.

Passing over the story about St. Clement, the fourth bishop of Rome, and some other idle tales of the dark ages, it appears that felt hats were invented at Paris by a Swiss, about the commencement of the fifteenth century. They were not generally known till Charles the Seventh made his triumphant entry into Rouen, in the year 1449, when from F. Daniel's account of that entry, it appears he astonished the whole city by appearing in a hat lined with red silk, and surmounted by a plume of feathers; from this entry their general use is dated.

How far the manufacture of hats was practised on the Continent before they were made in England we cannot say, but we learn that in the beginning of the reign of Henry the Eighth, Spanish felt hats were made in England by Spaniards and Dutchmen.

In the second year of James the First, the feltmakers of London obtained a corporation, and hired a hall near Christ-Church, the king granting them various privileges and liberties.

England is now become the grand mart for the manufacture of hats; and hence the article is exported to the Continent, America, and various other parts of the globe: our laws prohibit the introduction of foreign hats, to encourage, of course, our domestic manufacture.

The materials in general use for hat-making, are lambs'-wool, rabbits' and hares' fur, beaver, seal-wool, monkey-stuff, or neuter-wool, camels'-hair, goats'-hair, or estridge silk, and cotton. The best fur is from the backs of the different animals; it decreases in value as it approaches the belly.

As the process is nearly the same in all, it will be sufficient if we describe the method made use of in the manufacture of beaver hats.

The skin of the beaver is covered with two kinds of hair; the one long, stiff, and glossy; the other is short, thick-set, and soft, and is used alone for hats.

To tear off these kinds of hair and cut the other, women are employed, who make use of two knives: a large one, something like a shoe-maker's knife, for the long hair, and a smaller one, nearly in the form of a pruning-knife, with which they shave or scrape off the shorter hair.

Experience has shewn that the hair of fur cannot be evenly and well fitted together unless all the fibres be first separated, or put into the same state with regard to each other. This is the object of the first process of hat-making, and is called *bowing.* The material is laid upon a platform of wood or wire, about four feet square, called a *hurdle,* which is fixed against the wall of the work-shop, and is enlightened by a small window, and separated by two side partitions from other hurdles which occupy the rest of the space along the wall. The hurdle, if of wood, is made of deal-boards not quite three inches wide, disposed parallel to the wall, and at the distance of one-fortieth of an inch from one another, for the purpose of suffering the dust and other impurities of the stuff to pass through; a purpose still more effectually answered by a hurdle of wire. The workman is provided with a bow, a bow-pin, and a basket, and several cloths. The bow is a pole of yellow deal, or ash, about seven feet long, to which are fixed two bridges, somewhat like that which receives the hair in the bow of the violin. Over these is stretched a cat-gut about one-twelfth of an inch in thickness. The bow-pin is a stick with a knot, and is used for plucking the bow-string. The basket is a square piece of ozier-work, consisting of open straight bars, with no crossing or interweaving; its length across the bars is two feet, and its breadth eighteen inches. The sides into which the bars are fixed are slightly bent into a circular curve, so that the basket may be set upright on one of these edges near the right-hand end of the hurdle, where it usually stands. The cloths are linen. Besides these implements, the workman is also provided with brown paper.

The *bowing* commences by shovelling the material towards the right-hand partition with the basket, upon which the workman holding the bow horizontally in his left hand, and the bow-pin in his right, lightly places the bow-string, and gives it a pluck with the pin. The string, in its return, strikes upon the fur, and causes it to spring up in the air, and fly partly across the hurdle in a light open form. By repeated strokes the whole is thus subjected to the bow; and this beating is repeated till all the original clots, or filaments, are perfectly opened and dilated, and having thus fallen together in all possible directions, form a thin mass or substance for the felt. The quantity thus treated at once, is called a *batt*, and never exceeds half the quantity required to make one hat.

When the *batt* is sufficiently bowed, it is ready for *hardening;* which term denotes the first commencement of felting. The prepared material being

evenly disposed on the hurdle, is first pressed
down by the convex side of the basket, then covered with a cloth and pressed backwards and forwards
successively in its various parts by the hand of the
workman. By this process the hairs are twisted
together, and the lamellæ of each hair, by fixing
themselves to other hairs, which happen to be directed the contrary way, keep the whole in a compact state.

When the felt is thus managed the cloth is taken
off; and a sheet of paper with its corners doubled
in, so as to give it a triangular outline, is laid upon
the batt, which last is folded over the paper as it
lies, and its edges meeting one over the other, form
a conical cap. The joining is soon made good by
pressure with the hands on the cloth. Another
batt, ready hardened, is in the next place laid on
the hurdle, and the cap, here mentioned, placed
upon it with the joining downwards. This last
batt being also folded up, will, consequently, have
its place of junction diametrically opposite to that of
the inner felt, which it must therefore greatly tend
to strengthen.

The principal part of the intended hat is thus put
together; and now requires to be worked with the
hands a considerable time upon the hurdle, the cloth
being also occasionally sprinkled with clear water.
During the whole of this operation, which is called
basoning, the felt becomes firmer and firmer, and
contracts in its dimensions. It may be easily understood that the chief use of the paper is to prevent
the sides from felting together. A superior method
is said to be, that after the bowing, and previous to
the basoning, a hardening skin of leather, alumed, or
half-tanned, should be used instead of the cloth, and
pressed upon the batt, to bring it by an easier gradation to a compact appearance. This operation of
basoning derives its name from the process of working being the same as that practised on a wool-hat

after bowing; the last being done upon a piece of cast-metal, three feet across, of a circular shape, called a *bason;* the joining of each batt is made good here by the motion of the hand, that is, by rubbing the edges of each batt, folded over the other, to excite the progressive action of the filaments in felting, and to join the two together.

The basoning is followed by a still more effectual continuation of the felting, called *working.* This is done at an apparatus called the *battery,* (see the back part of the plate,) consisting of a kettle containing water slightly accidulated with sulphuric acid, to which, for beaver-hats, a quantity of wine-lees, or the grounds of beer are added, or else plain water for rinsing out, and eight planks of wood joined together in the form of a frustrum of a cone, and meeting in the kettle at the middle. The outer or upper edge of each plank is about two feet broad, and rises a little more than two feet and a half above the ground; the slope towards the kettle is considerably rapid, so that the whole battery is little more than six feet in diameter. The quantity of sulphuric acid added to the liquor is not sufficient to give a sour taste, but only renders it rough to the tongue. In this liquor, heated rather higher than unpractised hands could bear, the felt is dipped from time to time, and worked on the planks ; before which it is plunged gently into the boiling kettle till fully saturated with the liquor, which is called *soaking.* The imperfections of the felt present themselves in the course of this part of the work to the eye of the workman, who picks out knots and other hard substances with a bodkin, and adds more fur upon all such parts as require strengthening. The added fur is patted down with a wet brush, and soon incorporates with the rest. Many Hatters, to hurry this work, use a quantity of sulphuric acid, and then to make the nap rise and flow, they kill or neutralize the acid, and open the body

again by throwing in a handful of oatmeal; by this
means they expedite their work, but at the same time
they leave it quite grainy from the want of labour.
This, in handling the dry grey hat, when made, may
be in part discovered. The beaver for the nap is
laid on towards the conclusion of this kind of working. The hat now possesses the form of a cone,
and the several actions which it has undergone, have
converted it into a soft flexible felt, capable of being
extended, though with some difficulty, in any or
every direction; therefore, the next thing to be done
is to give it the form required by the wearer. For
this purpose, the workman turns up the edge or
brim, to the depth of about an inch and a half, and
then returns the point back again through the centre or axis of the cap, so far as not to take out this
fold of the same depth. The point being returned
back again in the same manner, produces a third
fold, and thus the workman proceeds until the whole
has acquired the appearance of a flat, circular piece,
consisting of a number of concentric undulations,
rings, or folds, with the point in the centre. This is
laid upon the plank, where the workman, keeping
it wet with the liquor, pulls out the point with his
fingers and presses it down with his hand, at the
same time turning it round on its centre in contact
with the plank, till he has by this means rubbed out
a flat portion equal to the intended crown of the
hat. In the next place he takes a block, to the
crown of which he applies the flat central portion of
the felt, and by forcing down a string from the sides
of the block, causes the next part to assume the
figure of the crown, which he continues to wet and
work until it has properly disposed itself round the
block. The brim now appears like a flounced or
puckered appendage round the edge of the crown;
but the block being set upright on the plank, the
requisite form is soon given by working, rubbing,
and extending this part. Water only is used in the

operation of fashioning or blocking; at the conclusion of which it is pressed out by the blunt edge of the copper implement used for that purpose, called a *stamper*.

Previous to the dyeing, the nap of the hat is raised or loosened out with a wire-brush, or carding instrument. The fibres are too rotten after the dyeing to bear this operation. The dyeing materials are logwood, a little oak bark, and a mixture of the sulphates of iron and of copper, commonly known under the names of green copperass, and blue vitriol. The hats are boiled with logwood in water, and afterwards immersed in the saline solution. The dyed hats are, in the next place, taken to the stiffening shop. One workman, assisted by a boy, does this part of the business. He has two vessels, or boilers, one containing the grounds of strong beer, and the other containing glue dissolved in water, a little thinner than that which is used by carpenters.

The beer-grounds are applied in the inside of the crown, to prevent the glue from coming through to the face, and also to give the requisite firmness at a less expence than could be produced by the glue alone. Were the glue to pass through the hat in different places, it would be more difficult to produce an even gloss upon the face in the subsequent finishing. The glue is therefore applied after the beer grounds are dried, and then only upon the lower face of the brim, and the inside of the crown. For this purpose the hat is put into another hat, called a stiffening hat, the crown of which is notched, or slit open in various directions. These are then placed in a hole in a deal-board, which supports the brim, and the glue is applied with a brush. In France, however, they use wine-lees instead of beer-grounds, and gum-water instead of glue.

The dry hat, after this operation, is always rigid, and its figure irregular. The last dressing is given by the application of moisture and heat, and the use of the brush, and a hot iron as before mentioned, somewhat in the shape of that used by tailors, but shorter and broader on the face. The hat being softened by exposure to steam, is drawn upon a block, to which it is securely applied by the former method of forcing a string down from the crown to the commencement of the brim. The judgment of the workman is employed in moistening, brushing, and ironing the hat, in order to give and preserve the proper figure; (see the front part of the plate) when the brim of the hat is not intended to be of an equal width throughout, as is sometimes the case for military hats, it is cut by means of a wooden or metalic pattern. The contrivance for cutting them round is very ingenious and simple. A number of notches are made in one edge of a flat piece of wood, for the purpose of inserting the point of a knife, and from one side or edge of this piece of wood there proceeds a straight handle, which lies parallel to the notched side, forming an angle somewhat like that of a carpenter's square. When the legs of this angle are applied to the outside of the crown, and the board lies flat on the brim of the hat, the notched edge will lie nearly in the direction of the radius, or line pointing to the centre of the hat. A knife being therefore inserted in one of the notches, it is easy to draw it round by leaning the tool against the crown, and it will cut the brim very regular and true. This cut is made before the hat is quite finished, and is carried entirely through; so that one of the last operations consists in tearing off the redundant part, which by that means leaves an edging of beaver round the external face. When the hat is completely finished, the crown is tied up in gauze paper, which is neatly ironed down. It is then ready for the subsequent operations of lining, &c. for sale.

These hats are, in the trade, commonly called *stuff-hats;* another kind much in wear, but of course inferior in quality, are called *plate-hats :* they consist, in the interior, of wool, and are merely covered with a better material on the outside. The commonest hats of all are called *cordies;* they are made wholly of wool, or some such coarse material. Another kind of hats is latterly got up in the trade, called *castor-hats,* but we believe this is only a name adopted to set off the article, rather than as conveying the quality absolutely designed by the term, *castor* being merely the Latin word for the beaver.

Silk hats have also within these few years come into wear. They are formed of a stout oil-case, and the fine pile of the silk is fixed by some process of glueing, or gumming, on the outside. They are very neat, and have the advantage of being waterproof, but the silk, without great care, soon wears off, and the hat immediately loses its beauty.

Hats of the finest quality are made in large quantities in London, and also at some of our provincial towns : but the cordies are made in vast quantities at, and in the neighbourhood of Bristol, as well as plate and castor hats. The cordies form a regular article of exchange with the London manufacturers for their stuff goods.

Hats are worn of various colours, but those most in use at present, are black, drab, and white. The white have a nap of rabbits'-fur, selected from the skins. Drab hats are made of stuffs of a natural colour selected for the purpose.

The master Hat-maker employs frequently a large capital, and numerous hands. The journeyman's earnings are good; but we fear, as in numerous other trades, that his habits are not calculated to induce him to make the most of them.

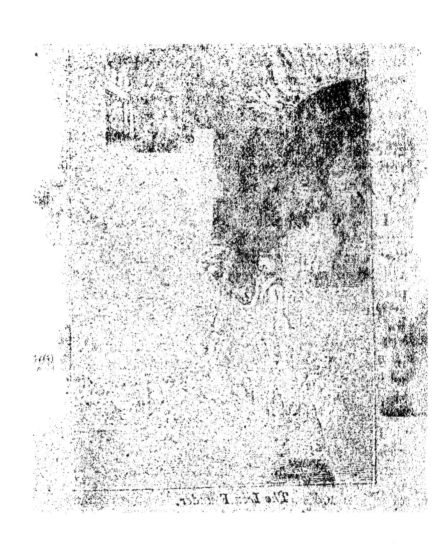

The Iron Founder.

———

THE art of founding in metal, or of melting it and forming it into various shapes, now occupies a space in our wants, which entitles it to considerable attention.

If the Greeks, and after them the Romans, perfected it as far as refers to casting in brass and bronze, we have extended it more than they did, inasmuch as we have turned it to all the great features of general utility.

Iron is the staple commodity in the modern foundery. The great abundance of this metal, with its consequent cheapness, together with the developements of chemistry, have, amongst us, opened to it a field, and created for it a demand, the extent of which is at present absolutely incalculable.

It is generally believed that cannon have been made use of in Europe ever since the year 1338, and that they were employed for naval purposes in the Baltic Sea, in 1350; at any rate, it is certain that they were used by the Venetians in 1366, at the siege of Claudia Jessa. Lamey ascribes the invention of brass cannon to J. Owen; he asserts there were none such known in England till the year 1535, and that iron cannon were for the first time cast in this country, in 1547. Specimens of great guns, as they were first used, and before the casting of them in founderies came into use, are still to be seen in

I 3

many parts of Europe, and some also in the Tower of London, and at Woolwich.

The uses to which cast-iron was applied, previously to the last century, are, comparatively, of trivial importance : it now enters more or less into the materials of almost every manufactory, forming wheels, cylinders, pipes, arches, grates, stoves, and innumerable other appendages and implements, without which, the mechanic would be almost undone, and the domestic concerns of mankind would suffer considerable disadvantage and inconvenience. If value be estimated by utility, iron is, unquestionably, the most valuable of the metals, for in addition to its use in the various arts of life, it is perfectly harmless in its effects upon the human constitution, when taken either in its crude state, or in the form of oxide, or rust, unless in immoderate quantity; a quality which few if any of the other common metals possess.

Iron is employed in three states, each having peculiar properties, by which it is applicable to various purposes : the first is *cast-iron*, the second *wrought*, or malleable iron, and the third is called *steel*.

Our business, at present, is with the cast-iron manufactory, of which we have a representation in the plate; the Founder has just taken from the furnace a ladle full of liquid metal, with which he is going to cast, perhaps the front of a stove, or some other article, the form of which is moulded out in stiff sand. It will be readily conceived that this business requires great strength, and a constitution that will bear a vast degree of heat.

Iron is dug out of the earth in the form of stones, and in this state it is called ore. The richest ores, that is, those which yield most pure metal, are heavy, and of a brownish colour, inclining to red.

Before the metal is extracted, the ore is sometimes roasted, or calcined; this is done by a different process, in different places: at the iron works in Staffordshire, after the ore is dug, they calcine it in the open air, with small charcoal, wood, or sea-coal, in order to break it in small pieces. This process requires three days. But at the Forest of Dean, in Gloucestershire, the ore is calcined in kilns, made like common lime-kilns: these are filled up to the top with coal and ore, one layer upon another, alternately; and then setting fire to the bottom layer of coal, it burns till the coal is wasted away. By these means the ore becomes brittle, but the metal is not fused.

It is now taken to the furnace to be melted, or, as it is usually termed, to be *smelted;* that is, to extract the metal from the dross.

The furnace, such as is represented in the plate, is built of brick, and is about twenty-four feet square on the outside, and near thirty feet in height within: the middle or widest part of which is not above eight or ten feet, the top and bottom being brought into a narrow compass, something like the shape of an egg. Behind the furnace are fixed two pairs of bellows, which are worked by means of a water-wheel; and they are contrived so as to play alternately, the one giving its blast whilst the other is rising. But in many founderies, the bellows used are constructed after Mr. Wilkinson's plan, by which a regular and uniform blast is continually produced. Holes are left in the furnace, which may be opened at any time to take away the scoriæ, or dross, or to permit the metal to flow out.

The furnace is filled with ore and charcoal, or coke; when coke is used, limestone is added, to promote more effectually the reduction of the metal, by supplying carbonic acid for that purpose. The ore gradually subsides into the hottest part of the furnace, where it is melted, and the metallic parts being the heaviest, fall to the bottom, where there is a passage made for taking off the scum. As soon as there is a sufficient quantity of metal in a complete and strong state of fusion, it is let out by a tap-hole into furrows, made in an immense bed of sand, which is prepared before the mouth of the furnace: the large mass which sets in the main furrow, is called by the Founders a *sow,* and the lesser or side furrows are termed *pigs* of iron. The metal is generally made so hot before it is drawn off, that it will not only run a great distance, but will keep boiling for some time in the sand.

For chimney-backs, hearths of ovens, the fronts of stoves, and other small articles, the Founder takes the metal out of the receiver in large ladles, from which he pours it into moulds of fine sand.

But for the more intricate cases of Iron-Foundry, as casting of cylinders for steam engines, or pipes with various branches, moulds are formed of loam or clay, which are made nearly in the same manner as the moulding of plaister for busts, &c.

When the furnaces are once at work, they keep them constantly employed for many months together, never suffering the fire to slacken night or day, but still supplying the wasting of the fuel and the ore, by fresh materials poured in at the top.

The excessive and long-continued ignition kept in these furnaces, gradually wastes the brick-work, till the sides, which are many feet thick, become unable to sustain the weight of the melted metal; so that it has sometimes been known to burst out suddenly in a violent and dreadfully-destructive stream. At certain intervals, therefore, the fire ought to be allowed to go out, whatever may be the expense of rekindling it, in order to examine and repair the furnace.

Three tons of iron are sometimes run off in twenty-four hours, with the application of the bellows, whilst the heat without these would scarcely melt a single hundred weight in the same time: indeed, we knew a well-conducted furnace at Redbrook, near Monmouth, where two tons of cast-iron

were regularly run out into pigs every eleventh
hour : the ore in this furnace was reduced entirely
by charcoal, and being in small lumps underwent
no previous roasting.

Cast-iron is now employed in the formation of
bridges of great extent; in roofs, and the girders,
and joists in buildings, as well as the sash-frames,
and sashes. It has also been used with success in
wheels and other machinery to our steam-engines.
Birmingham and its neighbourhood is the great
entrepôt for works of all kind in iron. The Soho of
Messrs. Boulton and Watt, near that town, is of
known celebrity. And the Colebrook-dale Company,
in Shropshire, have long been famous for a variety
of cast-iron materials for building both houses and
bridges. The Carron Iron-works in Scotland are
also well known: the guns known in war under the
name of carronades, derive their name from this last
foundery; for the mode of casting which, as well as
cannon generally, we refer to more voluminous writings, merely adding that cannon are always cast
with a large cap at their muzzle, which was originally cut off with a saw, but now a machine is used
for the purpose, which a man works by turning a
lathe, and as the turning goes on the turner uses a
chisel, with which he cuts into the gun to about one
inch and a half deep. The cap so cut is broken off
by being hammered.

THE JEWELLER.

It appears from history that the profession of a
JEWELLER is of very ancient date: for we read in
the Bible that Aaron had a breast-plate set with a
variety of precious stones; and in succeeding ages
there is frequent mention of rings and other ornaments being made of gold and set with stones.
Hence the name Jeweller, one who sets jewels or
precious stones, is properly derived.

There is scarcely a nation in the world who has
not employed Jewellers of some kind or another.

Cleopatra, Queen of Egypt, is said, as a proof of
her extravagance, in one of her feasts which she
gave to Mark Antony, to have melted pearls into
her drink. When Captain Cook visited the South
Sea Islands, where perhaps no civilized being had
been before, he found the natives with their ears,
noses, and arms ornamented with pearls, gold,
shells, and curious teeth of fish in a fanciful manner.

Civilized countries have greatly improved the art
of Jewellery. The French for lightness and elegance of design have surpassed their neighbours;
but the English Jewellers for excellence of workmanship have been, and still are superior to every
other nation. The name Jeweller is now commonly
applied to all who set stones, whether real or artificial; but properly speaking it belongs only to
those who set diamonds and other precious gems.
According to the general application of the term,
Jewellers make rings of all sorts in gold, lockets,

The Jeweller.

bracelets, broaches, ornaments for the head, earrings, necklaces, and a great variety of trinkets composed of diamonds, pearls, or other stones.

The diamond was called by the ancients *adamant:* as a precious stone, it holds the first rank in value, hardness, and lustre, of all gems. The goodness of diamonds consists in their *water* or colour, lustre, and weight. The most perfect colour is white, or rather a clear crystalline quality, which admits the rays of light very readily. The defects in diamonds are veins, flaws, specks of red and black sand, and a blueish or yellow cast.

In Europe lapidaries examine the goodness of their diamonds by day-light, but in the Indies they do it by night: for this purpose a hole is made in the wall, where a lamp is placed with a thick wick, by the light of which they judge of the goodness of the stone.

Diamonds are found in the East Indies; principally in the kingdoms of Golconda, Visapour, Bengal, and the island of Borneo. We likewise get them from Brazil; but the Brazilian diamonds appear to be of an inferior quality: they are known in commerce by the name of *Portugueze diamonds.* They are seldom above a certain size. The Indian Monarchs keep up the largest of them, to hinder their price from falling. Diamonds do not display all their lustre immediately after being taken out of the earth; they are brilliant only when found in water. All that are dug from mines are covered with an earthy crust. They are obtained from both mines and rivers.

Modern chemistry has proved, that the diamond can be completely decomposed by heat; in other words, it can be totally destroyed by that agent: its analysis proves it to approach the nearest to pure charcoal, or carbon, of any body yet known.

As the diamond is the hardest of all precious stones, it can only be cut and ground by itself, and in its own substance. To bring diamonds to that degree of perfection which augments their price so considerably, the workmen rub several against each other; and the powder thus rubbed off the stones, and received in a little box for the purpose, serves to grind and polish others.

The *pearl* is a hard, white, smooth, shining body, found in shell-fish resembling an oyster, and is ranked among the gems. The perfection of pearls, whatever be their shape, consists chiefly in the lustre and clearness of their colour, which Jewellers call their water. Those which are white are most esteemed in Europe; while many Indians, and the Arabs, prefer the yellow: some are of a lead-colour, some border on the black, and some are quite black. The *Oriental* pearls are the finest, on account of their largeness, colour, and beauty, being generally of a beautiful silver white; those found in the Western Hemisphere are more of a milk-white.

In various parts of the East are persons whose employment is to dive for pearls: it appears that the pearls obtained from shell-fish is merely an interior excrescence, arising from the shells being accidentally wounded: the divers, to increase the number of pearls, are in the habit of making holes in the shells of the fishes which produce them, and replacing them in the water; when, after a certain time, it is found that pearls are produced.

The finest pearls are brought from the East and West Indies: an inferior sort is sometimes met with in the shell-fishes of our own seas, particularly on the coasts of Scotland.

In Europe, *pearls* and diamonds are sold by *carat* weight, the carat being equal to four grains; but in Asia, the weights made use of are different in different states.

In the print we have a man at work, who will represent either a jeweller or a small worker in silver; one who makes rings, perfume boxes, &c. The

board at which he works is adapted also for a
second workman. The leathern skins fastened to
the board, are to catch the filings, and small pieces
of precious metals which would otherwise be liable
to fall on the ground. The tools on the board, and
in the front under the window, are chiefly files of
various kinds, and drills; beside which there is a
small hammer, a pair of pliers, and on a little block
of wood, a small crucible. On his left hand, above
the board, is a *drill-bow;* this is a flexible instrument, consisting of a piece of steel, to the end of
which is fastened a cat-gut : the cat-gut is twisted
round one of the drills which stand before the man,
and then it is fitted for the business.

Behind him is fixed the drawing-bench, on which
he draws out his wire to any degree of fineness.
The method of drawing wire for gold, or other
metals, is this: the metal is first made into a cylin-
dric form ; when it is drawn through the holes of
several irons, each smaller than the other, till it is as
fine as it is wanted, sometimes much smaller than a
hair. Every new hole lessens its diameter: but it
gains in length what it loses in thickness; a single
ounce is frequently drawn to a length of several
thousand feet.

In the front of the plate is represented a German
stove, which is rarely used for any other purpose
than that of heating the shop : for Jewellers cannot
work in winter, unless the temperature of the shop
be pretty high.

At the top of the stove is a crucible, and on the
floor is another; these are useful for many purposes ; they are not, however, heated in the stove,
but in a *forge,* which is an essential in a Jeweller's
shop, though not exhibited in the plate.

Another very material tool, found in every Jeweller's work-room, is the anvil and block.

A *flatting-mill* is also wanted ; and, indeed, cannot be dispensed with, where the business is consi-

derable. The flatting-mill consists of two perfectly round and very highly polished rollers, formed
internally of iron, and welded over with a plate of
refined steel; the circumference of these rollers
nearly touch each other; they are both turned with
one handle. The lowermost roller is about ten
inches in diameter; the upper one is much smaller.
The wire which is to be flattened, unwinding from
a bobbin, and passing through a narrow slit in an
upright piece of wood, called a *ketch*, is directed by
a small conical hole in a piece of iron called a guide,
to any particular width of the rollers; some of which,
by means of this contrivance, are capable of receiving forty threads. After the wire is flatted it is
again wound on a bobbin, which is turned by a
wheel fixed on the axis of one of the rollers, and
so managed that the motion of the bobbin just
keeps pace with that of the rollers.

Besides those which are already mentioned,
Jewellers require a great variety of other tools;
such as gravers, scrapers, spit-stickers, knife-tools,
straining-weights, brass-stamps, lamp, and blow-
pipe, ring-sizes, spring-tongues, piercing-saws, boil-
ing-pans, shears, &c. &c.

The trade of a Jeweller has always been considerable in London. The capital required to carry
on a business of this kind must be very great; a
single diamond being sometimes valued at twenty
thousand pounds: indeed there are a few diamonds
in possession of some of the Sovereigns of Europe,
which are valued at a much larger sum.

Some Jewellers will earn as journeyman four
guineas a week: but the general run of wages is
about twenty-eight or thirty shillings.

The Lace Maker.

THE LACE-MAKER.

—————

THE LACE-MAKER is a person, commonly a woman, who makes a kind of open net-work of thread, silk, &c. of various widths and fineness, with a variety of figures intermixed, used most commonly for trimmings to ladies' dresses.

The origin of the art of Lace-making cannot be distinctly traced; by some it has been supposed to be the same as that which is called in Latin authors the Phrygian art; but this probably consisted rather in needle-work, than in that sort of netting used in the making of bone-lace. Borders sewed upon cloths and tapestry, which are mentioned by ancient writers, were a kind of lace worked with a needle: this lace is undoubtedly of much older date than that made by netting. Of the former kind much is still extant among old church-furniture, which was probably the work of nuns or ladies of fortune, who devoted their time to the business on religious motives. But if it had been manufactured as an article of commerce, something more would have been found concerning it in cotemporary authors.

A lace manufactory was established in Paris under the auspices of the celebrated Colbert, in the year 1666; but this was done by the needle, and was similar to what is called point.

The Germans, however, claim the honour of having invented the art of Lace-making by means of the cushion and bobbins: they ascribe the invention to Barbara, the wife of Christopher Uttman, who died about the year 1575. At this period the mines in Germany were become much less productive than they had been for centuries; the wives and daughters, therefore, of the miners were induced to turn their hands to the making of lace, which, owing to the low price of labour, they were enabled to sell so cheap that it became fashionable, in opposition to the Italian lace worked with the needle, and even supplanted it in commerce.

The best laces are now made at Mecklin, Brussels, and Ghent, Antwerp, and Valenciennes, which still enrich the country around, and induce the farmers to cultivate flax on the poorest soils. In France lace was made formerly in large quantities in the convents.

In our own country the manufacture of lace is carried on to a greater extent and perfection in Buckinghamshire than in any other part of the United Kingdom, particularly in the town and neighbourhood of Newport-Pagnel, which is a sort of mart for that article, and flourishes considerably by its means.

The Lace-maker is represented in the plate busily engaged in her work in the open air, which, even in this country, is no uncommon sight during the summer months.

Lace is not woven, and of course it requires in the operation neither warp nor woof. It is made of silk, of thread, or cotton, which is wound on little bobbins made of bone or ivory, about the thickness of a skewer: hence the name bone-lace. The pattern to which the lace is made is drawn on paper or parchment, pricked with pin-holes, and then put on the pad or cushion which the woman holds on her knees. All the ends of the threads are first fastened together, and the Lace-maker twists them variously over and under one another round the pins, which are stuck into the holes of the pattern: these pins they remove from one part to another, as their work goes · on ; · and by these means are produced that multiplicity of eyes or openings which give to lace the desired figures.

For this operation much art and ingenuity are not necessary: it is, however, very tedious work: and when the thread is fine, and the pattern full and complex, it requires a degree of attention which can be rarely expected in persons of easy circumstances.

Lace-making is therefore consigned to the hands of indigent women and young girls, who by their skill and dexterity raise the value of materials, originally little worth, to almost any sum. But the time required to accomplish this beautiful manufacture is always in proportion to the value of the work; so that after all little money is earned in the business.

This is the usual method in which lace has been made in this country as well as on the Continent: but within these few years a considerable revolution in the manufacture of lace has been gradually taking place.

Cotton has been spun of so neat and fine a texture, that the use of it, even in the making of bone-lace, has completely in England superseded the use of flax; and great quantities of cotton finely spun are exported continually for the making of lace abroad, although we are not prepared to say that on the Continent cotton has wholly superseded the use of flax.

But a more important alteration has taken place in Lace-making by substituting the loom: at Nottingham, and some other places, is now manufactured a lace of finer quality, more even in its texture, and considerably more elegant in its appearance than any bone-lace whatever, and at about one-third the price of bone-lace.

This lace is made of two kinds: the coarsest is

called *Mecklin-net;* the other *bobbin-net,* because it is woven by bobbins in some such way as the bone-lace is made, and for which we believe a patent was obtained. Not only lace, but veils, cloaks, and handkerchiefs are made in this way, both of silk and cotton: the only inconvenience attending this mode of manufacture is, that the figures in the lace must be fixed by hand after the lace is woven: but notwithstanding this defect, the introduction of this method has considerably reduced the demand for bone-lace.

All these laces made by the loom are in the trade contradistinguished by the name of *British* lace, particularly that made of *black* silk, a lace which has lately most unaccountably gone a good deal out of fashion.

The Ladies' Dress Maker.

THE LADIES' DRESS-MAKER.

UNDER this head we shall include not only the business of a Mantua-maker, but also of a Milliner: for, although in London these two parts of in fact the same trade are frequently separate, they are not always so, and in the country they are very commonly united.

The history of dress would be as voluminous as the history of mankind : dress is a thing subject to almost daily fluctuation, so that a history of the ladies' dresses in England for merely half a dozen years would furnish matter for a bulky volume ; we shall therefore not attempt it, but merely observe that the best and perhaps the only excuse for such continual change in the empire of dress, is the opportunity which that change offers of employment to those persons who would otherwise have no immediate claim upon the rich and opulent; and thus what would be retained in their coffers is now scattered in a variety of ways amongst the community in the purchase of luxurious dress, and in the alterations which fashion is continually introducing.

In the Milliner taste and fancy are required, with a quickness in discerning, imitating, and improving upon various fashions, which are perpetually changing among the higher circles.

Silks and *Satins,* of various sorts, are much used in this business ; which were formerly imported into this country, but now are manufactured in great perfection in Spitalfields and its neighbourhood.

Gauze is a very thin, slight, transparent kind of stuff, woven sometimes of silk, and sometimes only of thread.

Crape is a very light transparent stuff; in some respects like gauze: but it is made of raw silk, gummed and twisted on the mill, and woven without crossing. It is used for mourning, and is now a very fashionable article in court dresses.

Spangles are small, thin, round leaves of metal, pierced in the middle, which are sewed on as ornaments to dress.

Artificial Flowers are made sometimes of very fine coloured paper, sometimes of the inside linings upon which the silk-worm spins its silk, but principally of *cambric,* which is a kind of linen made of flax, and was first manufactured at Cambray in France, whence its name.

Ribbands used by the Milliners are woven: of these there are different sorts, distinguished by different names; as the *China,* the *sarcenet,* and the *satin.*

Muffs and *fur-tippets* are sold by the Milliner; but the manufacture of them from the skin is a distinct business.

Velvet is also used by Milliners, and is now much in fashion: it is a sort of stuff or silk; the nap of which is formed of part of the threads of the warp, which the workman puts on a channeled ruler, and then cuts by drawing a sharp steel tool along the channel of the ruler to the end of the warp.

Muslin is a fine sort of cloth wholly made of cotton, so named from the circumstance of having a downy nap on its surface, resembling *moss,* which in French is called *mousse.*

The Ladies' Dress-maker's customers are not always easily pleased; they frequently expect more from their dress than it is capable of giving.

" Dress," says Mr. Addison, " is grown of universal use in the conduct of life. Civilities and respect are only paid to appearance. It is a varnish that gives a lustre to every action, that introduces us into all polite assemblies, and the only certain method of making most of the youth of our nation conspicuous: hence Milton asserts of the fair sex,

'———Of outward form
Elaborate, of inward less exact.'

" A lady of genius will give a genteel air to her whole dress by a well-fancied suit of knots, as a judicious writer gives a spirit to a whole sentence by a single expression."

The Dress-maker must be an expert anatomist; and must if judiciously chosen have a name of French termination; she must know how to hide all defects in the proportions of the body, and must be able to mould the shape by the stays, that, while she corrects the body, she may not interfere with the pleasures of the palate.

The business of a Ladies' Dress-maker and Milliner, when conducted upon a large scale and in a fashionable situation, is very profitable; but the mere work-women do not get any thing at all adequate to their labour. They are frequently obliged to sit up very late, and the recompense for extra work is in general a poor remuneration for the time spent.

The plate represents the Dress-maker taking the pattern off from a lady by means of a piece of paper or cloth: the pattern, if taken in cloth, becomes afterwards the lining of the dress.

THE LINEN-DRAPER.

THE LINEN-DRAPER sells cloths which are made of flax and hemp; as Irish linens, Russia towelling, Cambrics, &c. and also shawls, printed calicoes, muslin, &c. &c.

This business must have been in a great degree co-eval with the subdivision of labour, arising from civilization, modified of course by a variety of circumstances. In London it is in the number of its articles much more circumscribed than it is in the country. Linen-drapers frequently in the country combining with their trade that of a Silk-mercer, whereas in London these two trades are wholly distinct.

The Linen-draper is now comprehended under two, or at most three distinct branches. We have the *Linen-merchant*, a person whose more immediate province it is to import articles of linen manufacture from foreign countries, such as Irish cloths from Ireland, a variety of cloths made of hemp and flax, from Russia, Ticklenburghs, &c. from Germany; and nankins, calicoes, muslins, &c. from the East Indies.

We have also the *wholesale Linen-Draper;* a person whose business is to purchase linens from the merchant, and muslins, calicoes, printed-cottons, &c. from the different manufacturers in Manchester, Blackburn, Paisley, &c. and to sell them to the retail Linen-drapers throughout the kingdom, as well as frequently for exportation. For this pur-

The Linen Draper.

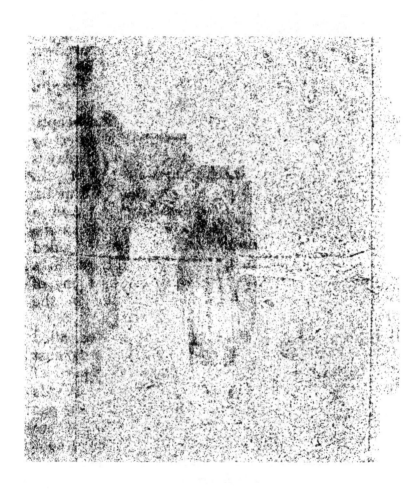

pose the *wholesale* Linen-draper generally keeps
one or two or more persons constantly travelling
throughout the country with patterns of his various
articles, by which means the retail dealer has an
opportunity of choosing his goods without the expensive and troublesome process of a journey to
London, or some other great market for that purpose. The business now done, or rather which
lately was done in this way, is beyond all precedent
or calculation.

The most striking part, however, is the *retail*
Linen-draper. We believe there is no trade in
England in which more efforts are made to capti-
vate the public, and more especially the ladies, by
a display of goods; and in London this display is
carried to a most costly and sumptuous extent. In
most of the principal streets of the metropolis,
shawls, muslins, pieces of ladies' dresses, and a
variety of other goods, are shown with the assistance of mirrors, and at night by chandeliers, aided
by the brilliancy which the gas-lights afford, in a
way almost as dazzling to a stranger as many of
those poetical fictions of which we read in the
Arabian nights' entertainment.

If some years ago our neighbours in sneer called
us a nation of shopkeepers, we think that they must
now give us the credit of being shopkeepers of
taste : we apprehend no place in the world affords
so great a variety of elegant amusement to the eye
as London in its various shops, and amongst these
those of the Linen-drapers are at all times conspicuous.

One of the principal things in this trade, in order
to be able to carry it on with success, is a knowledge
of the best markets for purchasing the different
articles of which a Linen-draper's shop is made
up; it may seem that immediate application to
the fountain head, the manufacturers in various
parts of the country, would be the best; but expe-

rience has frequently decided otherwise; and it is now well known that from a variety of circumstances linen and cotton goods can be often purchased in London cheaper than of the manufacturers themselves. The truth perhaps is, that the greatest quantity of floating capital is always to be found in the metropolis, and therefore the manufacturer will send his goods to that market, where they will be sure to obtain a ready sale, and that too generally for prompt payment, or for bills at a short date. Large sales, therefore, of muslin, calicoes, &c. are in London numerous, and the capitalist is generally sure of purchasing well. Hence it in general happens that no wholesale Linen-draper, residing in any other part of the empire, can effectually compete with the London houses; and this has been particularly the case for some years past, owing to the peculiarly depressed state of trade.

At *Manchester* are manufactured printed calicoes, checks, muslins, nankins, jeans, &c.

At *Blackburn* white calicoes are the staple commodity. At *Wigan* is manufactured a particular kind of check, known by its name *wigan*, of strong and durable quality.

At *Bristol, Birmingham*, and various other places, white calicoes are also manufactured.

In *Somersetshire* bed-tick of fine quality and dowlas are manufactured of a superior strength to most: *Yeovil, Langport*, and their neighbourhoods, are the chief seats of these manufactures: fairs in some of the towns of the county are held for the sale of these articles annually, and indeed oftener.

Paisley, in Scotland, has lately become eminent as a mart for printed cottons, calico, check, muslin, cambric, &c. &c.

Yorkshire has also its linen manufacture, and in the articles called huckaback and sheeting, it is well known.

London is, principally, in this trade, noted for getting up the most elegant articles in the printed calico and muslin departments; distinguished in the trade by the name of *London prints*.

Some of the retail Linen-Drapers in the metropolis transact daily so much business, as almost to exceed belief: there seems a disposition in the public to go to what are termed cheap shops, many of which have a name for doing business well, which, if conducted with any degree of prudence, soon insures a fortune. We have known persons in this line whose receipts have averaged five hundred pounds per day for a long period. In such a shop twenty or thirty persons, or more, are constantly employed, the average of whose salaries do not amount to forty pounds a year, exclusive of their board: of course a small per centage on three thousand pounds a week will cover those expences, and afford a good profit also. We cannot, however, avoid considering these overgrown and engrossing houses as a very great evil; but we suppose that as long as the British public are actuated by real or pretended cheapness, these houses must continue to monopolize the profits which would be more advantageous to the community if considerably subdivided.

This is a business in which, we believe, more persons have failed than in any other in the united kingdom, owing to its being liable to partake of the fluctuations unfortunately almost inherent in the manufacturing system, and to the great versatility in fashion and dress. It is a trade too in which, we are sorry to say, there is a trick at which the cheek of-honesty cannot fail to redden, but which is become so common as almost to be identified with the trade itself: we mean the bad practice of asking various prices for the same article, the same quantity of it, and on the same day, depending in a great measure upon the opinion which the shopman happens to conceive of the sagacity of his customer.

In this trade, in every branch, a considerable capital is generally required. Apprentice fees vary exceedingly: they are sometimes one hundred guineas; but more commonly young men make their way in this business without any fee at all. Experienced shopmen get, sometimes, fifty or sixty pounds a year and their board. We have known wholesale travellers, who were clever men and had good connexions, receive two hundred pounds a year as a salary.

The plate represents the interior of a retail Linen-Draper's shop in one of the most frequented streets of the metropolis.

THE LOOKING-GLASS MAKER.

———

THE LOOKING-GLASS MAKER is a person who lays
tin-foil on polished pieces of glass, by the assistance
of quicksilver, so as to produce reflection by effectually obstructing the rays of light, and, afterwards,
fits the glass to frames of various sizes, either for
the use of chambers and dressing-rooms, or for the
purpose of decoration in the houses and mansions of
the opulent.

Nature offered to mankind the first mirrors, in
representing objects upon the surface of water when
it was still. Human industry and ingenuity has,
from time to time, improved upon such suggestions,
and has not only equalled but very far exceeded the
original model. The discovery of metals considerably assisted man in the progress of this art. Mirrors were at first made of polished brass, of tin, or
of burnished iron, and also of a mixture of tin and
brass. A person named Praxiteles, not the sculp-
tor of that name, who was cotemporary with Pompey
the Great, made mirrors of silver. These last were
preferred to all the other kinds, and the use of
them was only abandoned, when glass coated with
tin, as we now have it, was introduced.

The precise time in which the ancients began to
use glass for mirrors is not known: the first, we
think, was furnished from the glass-houses of Sidon,
where glass was worked in a variety of ways, both
for use and ornament. As to the stone which the
Romans adapted to their windows, in order to keep

out the rain and weather, it does not appear that they ever employed it as mirrors.

In the thirteenth century, the Venetians were the only people who had the art of making looking-glasses of crystal. The great glass works at Murano, in the neighbourhood of Venice, furnished all Europe for centuries with the finest glasses that were made. The first plates for looking-glasses were made in England, at Lambeth, in 1673, by the encouragement of the Duke of Buckingham, who in 1670 introduced a few Venetian artists.

The polishing of the plates for this business is usually effected by other hands, before they come to the Looking-Glass Maker, but we can just mention that the usual mode of making glass smooth, and in every respect proper to receive the tin-foil and quicksilver, is to use first of all fine sand and water, then emery of different degrees of fineness; and, lastly, colcothar of vitriol, or as it is more commonly called, crocus martis, or purple brown. The polishing instrument is a block of wood covered with several folds of cloth and carded wool, so as to make a a fine elastic cushion. This block is worked by the hand; but to increase the pressure of the polisher, the handle is lengthened by a wooden spring, bent to a bow three or four feet long, which, at the other extremity, rests against a fixed point to a beam placed above. The plate is now fastened to a table with plaister, covered with colcothar, and the polisher begins his operation by working it backwards and forwards over the surface of the plate till one side is done; then the other is to be polished in the same manner.

It is well known that glass when smoothed and polished does not acquire the property of reflecting objects till it has been silvered, as it is called, an operation effected by means of an amalgam of tin and quicksilver. The tin-leaf, or as it is more commonly called, tin-foil, which is employed for the purpose, must be of the same size as the glass, because, when pieces of that metal are united by means of mercury, they exhibit the appearance of lines. Tin is one of those metallic substances which becomes soonest oxydated by admixture with mercury. If there remain a portion of the oxyde of a blackish grey colour on the leaf of tin, it produces a spot or stain in the mirror, and that part cannot reflect objects presented to it : great care, therefore, must be taken in silvering glass, to remove whatever portion of oxyde there might be from the surface of the amalgam.

The process is as follows : the tin-foil is laid on a very smooth stone table, usually prepared for the purpose, with grooves on its edges, or with ledges, to preserve the waste quicksilver, and mercury being poured over the metal, it is extended over the surface of it by means of a rubber made of bits of cloth. At the same moment the surface of the tin-foil becomes covered with blackish oxyde, which must be removed with the rubber. More mercury is then to be poured over the tin, where it remains at a level to the thickness of more than a line, without running off. The glass must be applied in a horizontal direction to the table at one of its extremities, and being pushed forwards, it drives before it the oxyde of tin, which is at the surface of the amalgam. A number of leaden weights covered with cloth, are then placed on the glass, which floats on the amalgam, in order to press it down. Without this precaution the glass would exhibit the interstices of the crystals resulting from the amalgam : in this state it is generally suffered to remain several days, till the mixture adheres firmly to the glass.

To obtain leaves of tin, which are, sometimes, six or seven feet in length, with a proportionate breadth, they are not rolled, but hammered after the manner of gold-beaters. The prepared tin is first cast between two plates of polished iron, or between

K 3

two smooth stones; not of a porous nature. Twelve of these plates are placed over each other; and they are then beaten on a stone with heavy hammers, one side of which is plain, the other rounded. The plates joined together are first beaten with the latter: when they become extended, the number of plates is doubled, so that they amount sometimes to eighty or more. They are then smoothed with the flat side of the hammer, and are beaten till they acquire the length of six or seven feet, and the breadth of four or five. The small block of tin from which they are formed is at first ten inches long, six in breadth, and a line and a quarter in thickness. When the leaves are of a less extent and thin, from eighty to a hundred of them are smoothed together.

This is a trade which is comparatively in very few hands; and is in consequence one of considerable profit: it is, however, not always carried on alone, but is often combined with that of a carver and gilder; some cabinet-makers also undertake it.

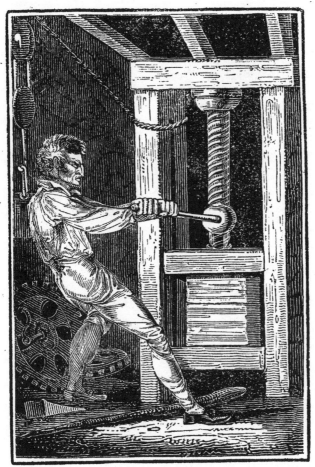

Mechanical Power.

THE MACHINIST.

If any thing is capable of persuading man that he is of a superior order of being to that of the animals which surround him, it is above all the beauty of his inventions, and the inexhaustible resources which he finds in his industry. He is born weak and absolutely naked. His weakness renders him even active and industrious. Upon a contemplation of his own poverty, he calls into activity all his senses. He applies force to force, opposition to resistance—velocity to weight—and weight to velocity. By the assistance of Mechanics this little being of five or six feet in height, with two arms, can expedite as much work as a giant whom we might imagine having a thousand. Take Mechanics from man, and you reduce him to barren thought. Mechanics have done what there is of most beautiful upon the earth.

The Machinist, who embodies in his profession the chief principles of Mechanics, and brings them into active use, is the follower of an occupation of very recent introduction amongst the social and useful arts. It is true, we had to a remote period the common smith, the founder, and the carpenter; and the optician has also been for some time known; but such has been the rapid improvement in mechanical machinery during the last fifty years, that the Machinist was wanting to unite the correct precision of the finer branches of Mechanics to the practical utilities of the common smith, the carpenter, &c.

As the *steam-engine* occupies so conspicuous a portion in this trade, indeed, is the chief moving power in it, we deem it necessary to say, that it is, unquestionably, one of the noblest monuments of human ingenuity. It was originally invented by the Marquis of Worcester, in the reign of Charles the Second. This nobleman published, in 1663, a small book called " A Century of Inventions," giving an account of a hundred different discoveries or contrivances of his own; amongst these is an account of raising water by the force of steam, which, now that we are possessed of the engine, appears to agree very well with its construction. But as there was no plate accompanying his description, we are entirely unacquainted with the particular mode in which he applied the power of steam. It does not appear, however, that he met with sufficient encouragement, and this useful discovery was long neglected.

Towards the end of the seventeenth century, Captain Savary succeeded in constructing a machine of this kind, having probably seen the Marquis of Worcester's account; obtained a patent for the invention, and erected several steam-engines, which he described in a book entitled the "Miner's Friend," published in 1696.

In the beginning of the eighteenth century, Newcomen and Crauly first conceived the project of applying a piston with a lever and other machinery. They were contented to share the profits of the invention with Savary, who procured a patent for it in 1705, in which they all three joined. But it was not till 1712, that the difficulties in working it were removed.

About 1762, Mr. Watt began to turn his attention to this machine, which he has since brought to so great a degree of perfection.

Perhaps we cannot better describe the trade of a Machinist than in enumerating some of the most important articles which he manufactures, which are, machinery constructed and manufactured for experimental and scientific elucidation, steam-engines, both of condensing and high pressure, to any required power. Digesters, chemical apparatus, philosophical and gas-light machines; conductors for protecting buildings and shipping from lightning. Pumps, both atmospheric and forcing, machines for soda and artificial waters; syphons, air and fluid cocks; exhausting and condensing syringes; garden engines, fountains, hydrostatic engines, and hydro-mechanical presses, cutting engines for screws, wheels, cylinders, and boring bars, stamping and cutting presses with dies and punches. Saw-mills, portable iron forges, mill work, and large framing in wood and iron. Mechanical modelling, and experimental machinery. Turning-lathes, lead and pewter pipe-moulds, all sorts of turning, in iron, steel, and brass, with screw cutting, and a great variety of other articles for mechanical movements, which it would not be easy to enumerate.

It is obvious that the person who carries on this business must be possessed of considerable ingenuity, and great mechanical knowledge; his employment being of a very complicated kind. He requires the talents and experience of the joiner, the brass and iron founder, the smith and the turner, in their most extended variety. It is by uniting the powers of these several occupations into one, together with the great assortment of excellent tools which he unavoidably requires, that the Machinist is furnished with those facilities of manufacture which peculiarly belong to his employment. The saw, the plane, the chisel, and the hammer; the furnace, and all the implements for casting; the forge, the anvil, the vice; and the products of these tools are, at last, submitted to the *turning-lathe.* This machine,

K 5

and its apparatus, as they are now found in the Machinist's manufactory, form the grand and rapid instrument that, by the assistance of the steam-engine to give it motion, produces the accuracy which we find in all the different machinery and instruments that the Machinist prepares.

The *turning-lathe*, and its various applications, would occupy much more space than we can spare to describe: we can only hint at them. Cylinders, both interior and exterior, are turned and bored; plain surfaces of any form, are smoothed; cones, globes, and every other figure that the skill of the workman, or the ingenuity of the apparatus can effect, are brought to their exact shape and polish by this machine, which ranks above all others in usefulness, as well as in the endless variety of its powers.

The plate represents the Machinist's work-shop, with the five mechanical powers, viz. the screw, the pulley, the wheel, the wedge, and the lever. There is also the turning-lathe, the steam-engine, and the saw-mill.

Able journeymen at this business, will get from thirty to fifty shillings per week.

We have obtained the principal part of this description from an inspection of the workshop of Mr. Alexander Galloway, the Machinist, West Street, Smithfield, who, we understand, was the first person who established himself under this designation, and who is a proof, in his own person, of the great power, activity, and ingenuity of man.

Mariner.

THE MARINER.

THE MARINER is, in common language, the same as sailor, or seaman ; although the art of the Mariner is not, strictly speaking, a trade, it is an occupation of so much importance in England, that we cannot pass it over.

What boldness must that man have possessed who first traversed the ocean in a ship! If nature has denied us wings, the industry and ingenuity of man has furnished ships with sails, which enable him to move over immense seas with the rapidity of the eagle : nothing more strongly proves the superiority of the genius of man, nothing more powerfully attests his sovereignty and his pre-eminence.

Navigation, which is in some way or another known even to the most savage nations, is a profession which requires considerable information, and, which contributes, in a very great degree, to the comforts, the convenience, the happiness and wealth of a nation, more especially in this country, in which it is so much fostered and encouraged.

The art itself is very ancient. The Tyrians and the Carthaginians are said to have practised it in the Mediterranean; but the Chinese, the Arabians, and Persians, navigated the East Indian seas a long time before. After the ruin of Carthage, navigation was adopted by many of the nations of Europe as a medium of commerce, which has been, indeed, the principal stimulus in the prosecution of voyages from the remotest period of time. It is amongst

European nations, during the last four centuries, that individuals have arisen, who have, by their enterprise and perseverance, very much contributed to distinguish them as periods of extraordinary importance in the history of the world.

A knowledge of the different seas, of the application of astronomy, the discovery of the compass, the invention of instruments to take the height of the sun and stars, or to measure the course of the ship; the observations of sailors themselves, the fidelity of charts; the better construction of ships, and the perfection of many other things, have brought the management of a ship on the ocean, to almost mathematical demonstration. Christopher Columbus, who discovered America, Bartholomew Diaz, who discovered the Cape of Good Hope, and Captain Cook, by his attempts to discover a north-west passage to India, and other geographical investigations, amidst a crowd of men big with enterprise, might be mentioned, who have contributed to this important art.

As the discovery of the compass forms an æra of the first importance in navigation, we shall present our readers with a short history of it.

The magnet, or loadstone, was certainly known to the philosophers of ancient Greece, for its quality of attracting iron; and in later ages, the few who were in possession of the secret were enabled to perform tricks, which the amazement of the ignorant ascribed to magic: but till about the end of the twelfth century we find no good authority to shew that its more valuable property, its polarity, or that power by which one point of it, or even of a needle or bar of iron touched with it, turns to the north pole, was known, at least in the western part of the world.

It has been asserted, that the Chinese knew the polarity of the magnet, and used the compass many centuries before it was known in Europe: but this point does not seem satisfactorily proved, since, after *asserting* that the compass was known, they fail in proving the knowledge of its most valuable use in conducting a ship across the ocean.

About the conclusion of the twelfth century, the earliest notice that is to be found of the polarity of the magnet, and its use by seamen, appears in the poetical works of Hugues de Bercy, called also Guiot Provins.

Jacob de Vitriaco, also, who lived at the same time, and was bishop of Acon in Palestine, mentions it under the name of adamant, but at the same time describes it as indispensably necessary to all who used the sea.

In defiance, however, of these authorities, the Italian writers claim the honour of the invention for Flavio Gioia, a citizen of Amalfi, on the coast of the Adriatic, who, they say, first used it in the year 1302, or 1320.

The truth, however, seems to be, that the very early Mariners, to whom the use of the magnetic needle was familiar, were accustomed to place it on a floating straw: while the addition of a circular card, on which the different winds were represented, affixed to the needle, and traversing with it, was apparently the improvement of Gioia.

Peter Adsiger, whose letter, dated in 1269, is said yet to remain in the library of the University of Leyden, not only wrote upon the various properties of the magnet, and the construction of the azimuth compass, but on the *variation* of the magnetic needle: a discovery, the credit of which was attributed to Columbus in 1492, and afterwards to Sebastian Cabot in 1500 : who seems only to have had greater opportunities than other persons, of remarking that the needle was not perfectly true to the north point, but diverged or varied a little from it.

The compass was long very rude and imperfect ; but at length received great improvement from the invention and experiments of Dr. Knight, Mr. Smeaton, and Mr. M'Culloch about the middle of the sixteenth century. The variation of the needle was not for a long time believed, but careful observations soon discovered that in England and its neighbourhood, the needle pointed to the eastward of the true north line, and the quantity of this deviation being known, Mariners relied upon their compass, upon making an allowance for the true variation, the exact course being readily obtained. Later observations prove that the deviation from the north was variable; that it gradually diminished till 1657, when it pointed due north at London; since then it veered to the westward, and is, at this time, 1818, again returning from the west towards the pole.

Mariners are sometimes employed on board merchant ships, and sometimes in men of war. In merchants' employ, the mariners are accountable to the master, the master to the owners of the vessel, and the owners to the merchant, for any damages that may happen. If a vessel is lost by tempest, the mariners lose their wages, and the owners their freight: this is intended to make them use their utmost endeavours to preserve the ship committed to their care.

Mariners on board the king's ships are subject to strict regulations, which, however, depend on certain fixed laws passed at different times by parliament. Mariners who are not in his Majesty's service are liable, during the time of war, to be impressed, unless they enter voluntarily, to which they are encouraged by bounties and high wages; and every foreign seaman who, during war, shall serve two years in any man of war, merchant-ship, or privateer, becomes naturalized.

The Mariner represented in the plate, is of a higher rank and estimation than common sailors; he understands the art of navigation, or of conducting a vessel from one place to another in the safest, shortest, and most commodious way. He ought, therefore, to be well acquainted with the islands, rocks, sands, and straits near which he has to sail. He should also know the signs which indicate the approach to land: these are the appearance of birds, the floating of weeds on the surface of the sea, the depth and colour of the sea. He should, moreover, understand the nature of the winds, particularly the times when the *trade* winds and monsoons set in; the seasons when storms and hurricanes may be expected, and the signs of their approach; the motion of currents and tides. He must understand, also, the working of the ship; that is, the management of the sails, rigging, &c.

Navigation is either *common* or *proper*. The former is usually called coasting; that is, where the ships are on the same or very neighbouring coasts; and where the vessel is seldom out of sight of land, or out of reach of *sounding*. In this case little more is required than an acquaintance with the lands which are to be passed, the compass, and the sounding-line.

To gain a knowledge of the coast, a good chart or map is necessary.

The *compass*, or Mariner's compass, as it is sometimes called, a history of which we have just given, consists of a circular brass box, which contains a card with the thirty-two points, fixed on a magnetic needle, which always turns to the north, or nearly so. The needle with the card turns on an upright pin fixed in the centre of the box. The top of the box is covered with glass to prevent the wind from disturbing the motion of the card. The whole is inclosed in another box of wood, where it is suspended by brass hoops to keep the card in a horizontal position, whatever the motion of the ship may be; and it is so placed in the ship, that the middle section of the box may lie over the middle section of the ship, along her keel.

. The method of finding by the compass the direction in which a ship sails is, the compass being suspended, the Mariner looks horizontally over it, in the direction of the ship's *wake*, which is a light-coloured track caused on the surface of the water by the course of the ship, by which he sees the point of the compass denoting the direction of the wake; the point opposite to this is that to which the ship is sailing according to the compass; and knowing how much the compass varies, he can tell the true point of the horizon to which he is going.

The sounding-line is a line with a plummet at the end: it is used to try the depth of the water and the quality of the bottom.

In *navigation proper*, which is where the voyage is long, and pursued through the main ocean, there are many other requisites besides those already mentioned. Here a considerable skill in mathematics and astronomy is required, and an aptness in using instruments for celestial observations.

One of these instruments the Mariner in the plate is represented holding in his right hand, while he is pointing to his ship with the other. The boat which is to carry him on board of ship, is drawn on shore.

To ascertain the velocity of the ship on the water, the Mariner is provided with an instrument called a *log*, which is a triangular piece of wood eight or nine inches long, to which is attached a small cord having knots in it at proper distances, and he has also a half-minute sand-glass: the rule is, that as many knots as run off the reel per half minute when the log is in the water, so many miles sails the ship per hour: thus when in nautical language the sailor says, We sailed *nine knots*, he means our progress was nine miles an hour. When the weather is so cloudy that no celestial observations can be made, the log and compass are of infinite importance: vessels sailing under these disadvantages, are said to sail by *dead reckoning.* A book of this reckoning is kept in which entries are made daily; it is called the *log-book.*

The wages of a Mariner depend upon his employment; that is, whether he be in the king's service or on board a merchantman: they depend also upon the size of the ship, and on the situation which he holds in it.

There is no profession of more importance to the interests of this country than that of the Mariner. Government, therefore, provides a place for numbers of those who are disabled, in Greenwich Hospital, or a pension out of it; and to the widows and children of those who are slain in defending their country, small pensions are granted. Greenwich Hospital is supported by the nation, and by sixpence a month deducted out of every seaman's wages.

THE MERCHANT.

THE MERCHANT is a wholesale dealer in all sorts of merchandise, who exports and imports goods to and from different parts of the world, who deals in exchange, and buys and sells goods in their original packages without breaking bulk. In England the term Merchant is usually restricted to a person who has commercial transactions with foreign countries, who is owner of a vessel or vessels, or who is engaged in sending on his own account goods in large quantities from one port to another. To this general definition there are, however, a few exceptions, as a Hop-merchant, &c.

The mercantile profession is very ancient, and generally esteemed noble and independent: in France, by two decrees of Louis the XIVth, the one in 1669, and the other in 1701, a nobleman was allowed to trade both by land and sea without any disparagement to his nobility; and we have frequent instances of Merchants having been ennobled in that country in consequence of the utility which their commerce produced to the state. In many other places, more especially in the republics of Venice, Holland, and Genoa, the value of commerce has been justly appreciated; and in Great Britain there is not a higher or more enviable character in the community than that of an honourable, upright, and intelligent Merchant.

To carry on the business of a Merchant with a high degree of credit, a man should possess a large

The Merchant.

stock of general knowledge and a considerable capital; the one will prevent him from falling into errors, and the other will enable him to give credit to his customers both at home and abroad.

The Merchant should be perfectly acquainted with all the departments of writing, arithmetic, and the keeping of books. He should be expert in the forms of invoices, account of sales, policies of insurances, in the nature of charters, bills of lading, and bills of exchange. He should understand the agreement and difference which subsist between the monies, weights, and measures of different countries, or of different counties in his own country. He ought to have a general and accurate knowledge of the different manufactures in which he deals, at least of the places where they are best made, and of the materials of which they are composed. He should know the best season for bringing his own goods to market, and be well acquainted with the nature of *exchange,* according to the course of different places, and with the causes of its rise and fall. He should know what merchandizes are permitted or prohibited, as well on entering as in going out of the kingdom or states where they are manufactured. He should know the customs due on the importation or exportation of goods, according to the usage and regulations of the places to which he trades. He should understand the best methods of packing merchandizes, either to preserve them in warehouses, or to adapt them for short or long voyages. He should know the price and condition of freighting and insuring ships and goods; and if the vessels or any part of them are his own property, he should be acquainted with their value; the expense of first building and subsequent repairs; the wages given to the several officers and sailors who work them, and the best method of engaging them in his service. He ought to be able to write letters with ease and elegance, and to understand as, many foreign languages as he can. The following are, however, the most important for him to know: the *Spanish*, which is used not only in Spain, but on the coast of Africa, from the Canaries to the Cape of Good Hope; the *Italian*, which is understood on all the coasts of the Mediterranean, and in many parts of the Levant; the *German*, which is understood in almost all the Northern countries; and the *French*, which is current in most parts of Europe. Finally, the Merchant should be well acquainted with the laws, customs, and regulations of the countries to which he does or may trade.

, The business carried on by Merchants in this country may be divided into *inland* and *foreign*. The *inland* trade consists in transporting the commodities of one part of the kingdom to another, but this is rather the cent. more or less upon condition that he pay the business of the wholesale dealer, than of professed Merchants, unless goods are conveyed by ships.

The foreign trade consists of exports to, and imports from almost all parts of the world.

Merchants are distinguished from one another either by the goods in which they traffic, or by the countries with which they have their chief correspondence. Thus a Merchant who deals chiefly in tobacco is called a Tobacco-Merchant, a wholesale dealer in wines a Wine-Merchant, &c.

: The West India Merchant exports and imports goods to and from the West Indies. A Turkey Merchant exports and imports goods to and from Turkey. A Russian Merchant exports and imports goods to and from Russia, &c.

Merchants have in their dealings much business with the Custom-House, which may be readily explained. Rum, sugar, and almost all articles imported from abroad pay certain duties to government before they can be sold in England: these duties are to be paid at the Custom-House.

Many articles manufactured in England, as glass, leather, &c. are subject to heavy taxes; but to encourage trade these taxes, or part of them, are often returned, when the same articles are exported to foreign countries, and such returns of taxes are called *drawbacks.* Sometimes more is allowed than the tax; such allowance is called a *bounty* on exportation.

Ships are also entered *inwards* and *outwards,* when they bring home or proceed abroad with cargoes; they also pay a tonnage duty in this country on their arrival, the master being required to carry an account of his cargo to the Custom-House, which is called a manifest report.

Factors or *Brokers* are a species of Merchants who deal by commission, and sell the goods of other people, consigned from the place of growth or manufacture to them, for a certain premium per cent. Thus a farmer in the country has a thousand quarters of wheat to sell at the London market; he cannot conveniently come to town, therefore he sends his wheat to a corn-factor, who sells it to the best advantage, receives the money, and remits it to the farmer, after having deducted his commission-money for trouble and expense.

There are, also, factors or brokers who deal in foreign commodities or colonial produce in the same manner. These are distinguished either by the countries with which they deal, or by the goods usually assigned to them; as sugar-brokers, Sheffield-factors, wine-brokers, &c. &c.

Insurers, Underwriters, are a species of Merchants who insure goods from one port to another for a certain premium per cent. If I have a ship bound with goods for the East Indies, there is a risk of its being lost at sea or being burnt; or in time of war, of being taken by an enemy; I therefore go to an *Underwriter,* and pay him 5, 10, or 20 per me, as many hundred pounds as I have insured in the event of the vessel's being lost or captured by the enemy. The Insurers are called *Underwriters,* because they write their names *below* the articles in the instrument called a policy, by which I become legally intitled to the sum which I have insured. To effectuate which insurances there is a class of persons denominated Insurance-brokers.

' To form an adequate idea of the mercantile transactions of the city of London alone, it has been computed that upon an average about five thousand vessels sail from this port every year. These measure upwards of one million of tons, and are navigated by about sixty thousand seamen.

The Musical Instrument Maker.

THE MUSICAL-INSTRUMENT MAKER.

THE MUSICAL INSTRUMENT MAKER requires no further definition than that which the name itself imports.

Music, as well as painting, can be traced to the most remote antiquity. The most savage nations are not strangers to the pleasure which it affords. We find in every country the art more or less perfect, the instruments more or less rude, in proportion to the degree of civilization to which the people have arrived.

After the ordinary exercise of speech, to express our wants and our intentions, it is a great pleasure to hear from the same voice a melodious song, and this melody is frequently such, that the most perfect instruments are still, in expression, far below it.

However, the art and ingenuity of man have now brought musical instruments to a surprising degree of perfection, and considerably added to the elegant luxuries and refinements of the age.

It will be impossible for us to mention all the instruments which are made, either of the wind or stringed kind, but we shall describe some of the principal ones, in order to give some idea of the whole, and of the trade of which we now treat.

The *organ* is an instrument of the highest antiquity, in the structure of which the greatest ingenuity has been displayed. The most difficult part of this instrument in its manufacture is the wind-

5

chest, which is a large horizontal box, so closely
fitted and prepared as to retain the wind forced
into it, by various large bellows, which must be numerous, and capacious in proportion to the size of the
wind-chest. The quantity of wind in it is always
known to the organist, by means of a tell-tale, or
index attached to the bellows, which rises and falls
in proportion to the quantity of air, and apprizes
the performer in what degree the wind is exhausted.
The top of the wind-chest is bored with several lines
of apertures, proportioned to the sizes of the pipes
which they are to receive, those of the bass notes
being of course the largest; but all the pipes in
each row being different as to their interior construction, and consequently producing very different sounds, each row is called a *stop*, and has a
plug appropriate to it, acting upon a slide, which
shuts or opens the whole of that row at pleasure;
this is called a register. There are as many of such
rows of apertures, or registers, as there are kinds
of tones, or stops on the organ: some having few,
others having numerous stops. The wind is prevented from escaping from the wind-chest into the
pipes by valves, which are opened only when the
performer presses the keys respectively; when, by
means of communicating wires, the valves are
pressed down, and the wind passes into the pipes.
When the key is quitted, the pressure of the wind,
aided by a spiral wire-spring, shuts the valve, and
the sound of that pipe instantly ceases. In order
to regulate the force of the sound, most church-
organs have either two or three rows of keys whereby a greater or less number of pipes may be filled,
and the powers of the instrument be controlled into
what is called the small organ, or be let loose, so as
to become the full organ. The pipes suited to the
higher notes are made of mixed metals, chiefly tin
and lead; they increase in length and diameter, in
proportion to the note; until metal pipes being no

farther applicable, square ones of wood are substituted in their stead, for all the lower notes. The dimensions of all the pipes of an organ are regulated by a scale, or diapason, formed for the use of the manufacturers in this line, and apportioned to every size of the instrument usually made.

The *stops* usually made in a great organ, are the *open diapason*, in which all the pipes are open at the top ; this is a metallic stop ;—the *stopped diapason*, the bass-notes of which, up to the tenor C, are always made of wood, and are stopped at their summits with wooden plugs, by which the tone is very much softened ;—the *principal* is the middle stop, which serves, when tuned, as the basis for tuning all the other parts, above and below ; it is metallic ;— the *twelfth*, which is metallic also, derives its name from being a twelfth, or an octave and a half above the diapason ; the *fifteenth*, so called because it is two octaves above the diapason ; the *sesquialtera* is composed of various pipes, turned in the parts of the common chord ; the upper part is often called the cornet ; the *furniture* stop is very shrill, and in some passages has a peculiarly fine effect ; the *trumpet* is a metallic stop, and derives its name from the instrument which it so admirably imitates ; this peculiar tone is produced by what is called a reed, but in reality a piece of brass, on which the wind acts forcibly, giving a roughness of sound, which is further changed by all the pipes of this stop having bell-mouths like trumpets ; the *clarion* is a reed-stop also, but an octave higher than the trumpet : the *tierce* is a third above the fifteenth. The octave above the twelfth is too shrill to be used, but in the full organ ; the *cornet* is a treble stop ; the *dulcimer* takes its name from the sweetness of its sound ; there are also the *flute*, the *bassoon, vox-humana, haut-boy,* and *cremona* stops.

The fingering of an organ is precisely the same as that of the piano-forte, so far as relates to the situation of the keys, &c.; but on account of the great number of holding notes in organ music, the fingers are never kept down, whence it is considered highly injudicious to piano-forte performers to practise the organ, they being subject to lose that lightness and that delicacy of touch required for the former instrument.

Organs are also made with barrels, on which are a great number of pins, and staples, of flat brass wire, and of different lengths. The barrel being turned by means of a crank, or winch, the wires that communicate with the valves in the wind-chest, are acted upon by the pins and staples, which hold down the valves for a longer or shorter time, according to the duration of the notes which they are designed to give. On these barrels, which are made to shift at pleasure, from ten to fifteen tunes are usually made. The winch not only turns the barrel, but also works a pair of bellows, by which the wind-chest is supplied. This instrument is called the hand, or barrel organ, and is very common in the streets of London.

Before we quit the organ, we may just observe, and the observation will be equally applicable to the manufacturers of other musical instruments, that the organ-builder should possess a nice, accurate, and highly-cultivated ear, and a sound judgment in the vibratory qualities of wood and metal. He should also be acquainted with the science of pneumatics, and practical mechanics; and he should be so far informed in the simple elements of musical composition as to be capable of trying the different stops and combinations of his own instruments, and of deciding for himself on the effects in performance.

Having been so diffuse in the account of the organ, our notice of the other instruments must be somewhat circumscribed. But we may remark generally, that in the structure of all kinds of musical instruments, both wind and stringed, the use of well-seasoned wood is of the utmost importance, and that to the preparing and seasoning it, the attention of the musical instrument manufacturer must be particularly directed : for with every precaution in this particular, from the alterations of the atmosphere, the best instruments will sometimes get out of tune; and, with neglect, the artist's labour will often be in vain.

The other principal wind-instruments now in use, are the mouth-organ, or *Pandean-pipes*, frequently played as an accompaniment to other music in the streets; they consist of a range of pipes, bound together, side by side, gradually lessening with respect to each other in diameter, and shortening in length. The longest is about six inches, and the shortest about two inches in length.

The *Eolian harp* consists of a long box, in which four or more strings are stretched its whole length, and tuned to the component parts of any common chord, such as C. E. G. C. E. G, &c. opposite the line of strings, which are placed over a slanting sounding-board, and two slits, one on each side, running parallel with the entire strings, or a circular hole with ornamental openings, is made in the centre of the box, under the strings; when this instrument is placed in a confined passage, a window for example, the air rushing between the strings, and through the apertures in the box, produces a variety of harmonious and beautiful sounds.

The *Trumpet* may be next mentioned. It is made of metal: those of silver are by far the softest in tone, but brass is in general use. It has a mouthpiece about an inch in diameter, concave, for the lips to act within, and closing to a very narrow tube. Trumpets with slides to lower or raise the pitch one or two notes, are the best and most useful instruments of this class.

The *French Horn* consists of a long tube twisted

into several circular folds, gradually increasing in diameter, from the end at which it is blown, to that at which the wind issues. Those intended for concerts have, like the trumpets, various crooks and a slide, whereby they may be brought to accord with the most scrupulous exactness.

The *Serpent* is so called from its form: its mouthpiece is very similar to that of the trumpet, but it is made of ivory. This is the deepest bass instrument of all that have five finger holes. It is made of very thin wood, covered with buckram and leather, so as to become very firm.

In the *common flute* there are seven fingers above, and one for each thumb below; some have only one thumb-hole, others two small ones: the sound is generated by blowing through a slit into the bore, the superfluous wind passing out at a vent made on the top close to the upper end. All the flageolet tribe, which are of various sorts and sizes, belong to this species; one lately introduced, called the double flageolet, is a very pleasing instrument.

The *German flute* is also a very agreeable instrument, it is usually made of box, or some very hard and seasoned wood.

The *Bassoon* is not, we believe, so much in use as it formerly was. It has two bodies, and a swanneck brass tube, with a reed attached to it, through which the sound is generated.

The *Hautboy* and *Clarionet* have mouth-pieces of different forms, made of reeds, or canes.

The principal varieties of stringed instruments, are found in the harp, the piano-forte, the guitar, the violin, and the Eolian harp, before mentioned, &c.

In the *Harp*, each note has a separate string; in the Welch harp, there are two strings to each note of the principal scale, with an intermediate row for the semitones. In the pedal harp, the half notes are formed, by pressing pins against the strings, so as to shorten their effective length.

In the *Harpsichord* and *Spinnet*, instruments gone very much out of fashion; the quill acts like the finger in the harp, or the plectrum in the lyre.

In the *Piano-forte* the sound is produced by a blow of a hammer, raised by a lever, which is as much detached from it as possible. The *Grand Piano* resembles the Harpsichord in form, but its action and tone are much superior. Its wires run longitudinally along the belly, or sounding-board, supported, at about two-thirds of an inch distance, by small, low, curved battens of beech, or other wood, into which pins are firmly driven, for the purpose of keeping the wires perfectly parallel. These battens, called bridges, determine the lengths of the several wires; though the latter pass beyond them for some distance, being hooked on at their farther ends to stout pins, driven into a solid part of the frame-work, and coming over the bridge, which is next to the keys, with which it is parallel, and winding on a set of iron pegs, which, being driven into a solid block of hard wood, are turned either right or left by means of a small instrument, called a *tuning hammer*, and are thus tightened or relaxed at pleasure. The shortest wires are the thinnest, which lie to the right, and give the upper notes; the longest are to the left, and give the lowest notes; those between them are longer or shorter according to their vibration, their several lengths increasing as they approach towards the left side of the instrument, forming, by means of the bridges which lie obliquely, a triangular figure. Each note has three wires lying within somewhat less than half an inch in breadth: these are equi-distant, and proceed to three rows of tuning-pins, so that the tuner cannot mistake as to which of the three wires he acts upon. The wires are imported from Germany, our artisans not having acquired the mode of giving them a due degree of temper. Those of the higher notes are of brass, and commonly begin with No. 8, 9, or 10, gradually increasing in thickness, until they reach the extent of about four octaves, when they give place to copper, wires, which produce a deeper sound.

Most grand piano-fortes have two pedals, one for each foot, communicating with the interior; one is designed to raise all the dampers completely, the other to throw the whole of the key-frame to the right, more or less, by which means the hammers are slid at the same moment in a body, about a quarter of an inch to the right, also so as to quit either one or two, at pleasure, of the left-hand wires of each note, and to strike upon only one or two, as is judged proper for the greater or less diminution of sound. The sounding-board, or belly, is made of very fine narrow deals, chiefly imported from the continent, and so closely joined, that in many, no line or indication of junction, can be distinguished.

The square piano-forte is very different in form from the grand. It however has an action and movements nearly similar.

The *Piano-forte* is of German origin, and derives its name from its equal command, both of softness and strength of tone.

The *Guitar* is played with the fingers like the harp. It has a broad neck, on which are various frets, made of wires, fixed into the finger-board, at right-angles with the wires, these being the guides for the fingers to make the several notes by passing between the frets. The bridge is very low, and stands behind a circular sound-hole, covered with an ornamental and perforated plate; the body of the guitar is of an oval form, the sides perpendicular to the belly and back.

The *Violin* is an instrument universally known. All the violin class have four strings fastened at one end to a small piece of ebony, called the tail-piece, and after passing over a raised bridge, made of seasoned wood, and over a little ridge, called the nut, are fastened respectively to four pegs, made of very hard tough wood, by the turning of which the strings are put in tune. All the strings give fifths to their neighbours throughout; thus the first string is E; the second A, the third D, and the fourth, which is a covered one, is G; the tenors and basses have no E string, but a C one added below the G. The notes are made by compressing the strings on a rounded slip of ebony, called a finger-board, which proceeds from the nut, full four-fifths of the distance between that and the bridge, the latter being always placed on the belly or sounding-board, exactly between the centres of the two sound-holes, which are in the form of an S; the belly is supported by a small piece of rounded deal, called the sounding-post, without which the tones would be imperfect and harsh.

Violin strings were formerly obtained from Rome, Naples, and some parts of Germany; but latterly they have been manufactured in England, of equal quality with those procured from abroad.

Of *Drums* we have an abundant variety. The side or military drum is well known. The *Kettle* drum derives its name from its form, the bottom being made of copper, and the head being vellum, or goat's skin.

The *Tabor* is a small drum, so flat, that the two heads are not more than three inches asunder.

The *Tambourine* is a kind of drum, with only one head, the other end of the hoop, which is not more than four inches in breadth, being open.

The *Triangle* is known from its name; but we must not swell our article with any further notice.

The business of a Musical-Instrument Maker is a very lucrative one. The trade in piano-fortes alone is one of considerable magnitude, seventy guineas being frequently paid for a good article of this kind. The price of an organ frequently amounts to many hundred pounds. Of course considerable capital is necessary in this trade, and the wages of journeymen are good.

The plate represents the Musical-Instrument Maker's shop.

THE NEEDLE-MAKER.

THE needle is a very common little instrument, made of steel, pointed at one end and pierced at the other, used in sewing, embroidery, tapestry, &c.

Needles were first made in England by a native of India, in 1545, but the art was lost at his death; it was, however, shortly after recovered by Christopher Greening, who, with his three children, were settled by Mr. Damer, ancestor of the present Lord Milton, at Long Crendon, in Bucks, where the manufactory has been carried on from that time to the present.

Needles make a very considerable article of commerce, although there is scarcely any commodity cheaper, the consumption being almost incredible. The sizes of common sewing needles, are from No. 1 the largest, to No. 25 the smallest. They are, also, of three kinds, *sharps*, *betweens*, and *blunts*. They are distinguished as *Common* and *Whitechapel*, from the latter being of better quality, and having a C cut upon each needle, we apprehend from *Whitechapel* being the residence of the first and best makers of the articles. *Whitechapel* needles are now, however, made in different parts of England. There are, also, many other kinds of needles, as *darning* needles, *double longs*, No. 50, &c. Besides which, there is the netting-needle, and the knitting-needle: the glover's needle with a triangular point; the tambour-needle, which is made like a hook; being thrust through the cloth, the thread is caught under the hook, and the needle is drawn back, taking the thread with it.

Surgeons' needles are generally made crooked, and their points triangular: they are of different forms and sizes, and bear different names, according to the purposes for which they are used.

In the manufacture of needles, the German and Hungarian steel is most in repute. The first thing in making needles is to pass the steel through a coal fire, and by means of a hammer to bring it into a cylindrical form. This being done, it is drawn through a large hole of a wire-drawing iron, and returned into the fire, and drawn through a second hole of the iron, smaller than the first, and so on till it has acquired the degree of fineness necessary for the kind of needle wanted. The steel thus reduced to a fine-wire, is cut in pieces of the proper length; these pieces are flatted at one end on the anvil, in order to form the head and the eye. They are then softened and pierced at each extreme of the flat part on the anvil, by a punch of well-tempered steel, and laid on a leaden block to bring out, with another punch, the little piece of steel remaining in the eye. When the head and eye are finished, the point is formed with a file, and the whole filed over: the needles are then made red hot, by being laid on long narrow iron, crooked at one end, in a charcoal fire; and when taken out from thence they are thrown into a bason of cold water to harden. They are next placed in an iron shovel on a fire, more or less brisk in proportion to the thickness of the needles, taking care to move them from time to time. This serves to temper them and take off their brittleness.

They are now to be straightened one after another with the hammer. The next process is the polishing. To do this, twelve or fifteen thousand needles are ranged in little heaps against each other, in a piece of new buckram sprinkled with emery-dust. The needles being thus disposed, emery-dust is thrown over them, which is again sprinkled with oil of olives; at last, the whole is made up into a roll, well bound at both ends. This roll is laid on a polishing table, and over it a thick plank loaded with stones, which men work backward and forwards for two days successively; by these means the needles become insensibly polished. They are now taken out and the filth washed off with hot water and soap, they are then wiped in hot bran a little moistened, placed with the needles in a round box suspended in the air by a cord, which is kept stirring till the bran and needles are dry. The needles are now sorted; the points are turned the same way and smoothed with an emery-stone turned with a wheel; this is the end of the process, and nothing remains to be done but to put them up in papers, some of which contain a quarter of a hundred, and others, one hundred in a paper, according to the convenience or wishes of the purchaser.

An improvement in the usual mode of tempering needles has been latterly adopted by using oil, or tallow and other ingredients, instead of water, which substances are supposed to improve the process. The needles thus hardened are returned to the furnace with the oil upon them, and remain there till the oil inflames, when they are withdrawn, and again cooled in water. This second process tempers them: at first they are quite hard, and so brittle as to break with the slightest touch; the tempering takes off the brittleness, but leaves them hard enough to take a good point. When they are hardened in water according to the old method, the heat for tempering them can only be guessed at, or estimated by experience, but the flaming of the oil is a much more certain method.

Mr. W. Bell, of Walsal, has obtained a patent for the manufacture of needles of all sorts: the principal difference between which, and the usual method, is, that the needles are cast, and we suppose, that by this process, needles may be made still cheaper than they now are.

The Mathematical Instrument Maker.

THE OPTICIAN.

THE OPTICIAN makes telescopes, microscopes, spectacles, opera-glasses, reading-glasses, &c. &c.

The history of this important art will, in effect, be an account of the art itself, which we shall endeavour to give in as concise and perspicuous a manner as we can, consistent with the design of this work.

Although the ancients made few optical experiments, they nevertheless knew that when light passed through media of different densities, it did not move in a straight line, but was bent or refracted out of its original direction. This was probably suggested to them by the appearance of a straight rod partly immersed in water; and accordingly we find many questions concerning this and other optical appearances in the works of Aristotle. It appears also from Pliny, and Lactantius, that burning-glasses were known to the ancients.

Archimedes is said to have written a treatise on the appearance of a ring or circle under water, and therefore could not have been ignorant of the common phenomena of refraction.

The ancients, however, were not only acquainted with these more ordinary appearances, but also with the production of colours by refraction. Seneca says, that if the light of the sun shines through an angular piece of glass, it will shew all the colours of the rainbow. The first treatise of any consequence, on the subject of optics, was written by Ptolemy;

this treatise is now lost, but from the accounts of others, we find that he treated of astronomical refractions.

The nature of refraction was afterwards considered by Alhazen, an Arabian writer; and his observations were afterwards confirmed by Vitellio, Tycho Brahe, and others.

In the writings of Roger Bacon, in the thirteenth century, we find the first distinct account of the magnifying power of glasses, and it is not improbable that what he wrote upon this subject gave rise to the useful invention of *Spectacles*. From this time to that of the revival of learning in Europe, we have no treatise on optics. One of the first who distinguished himself in this way, was Maurolycus, teacher of mathematics at Messina, in 1578. Baptista Porta, who died in 1515, was the inventor of the camera obscura, which throws more light on these interesting subjects. From this period the writers on optics have been numerous and important, amongst whom Sir Isaac Newton ranks as one of the most eminent.

Glass globes, and specula, seem to have been the only optical instruments known to the ancients. Alhazen gave the first hint of the invention of spectacles. From the writings of this author, together with the observations of Roger Bacon, it is not improbable that some monks gradually hit upon the construction of spectacles. It is certain that spectacles were well known in the 13th century, and not long before. It is said, that Alexander Spina, a native of Pisa, who died in 1313, happened to see a pair of spectacles in the hands of a person who would not explain them to him, and that he succeeded in making a pair for himself, and immediately made the construction public. It is also inscribed on the tomb of Salvinus Armatus, a nobleman of Florence, who died in 1317, that he was the inventor of spectacles.

But although convex and concave lenses were sufficiently common, yet no attempt was made to combine them into a telescope till the end of the sixteenth century. We are informed, that as James Metius was amusing himself with mirrors and burning-glasses, he thought of looking through two lenses at a time; and that happening to take one that was convex, and another that was concave, and happening also to hit upon a pretty good adjustment of them, he found that by looking through them, distant objects appeared very large and distinct. In fact, without knowing it, he had made a *Telescope*.

But the honour of having exhibited this arrangement of glasses in a tube, appears due to Jansen, a spectacle-maker of Middleburgh, in 1590. Jansen, directing his telescope to celestial objects, distinctly viewed spots on the surface of the moon, and discovered many new stars.

Galileo having made many improvements in the telescope, has by some been considered as the inventor, but he himself acknowledges that he first heard of the instrument from a German. The first telescope which Galileo constructed, magnified only three times; but soon after he made another, which magnified eighteen times; and afterwards, with great trouble and expence, he constructed one which magnified thirty-three times, and with this he discovered the satellites of Jupiter, and the spots on the sun.

The honour of explaining the principles of the telescope is due to Kepler.

The principal effects of telescopes depend upon these simple principles, viz. that objects appear larger in proportion to the angles which they subtend at the eye; and that the effect is the same whether the pencils of rays by which objects are visible to us, come directly from the objects themselves, or from any place nearer to the eye where they may have been conveyed, so as to form an image of the object; because they issue again from those points when there is no real substance in certain direction, in the same manner as they did from the corresponding points in the objects themselves.

In fact, therefore, all that is effected by a telescope, is first to make such an image of a distant object by means of a lens or mirror; and then to give to the eye some assistance for viewing that image as near as possible: so that the angle which it shall subtend at the eye, may be very large compared with the angle which the object itself would subtend in the same situation. This is done by means of any eye-glass which so refracts the pencil of rays, that they may afterwards be brought to their several foci by the humours of the eye. But if the eye was so formed as to be able to see the image with sufficient distinctness at the same distance without an eye-glass, it would appear to him as much magnified as it does to another person who makes use of a glass for that purpose, though he would not in all cases have so large a field of view.

Such is the telescope which was first discovered and used by philosophers. The great inconvenience attending it is, that the field of view is exceedingly small. This inconvenience increases with the magnifying power of the telescope, so that it is a matter of surprise how, with such an instrument, Galileo and others could have made such discoveries. No other telescope, however, than this, was so much as thought of for many years after the discovery.

It is to the celebrated Kepler that we are indebted for what we now call the astronomical telescope. The principles of this instrument are explained, and the advantages of it are clearly pointed out by this philosopher in his Catoptrics; but what is very surprising, he never actually reduced his theory to practice.

The first person who made an instrument of Kepler's construction was Scheiner, who has given a description of it in his Rosa Ursina, published in 1630. If, says he, you insert two similar lenses in a tube, and place your eye at a convenient distance, you will see all terrestrial objects inverted, indeed, but magnified and very distinct, with a considerable extent of view. He afterwards subjoins an account of a telescope of a different construction with two convex eye-glasses, which again reverses the images, and makes them appear in their natural position. This construction, however, answered the end very imperfectly, and Rheits soon after discovered a better construction, using three eye-glasses instead of two.

But these improvements, and many others since made, have diminished in value by the discovery of the *reflecting* telescope; for a reflecting telescope even of one 1,000 feet focus, supposing it possible to be made use of, could not be made to magnify with distinctness more than 1,000 times, whereas a reflecting telescope not exceeding nine or ten feet, will magnify 1200 times.

Mr. James Gregory of Aberdeen was the first inventor of the reflecting telescope, but his construction is quite different from Sir Isaac Newton's, and not nearly so advantageous.

But in constructing reflecting telescopes of extraordinary magnifying powers, Sir William Herschel has displayed skill and ingenuity surpassing all his predecessors in this department of mechanics. He has made them from 7, 10, 20, to even 40 feet in length, and with instruments of these dimensions made several important discoveries in astronomy. To describe these instruments would far exceed the limits to which we are confined; but we may mention that the concave face of the metallic mirror of Sir William's largest telescope, which is fixed at the bottom of a forty-feet tube of iron, is forty-eight inches of polished surface in diameter. The thickness, which is equal in every part of it, is about three inches and a half, and its weight, when it came from the cast, was 2,118 pounds, of which it must have lost a small quantity in the polishing. The metal is an amalgam supposed to be composed of 32 parts of copper, 15 of tin, 1 of brass, 1 of silver, and 1 of arsenic: for Sir W. Herschel has not made the composition public; but Mr. Edwards, an intimate friend of his, after repeated trials, found this proportion the best for receiving a fine polish, and producing the most perfect reflection.

This instrument, with proper eyé-glasses, magnifies above 6,000 times, and is the largest which has ever been made.

The *achromatic* telescope was the invention of Mr. Peter Dollond.

The *micrometer* is an instrument which is used with a telescope for the purpose of measuring small angles, and by the help of which the apparent magnitudes of objects viewed through a telescope or microscope, are measured with great correctness.

The *microscope* is composed of lenses or mirrors, by means of which small objects are made to appear larger than they really are to the naked eye. Microscopes are distinguished into simple, compound, and double. Simple microscopes consist of a single lens or spherule. The compound microscope consists of several lenses duly combined. As optics have been improved, other varieties have been contrived in this instrument: hence we have reflecting microscopes, water microscopes, botanical microscopes, solar microscopes, &c.

The *kaleidoscope* is an instrument which has lately obtained great celebrity on account of the very amusing and new forms which, by turning it round,

it constantly presents to the eye. Dr. Brewster of
Edinburgh has obtained a patent for the invention,
an account of which may be seen in the Monthly
Magazine for January, 1818. It is asserted, however, that the discovery is not a new one : for that
a person named Bradley, a gardener at Hampton
Court, mentions such an instrument in a work published by him more than one hundred years ago.

The mode in which the kaleidoscope is made is
very simple: take a hollow tube of any dimensions,
and of any length, two inches in diameter, and
twelve long is a convenient size : take two pieces of
plate glass about one inch and a half in diameter,
and one line in thickness, of a length somewhat
shorter than the tube itself, and let them be fixed
so that one edge may touch the other, and so as to
form an angle with each other of $22\frac{1}{2}$ degrees; a
few bits of cork may be so notched as to keep the
pieces of glass in their places : the glasses are to be
darkened by black painting, or some other convenient method on the exterior sides. At one end of
the tube provide two circular pieces of plain clear
glass, exactly the diameter of the tube into which
they are to be fitted. Place between these two
glasses a quantity of broken pieces of different
coloured glass, the more intense and various the
colours, the more brilliant will the forms be, and
let the pieces of broken glass be so placed as to
move freely as the tube is turned round. At the
opposite end of the tube let there be a small hole
for the sight: the instrument will be complete ; a
succession of beautiful forms will then be visible,
which till experienced would be believed absolutely
impossible to be produced by any art or contrivance
of man. The uses to which this instrument may be
put, both useful and ornamental, it would not be
easy to enumerate ; it can never cease to be a constant source of amusement and delight.

Telescopes are made of various dimensions, and at a great variety of prices.

Spectacles are also an article, as is well known, in considerable request. They are made to suit eyes of different ages and of different capacities of vision. Their prices are various, depending principally upon the style in which they are mounted.

From what has been said, it is evident that an Optician should be conversant with mathematics and mechanics, and many other branches of science with which optics are connected. He should also know the history of what has been hitherto done in this art, as well as what is now doing, in order to be able to apply himself to the construction of the various instruments which it is his business to make.

The plate represents the Optician's shop, in which are seen the telescope, the microscope, spectacles, opera-glasses, &c.

Painter.

THE PAINTER.

THIS artist paints portraits, historical pieces, landscapes, sea pieces, with shipping, &c. Some Painters have peculiar talents for one department, and some for others; but it rarely happens that the same man excels in them all, or even in more than one or two. A Portrait Painter in large, is, however, frequently well skilled in history, but an artist who paints in miniature is often unacquainted with any other part of the profession. Some Painters, who can execute almost any thing else in a masterly manner, have no idea of shipping, which requires a considerable degree of nautical knowledge.

Painting, which at the present time has arrived at a high degree of perfection, appears to have been invented by the Egyptians, at least as to the four principal colours; the knowledge which they had of chemistry seems to confirm this opinion, but we cannot infer from their monuments, or from what is said of them by ancient writers, that they were good Painters; on the contrary, Petronius says distinctly, that their painting was bad, and that they corrupted the art.

Painting passed very soon from Egypt into Greece, where were formed in process of time the famous schools of Scio, Rhodes, and Athens. What is most astonishing is, that the first Painters, amongst whom we reckon Polygnotus, used but the four principal colours. It was Echion, Nichomachus, Protogenes, and after them Apelles, who imitated with compound colours all the shades of nature.

The Greeks, with all their skill, were not able to retain painting in that perfection which it had acquired in the time of Apelles: for in the age of Augustus, as we are informed by Dionysius of Halicarnassus, it had very much degenerated.

The art of painting was a long time buried in the West, under the ruins of the Roman empire. The Orientals preserved it with more care, but entirely divested it of its former splendour. In the thirteenth century it again appeared in Italy, beneath the pencil of Cimabué. Many Painters acquired repute in the two succeeding ages, but their works are no longer inquired after.

At the end of the fifteenth century, painting was still a coarse art in Italy, two hundred years after its revival. The method of painting in oil had been discovered, but it was in a very rude way.

Ghirlandajo painted in this style, although he surpassed all the Painters of his time: his chief merit · consists in having formed the celebrated Michael Angelo.

The arts and sciences generally began to appear with considerable lustre under the pontificate of Julius the Second, Leo the Tenth, and Clement the Seventh. Painting, architecture, and sculpture, had their distinguished men, as well as the belles lettres; and Michael Angelo, excited by the reward of Julius, perfected his pencil, and became a great master of his art.

From this period, the progress of painting in many countries of Europe, particularly Italy, Holland, France, and England, has been of the most brilliant kind. Academies have been instituted, societies have been formed, collections have been made, and exhibitions opened, an account of which, and of the illustrious men who have contributed by their works to fill them, would require volumes.

The implements made use of in this art are a stone and a muller to grind the colours ; an operation which is sometimes performed with oil, and sometimes with water: hence the distinction between *painting in oil* and painting in water colours. A palette and palette knife are also required ; the *latter* to take off the paint from the stone, and the *former*, which is made of walnut-tree or mahogany, is that on which the artist puts his colours for immediate use. The pencils or brushes are made of camel's hair, badger's hair, or hog's bristles.

The stick in the Painter's hand *(see the plate)* is about a yard long, with cotton wool tied round the end in a piece of soft leather to prevent its scratching the picture. On this the artist rests his right hand to keep it steady. The canvas for the intended picture is placed on a wooden frame, called an *easel,* which is so constructed, by means of holes and pegs, that it may be raised or lowered at pleasure.

The cloths prepared for receiving the colours of the Painter are usually denominated *primed* cloths, and in the general way are got up as a separate branch of business, ready to the Painter's hands.

It will be impossible to describe in the limits of this work the great variety of different articles used for colours in painting, but to give some idea of them we may mention that in painting landscapes, for instance, flake white, white lead, fine light ochre, brown ochre, brown pink, burnt umber, burnt ochre, ivory black, terra de Siena, Prussian blue, ultramarine, terre-verte, lake, Indian red, vermillion, king's yellow, &c. &c. are commonly used.

The earnings of an artist cannot be defined : he is paid according to his talents, and to the celebrity which he has acquired. Some persons will require a hundred guineas for a piece, which another of inferior merit, or little known to the public, would be glad to perform for a twentieth part of the sum.

To give some idea of the present art of painting in England, according to a list inserted in the seventh number of the Annals of the Fine Arts, there are five hundred and twenty three Painters in the different departments of the art, amongst whom, it deserves to be especially noted, are forty three ladies!

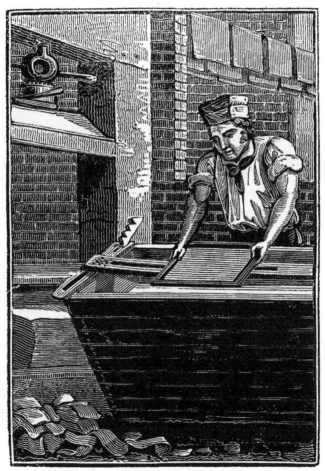

Paper Maker

THE PAPER-MAKER.

———♦———

THE art of making paper, as at present practised, is not of a very ancient date; paper made of linen rags appears to have been first used in Europe towards the beginning of the thirteenth century, but of its origin nothing can with certainty be affirmed.

The ancients, as substitutes for paper, had recourse successively to palm-tree leaves, to table-books of wax, ivory, and lead; to linen and cotton cloths, to the intestines or skins of different animals, and to the inner bark of plants. In some places and ages they have even written on the skins of fishes, on the intestines of serpents, and in others, on the backs of tortoises. There are few plants but have, at some time, been used for paper or books, and hence the several terms bibels, codex, liber, folium, tabula, &c. which express the different parts on which they were written; and though in Europe all these disappeared upon the introduction of the papyrus and parchments, yet in some other countries the use of them remains to this day. In Ceylon, for instance, they write on the leaves of the tallipot; and the Bramin, MSS. in the Tulinga language, sent to Oxford from Fort St. George, are written on leaves of plants.

The paper which had been for a long time used by the Romans and Greeks, was made of the bark of an aquatic plant called papyrus, whence the name *paper.*

M

The internal parts of the bark of this plant were the only ones that were made into paper, and the manner of the manufacture was as follows :—

Strips or leaves of every length that could be obtained being laid upon a table, other strips were placed across, and pasted to them by means of water and a press, so that this paper was a texture of several strips ; and it even appears that in the time of the emperor Claudius, the Romans made paper of these layers. The Roman paper received a size as well as ours, which was prepared with flour of wheat diluted with boiling water, on which were thrown some drops of vinegar; or crumbs of leavened bread diluted with boiling water, and passed through a bolting-cloth, being afterwards beaten with a hammer.

Paper made in this manner with the bark of the Egyptian plant, was that which was chiefly used till the tenth century, when cotton was used for making paper by pounding it, and reducing it to a pulp. This method, known in China some ages before, appeared at last in the empire of the East, yet we are without any certain knowledge of the author, or the time and place of this invention.

Father Montfaucon says, that cotton paper began to be used in the empire of the East about the ninth century. There are several Greek manuscripts, both on parchment and cotton-paper, that bear the date of the time in which they were written; but the greatest part are without date. The most ancient manuscript on cotton-paper, with a date, is that in the library of the king of France, numbered 2,889, written in 1050: another in the emperor's library, dated 1095.

Chinese paper is of various kinds : some is made of the bark of trees, especially the mulberry-tree and the elm, but chiefly of the bamboo and cotton-tree. In fact, almost each province has its several sorts of paper.

The inventor of the linen-rag paper, whoever he was, is entitled to the gratitude of posterity, who are enjoying the advantages of the discovery. The cotton-paper, though an improvement, was but a rude and coarse article, unfit for any of the nice purposes to which paper is now applied. The perfection of the art of paper-making consisted in finding a material which could be procured in sufficient quantities, and would be easy of preparation. Such paper is now in use, of which we shall endeavour to describe the manufacture.

Linen, such as our shirts are made of, is spun from flax which grows in the fields; and from linen rags, that is, from shirts and other articles of dress, when worn thread-bare, fine white paper is manufactured: of course every piece of rag, however small, should be preserved, and not thrown into the fire; and latterly, indeed, from the increased use of *calico* as an article of clothing, cotton rags are become of almost as much importance as linen rags, and should have equal care devoted to their preservation.

The first thing to be done towards the formation of paper, is to put the rags into a machine or cylinder formed of wire, which is made to turn round with great velocity, to whirl out the dust; they are then sorted according to their different qualities; after which they are put into a large cistern or trough, perforated with holes, through which a stream of clear water constantly flows. In this cistern is placed a cylinder about two feet long, set thick with rows of iron spikes. At the bottom of the trough there are corresponding rows of spikes. The cylinder is made to whirl round with inconceivable rapidity, and with the iron teeth rends and tears the cloth to atoms, till, with the assistance of the water, it is reduced to a thin pulp. By the same process all the impurities are cleared away, and it is restored to its original whiteness. This fine pulp

M 2

is next put into a copper of warm water, and here
it becomes the substance of paper, and ready for
the mould; for which purpose it is conveyed to the
vat. This vat, of which we have a representation
in the plate, is made of wood, generally about five
feet broad, and two or three feet in depth. It is
kept to a proper temperature by means of a charcoal fire.

The mould which the Paper-Maker has in his
hand is composed of many wires set in a frame close
together, and of another moveable frame equal in
size to the sheet of paper to be made. These wires
are disposed in the shape of the figure which is
discovered in a sheet of paper when we hold it up
to the light.

The workman holds the frame in both his hands,
plunges it horizontally into the tub, and takes it up
quickly; the water runs away between the wires,
and there remains nothing but the beaten pulp, in a
thin coat, which forms the sheet of paper. -

- Another person, called the *coucher*, receives the
mould, and places the sheet of paper on a felt or
woollen cloth, during which the workman makes
another sheet. They proceed in this manner, laying
alternately a sheet and a felt, till they have made
six quires of paper, which are called a post: such is
the heap on the right hand of the vat. When the
last sheet of the post is covered with the last felt,
the workmen employed about the vat unite, and
submit the whole heap to the action of the press,
which is on the Paper-maker's right hand. After
this operation another person separates the sheets
of paper from the felts, laying them in a heap; and
several of these heaps collected together are again
put under the press. They are turned and pressed
several times, and then the sheets are hung up three
or four together, on lines, to dry.

The paper is now to be *sized*, because in its present state it will not bear the ink. The size is made of

shreds and parings collected from the tanners, curriers, and parchment-makers; and, immediately before the operation, a certain quantity of alum is added to it. The workman then takes a handful of the sheets, smoothed and rendered as supple as possible, and dips them into the vessel containing the size; and when he has finished ten or a dozen of these handfuls, they are submitted to the action of the press; the superfluous size is carried back to the vessel by means of a small pipe. The paper is now to be hung sheet by sheet on lines to dry.

When the paper is sufficiently dry, it is carried to the finishing room, where it is pressed, selected, examined, folded, made up into quires, and finally into reams. It is here submitted twice to the press; first when it is at its full size, and secondly after it is folded.

. Every quire of paper consists of twenty-four or twenty-five sheets; the larger number refers to paper made use of in printing : and each ream contains twenty quires.

In the manufacture many sheets are damaged; these, in the sorting-room, are put together, and two of the worst quires, containing only about twenty sheets, are placed on the outsides of the ream, called *outside* quires. The reams are tied up in wrappers made of the settling of the vat, and they are then fit for sale.

Some paper is made smooth and glossy like satin, by means of hot plates; this is called hot-pressing. The process of paper-making takes about three weeks.

Pasteboard is made in a similar way to that of paper, and when it is wanted very thick, it is made by having sheets pasted one upon another. There is, however, a kind of thick paper, called *millboard*, used for covers of books, which is made at once : it is composed, like brown papers, of very coarse rags, old ropes, &c.

Blotting-paper, and paper used for filtering fluids, is paper not sized, into which, therefore, the ink readily sinks. The best filtering paper is made of woollen rags, chosen for the purpose.

Wove or woven paper is made in moulds, the wires of which are exceedingly fine, of equal thickness, and woven or latticed one within another. The marks, therefore, of these, are easily pressed out, so as to be scarcely visible.

The greatest modern improvement in paper-making, is the bleaching of the rags. This enables the manufacturer to produce the finest paper, in point of colour, from any kind of rags. He has therefore only to find such materials as will make a paper of a strong texture, and a fine even surface, knowing that he can produce colour at pleasure. Bleaching is conducted by different methods, either by bleaching the rags immediately after they are sorted, bleaching them in the half-stuff, that is, after they have been once ground in the washing-engine, or while they are in the engine. For the first of these methods Mr. Campbell obtained a patent in 1792. It consists in having a chamber which is air-tight, into which the rags must be introduced, and with proper retorts, containing a mixture of manganese, sea-salt, and sulphuric-acid, heated to a certain extent; a gas will be discharged from the mixture, which destroys all the colour that the rags may contain.

Another important alteration has been recently made in the art of paper-making, by the adoption of machinery for fabricating it from the pulp, and at one operation pressing it between the felts, and rendering it fit for the second pressure, by which an immense saving of labour is made, and the quality of the paper improved. Messrs. Fourdriniers have a patent for these machines, of which they have erected a great number in different parts of the kingdom.

Paper has been occasionally made of straw, and

other materials not commonly in use, and Mr. Koop, in 1802, obtained a patent for making straw-paper, but we have not heard that the use of this article is become common.

Paper is subject to heavy excise duties, the particulars of which we have not room to enumerate; and the manufacturer of paper must also take out an annual license.

The manufacture of paper is so curious, and so well worth the attention of young persons, that we recommend them to take some pains to obtain a sight of the whole process, which may easily be done wherever there are paper-mills.

THE PEWTERER.

———

THE PEWTERER is a person who makes plates, dishes, pots, syringes, funnels, worms for stills, and a variety of other articles of pewter.

The trade of a pewterer is very ancient, and although little mention is made of it in books of history, there is no doubt, from the economy of its materials for culinary purposes, that it must have existed in this kingdom for many centuries.

We find in the reigns of Henry the Seventh and Eighth, that many statutes were enacted relative to the Pewterer: by 19 of the former king, cap. 6, and 4 of the same, cap. 4, the weights and standard of Pewterers' metal were limited. We find also by other statutes of Henry VIII. that their goods were liable to be searched and sold in open places; and by the 25th of Hen. VIII. c. 9, s. 3, no stranger born shall work pewter, &c. all which proves, that in Henry the Eighth's time, the Pewterer must have been a trade of considerable importance: indeed, we apprehend much more so than at the present day, for pewter, in domestic use, except the article of pots for porter, is by no means so common as it was forty years ago, earthenware having in a great degree superseded it.

Pewter is a factitious metal, and very uncertain in its composition. It is generally kept of different standards: that which is called plate-metal, is said to be formed of tin and regulus of antimony, in the

The Pewterer.

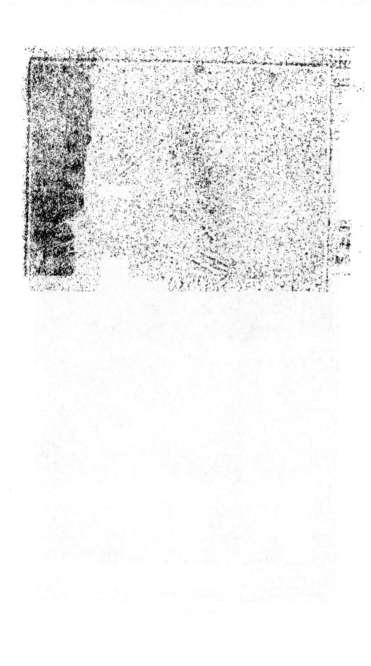

proportions of 112 pounds of the former, to six or seven pounds of the latter.

The next inferior to this is called trifling metal, and is lowered by alloying it with lead: of this metal ale-house pots are made. Lead may be mixed with tin in any proportion, without destroying its malleability. Hence, lead and tin, with or without other smaller additions, form the pewter of ordinary use. Lead being the cheapest of the two metals, the manufacturer finds it his interest to employ it in as large a proportion as possible. But as lead is well known to be a very noxious metal, experiments have been made to ascertain in what proportion it may be mixed with tin without injury to the liquors for which pewter is commonly used. It has been found, when wine or vinegar was allowed to stand in vessels composed of an alloy of tin and lead, that the tin is first dissolved, whilst the lead is not acted upon by the liquors, except at the line of contact of the air and liquor; and that no sensible quantity of lead is dissolved, even by vinegar, after standing for some days in vessels that contained no more than eighteen pounds in the hundred of lead. Hence it was concluded, that as no noxious effect is produced by the very minute quantity of tin which is dissolved, pewter may be considered as perfectly safe which contains about 80 or 82 per cent of tin. And when vessels are employed for measures, a much less proportion of tin may be used. But it has been found that the common pewter at Paris contains no more than about 25 or 30 per cent. of tin, the remainder is lead; and there is great reason for believing that the pewter commonly used in England is of no better quality. It is evident, therefore, that the use of pewter vessels, unless the proportion of its alloy could be ascertained, is by no means desirable.

The pewterer must have an iron pot to melt the metal, a ladle to take it out, and suitable moulds for making the various articles which he manufactures: he must also have a turning lathe, for the purpose of finishing those articles which require to be rounded and true.

Pewterers have two sorts of moulds, which are commonly made of copper: those which they use for flat pewter, as dishes, plates, &c. and those which they use for hollow vessels, such as pots, &c. &c.

The moulds for flat pewter are composed of two pieces, one of which forms the upper, the other the under part of the article. These two pieces are so far apart as to permit the metal to be run, when melted, between them, to the exact shape and thickness of the article wanted.

The moulds for pots, &c. are composed of four pieces, two for the bottom and two for the sides. Before the moulds are used, it is necessary to rub them with fine coal-dust, mixed with the white of an egg, and laid on with a brush; they are afterwards to be heated.

The propriety of casting consists in the knowledge of the due degree of heat, not only of the melted metal, but also of the moulds; and this is acquired principally by experience. The finer the pewter the hotter in general should the metal be when it is cast.

As soon as the mould is sufficiently hot, it is to be laid hold of with bits of hat, and the pieces are laid horizontally one upon the other; they are then fixed firmly together by an iron ring prepared for the purpose: it is afterwards placed on edge in such a way, that the hole of the mould having a funnel shape to it, may be easily come at. The pewter is then taken from the melting pot with an iron ladle, which will contain a sufficient quantity of it to make the article at once, without a second dipping. As soon as the article is cast, the mould is laid down, and the sides struck with a wooden mallet. The mould is now to be opened, and the article is taken

2

away on the blade of a knife. And in this way the workman proceeds till he has obtained as many of the kind as are wanted.

There are many statutes relating to the manufacture and sale of pewter: one clause in the 19 Hen. 7. c. 6, we think it necessary to quote.

" No person shall make any hollow wares of pewter, to wit, salts and pots made of pewter called lay-metal, but the assize of pewter and lay-metal within London; and the makers shall mark them with their own mark, that they may avow the same by them wrought; and the same, not sufficiently made and wrought, and not marked, found in the possession of the maker or seller, shall be forfeited; and if the same be sold, the maker shall forfeit the value thereof, half to the king, and half to the finder or searcher."

The plate represents the pewterer in the act of casting some article on a bench, with dishes, syringes, &c. around him: the pot in which is the melted metal, is on the ground by his side.

THE PIN-MAKER.

THE PIN-MAKER is a person who makes small instruments of brass wire, with a head at one end and a point at the other, which are used by females in adjusting their dress.

It is not easy to trace the invention of this very useful little implement. It is first noticed in the English statute book in the year 1483, prohibiting foreign manufactures: and it appears from the manner in which pins are described in the reign of Henry the Eighth, and the labour and time which the manufacture of them would require, that they were a new invention in this country, and probably brought from France.

At this period pins were considered in Paris as articles of luxury; and no master pin-maker was allowed to open more than one shop, for the sale of his wares, except on New Year's day, and the day before that; it should seem, therefore, that pins were given away as New Year's gifts; hence arose the phrase pin-money, the name of an allowance frequently made by the husband to his wife for her own spending.

The art of making pins of brass wire was not known in England before the year 1543: prior to that period they were made of bone, ivory, or box.

The pin manufactory was introduced into Gloucester in 1626, by John Tilsby. There are now in Gloucester nine distinct pin-manufactories, which

Pin Maker.

employ together at least 1,500 persons. The pins sent annually to the metropolis amount to the value of 20,000*l.*, but the chief demand is from Spain and America.

Pins are also manufactured in other places in England : some are made in Bristol.

There is scarcely any commodity cheaper than pins, and but few which pass through more hands from their first state of rough wire to their being stuck in paper for sale : it is reckoned that twenty-five workmen are successively employed from the commencement to the finishing of this simple article.

. Pins are now made wholly of brass wire; formerly iron wire was made use of, but the ill effects of iron have nearly discarded that substance from the pin-manufactory. The excellence and perfection of pins consist in the stiffness of the wire and its blanching ; in the heads being well turned and the points accurately filed. The following are some of the principal operations.

When the brass wire of which the pins are form-ed, is first received, it is generally too thick for the purpose of being cut into pins. It is therefore wound off from one wheel to another with great velocity, and made to pass between the two through a hole in a piece of iron of smaller diameter than the wire itself is, which operation is called *wire-drawing.* This operation is repeated with holes of different diameters, till the wire is reduced to the size which it may be wanted : what it loses in bigness, it of course gains in length. The wire is then straight-ened, and afterwards cut into lengths of three or four yards, and then into smaller ones, every length being sufficient for six pins ; each end of these is ground to a point, which is performed by a boy, who sits with two small grinding stones before him, turned by a wheel. Taking up a handful he ap-plies the ends to the coarsest of the two stones, being careful at the same time to keep each piece moving round between his fingers, so that the points may not become flat; he then gives them to the other stone; and by that means a lad of twelve or fourteen years of age is enabled to point about 16,000 pins in an hour. When the wire is thus pointed, a pin is taken off from each end, and this is repeated till it is cut into six pieces. The next operation is that of forming the heads, or as the pin-maker terms it, *head-spinning*, which is done by means of a spinning-wheel, one piece of wire being thus wound round another with astonishing rapidity, and the interior one being drawn out, leaves a hollow tube; it is then cut with shears, every two turns of the wire forming one head; these are softened by throwing them into iron pans, and placing them in a furnace till they are red hot. As soon as they are cool they are distributed to children, who sit with their anvils and hammers before them, which they work with their feet by means of a lathe; and, taking up one of the lengths, they thrust the blunt end into a quantity of the heads which lie before them, and catching one at the extremity, they apply them immediately to the anvil and hammer; and, by a motion or two of the foot, the point and the head are fixed together in much less time than it can be described in, and with a dexterity only to be acquired by practice, the spectator being in continual apprehension for the safety of the fingers' ends.

The pin is now finished as to its form, but still it is merely brass; it is therefore thrown into a copper containing a solution of tin and lees of wine. Here it remains for some time, and when taken out it assumes a white though dull appearance. To give it a polish it is put into a tub containing a quantity of bran, which is set in motion by turning a shaft that runs through its centre, and thus by means of friction it becomes perfectly bright. The pin being complete, nothing remains but to separate it from the bran, which is performed by a mode exactly similar to the winnowing of corn, the bran flying off, and leaving the pins behind fit for immediate sale.

The pins most esteemed in commerce are those of England; those of Bordeaux are next; then those made in some of the other departments of France. The London pointing and blanching are most in repute, because our pin-makers, in pointing, use two steel mills, the first of which forms the point, and the latter takes off all irregularities, and renders it smooth, and as it were polished; and in blanching they use block tin granulated; whereas in other places they mix their tin with lead and quicksiver, which not only blanches worse than the former, but is also dangerous, as any puncture made with pins of this sort is not readily cured.

Mr. W. Bunby, of Camden Town, obtained in the year 1809 a patent for a new instrument for heading pins, which we have not room to describe.

Besides the brass pin above described, pins are sometimes made of iron wire, rendered black by a varnish of linseed oil with lamp-black. These are, of course, designed for persons in mourning.

Pins are distinguished by numbers; the smallest are called minikins, the next short whites. The next larger ones are numbered 3, $3\frac{1}{2}$, 4, $4\frac{1}{2}$, and 5, to the 14th, whence they go by two's, viz. No. 16, 18, and 20, which is the largest size.

Pins are not only sold in papers and packets as in the above numbers, but they are also sold by the pound weight, being tied up in pound papers, and having a great variety of sizes mixed together in each paper for convenience.

There are also pins with double heads, of several numbers, used by ladies to fix the buckles of their hair for the night, without the danger of pricking.

THE PLUMBER.

The business of the Plumber consists in casting and working of lead, and using it in buildings. He furnishes us with a cistern for water, and with a sink for a kitchen; he covers the house with lead, and makes the gutters to carry away the water; he makes pipes of all sorts and sizes, and sometimes he casts leaden statues as ornaments for the garden. The plumber also is employed in making coffins for those who are to be interred out of the usual way. He also fits up water closets, and makes pumps.

Lead is an article which has been in use from a very remote period amongst different nations of the world. We have not been enabled to ascertain the commencement of the trade under our immediate consideration, but workers in lead must have been coeval with the discovery of the metal. That the plumber must be an ancient trade is evident: for we find that in France, as early as the middle of the seventeenth century, plumbers in that country form-ed one of the incorporated companies, with statutes for their particular government.

Lead is obtained from mines, and is frequently combined with sulphur, hence it is called a *sulphuret.* The operation of roasting the ore, or smelting it, as it is called, to obtain the pure metal, consists in picking up the mineral to separate the unctuous rich or pure ore, and the stony matrix and other impuri-ties,—in pounding the picked ore under the stam-pers,—in washing the pulverized ore, to carry off the

The Plumbers.

matrix by the water;—in roasting the mineral in a reverberatory furnace, taking care to stir it to facilitate the evaporation of the sulphur. When the surface begins to become of the consistence of paste, it is covered with charcoal, the mixture is shaken, the fire increased, and the lead flows down on all sides to the bottom of the basis of the furnace, from which it is drawn off into moulds or patterns prepared to receive it, the moulds are made so as to take a charge of metal equal to one hundred and fifty pounds. These are called in common *pigs* of lead.

Plumbers use a great deal of sheet lead; of this they have two kinds, one which they call *cast*, and the other *milled* lead. The cast lead is used for covering the flat roofs of terraces, buildings, gutters, lining reservoirs, &c. It is technically divided into 5, $5\frac{1}{2}$, 6, $6\frac{1}{2}$, 7, $7\frac{1}{2}$, 8, $8\frac{1}{2}$ lbs. by which is understood that every *foot* superficial of such cast lead is to contain these several weights of metal in each foot respectively.

Every plumber who does any business of consequence casts his sheet lead at home : which he does from the pigs. To perform which he provides a copper well fixed in masonry, and placed at one end of the casting shop, and near to the mould or casting table. The casting table is generally in its form a parallelogram, varying in its size from six feet in width to eighteen or more feet in length; it is raised from the ground as high as to be about six or seven inches below the top of the copper which contains the metal, and stands on strongly-framed legs, so as to be very steady and firm. The top of the table is lined by deal boarding, laid very even and firm, and it has a rim projecting upwards four or five inches all round it. At the end of the table, nearest to the copper in which is the heated lead, is adapted a box equal in length to the width of the table; at the bottom of this is made a horizontal slit, from which the heated metal is to issue, when it is to be cast into sheets. This box moves upon rollers along the edges of the projecting rim of the table, and is set in motion by ropes and pulleys, fixed to beams over the table. As soon as the metal is found to be adequately heated, every thing is gotten ready to cast it on the table, the bottom of which is then covered with a stratum of dry and clean sand, and a rake applied to smooth it regularly all over the surface. When this is done the box is brought up close to the copper. It must be observed, that these boxes are made in their capacity, equal to the containing of as much of the melted lead as will cast the whole of the sheet at the same time, and the slit in the bottom is adjusted so as to let as much and no more out during its progress along the table, as will be sufficient to cover it completely of the thickness and weight per foot required. When the box has dispersed its contents upon the table, the lead is suffered to cool, when it is rolled up and removed away, and other sheets are made till all the melted metal is used. The sheets so formed are rolled up and weighed.

Milled lead is not manufactured by the plumber, but is purchased of the lead merchant, as it is cast and prepared at the ore and roasting furnace. Such kind of lead is very thin, and has commonly not more than four pounds of metal to the superficial foot. In the operation of making it, a roller or a flatting mill is used, whence its name.

If a cistern is wanted the four sides are measured out, and the figures intended to be raised on the front are formed in the sand, and the lead cast as before; the sides are then soldered together, after which the bottom is soldered in.

Pipes are cast in a kind of mill with arms or levers to turn it. The moulds are of hollow brass, consisting of two pieces about two feet and half long, which open and shut by means of hinges and hooks. In the middle of these moulds is placed a core, or round solid piece of brass or iron, somewhat longer than the mould. This core is passed through two copper rundles, one at each end of the mould, which they serve to close; to these is joined a little copper tube two inches long, and of the thickness of the intended leaden pipe. These tubes retain the core exactly in the middle of the cavity of the mould, and then the lead is poured in through an aperture in the shape of a funnel. When the mould is full a hook is put into the core, and, turning the mill, it is drawn out and the pipe is made. If it is to be lengthened, they put one end of it in the lower end of the mould, and the end of the core into it, then shut the mould again, and apply its rundle and tube as before, the pipe just cast serving for a rundle, &c. at the other end. Metal is again poured in, which unites with the other pipe, and so the operation is repeated, till the pipe is of the length required.

Large pipes of sheet lead are made by wrapping the lead on wooden cylinders of the proper length, and then soldering in the edges.

Solder is used by the Plumber for the purpose of securing the joints of lead-work in cases in which a lap or roll joint cannot be employed. It is a general rule with respect to solder, that it should always be easier of fusion than the metal which is intended to be soldered by it: next to this care must be taken that the solder be, as far as it be possible, of the same colour as the metal intended to be soldered. *Soft solder* is composed of tin and lead in equal parts fused together: after which it is run into moulds, in shape not unlike a gridiron. For common purposes, however, a mixture of pewter and lead is more commonly used. The iron used in finishing or melting, in order to finish a joint in the process of soldering is called a grozing-iron.

The different kinds of pumps and water-closets

we have not room to describe; we must therefore refer the student to more elaborate works.

The lead which lines the Chinese tea-chests is reduced to a thinness which, we are informed, Europeans cannot imitate. The following account of the process in China is by an intelligent mate of an East Indiaman. The caster sits by a pot containing the melted metal, and has two large stones, the under one fixed, the upper moveable, directly before him. He raises the upper stone by pressing his foot upon the side of it, and with an iron ladle pours into the opening a proper quantity of the fluid metal. He then immediately lets fall the upper stone, and by that means forms the lead into a thin irregular plate, which is afterwards cut into a proper shape. The surfaces of the stones, where they touch each other, are exactly ground together.

In the country it is not unfrequent to find that the business of a plumber, glazier, and painter, is united in the same person; but the plumbing trade is of itself in London reckoned a very good one for the master. The health of the men is often injured by the fumes of the lead.

Journeymen earn about thirty shillings a week; and we recommend earnestly to lads brought up to either of the before-mentioned trades, that they cultivate cleanliness and strict sobriety, and that they never on any account eat their meals or retire to rest at night, before they have well washed their hands and face.

The Potter.

THE POTTER.

———

THE POTTER converts clay of various kinds, and mixed also with various ingredients, into utensils of innumerable shapes and sizes, for domestic and a variety of other purposes.

Vessels capable of holding liquid food and drink for the use of man would be so essential to his immediate necessities, that the fabrication would doubtless be prior to the humblest cottage. Vessels formed by excavating pieces of wood and leather were in all probability prior to those of earthenware. This manufacture is so ancient that we have no traces to the period of its invention. It was very common at different periods of Scripture History, as the well-known simile, of *being broken in pieces like a potter's vessel*, sufficiently indicates.

The ancient Greeks and Etruscans particularly excelled in it; but Porcelain, the most perfect species of pottery, has been made in China from time immemorial. It is very remarkable that the oldest specimen of China Porcelain does not differ in its essential qualities from the most recently manufactured: a strong proof that many centuries must have elapsed in bringing it to that state, unless contrary to the usual progress of most arts it was practised at once in the state in which it now is ; a most improbable supposition.

There is strong ground for supposing that the art of pottery had been brought to great perfection in the East before it was known either in Africa or Europe. It was afterwards cultivated by the Egyptians, from whom it descended to the Greeks and Romans.

A species of earthenware was manufactured in Persia, which was considered a great curiosity on account of its metallic lustre.

The Romans appear to have cultivated this art to a considerable extent. The taste and elegance displayed in their vessels for ornamental decoration were doubtless borrowed from what the Greeks had long before practised: the country most celebrated for this art was the ancient Etruria.

It was the ambition of the late Mr. Wedgewood to equal the manufacture of Etruria, after which he named the village which has grown out of his genius and industry. The potteries of this country, prior to his exertions and example, produced nothing but of a flimsy fabric, destitute of taste, and scarcely fit for domestic use. Since his time the manufactures of Staffordshire have been celebrated both at home and abroad. Stoke upon Trent, and Etruria above-mentioned, both in Staffordshire, are amongst the principal places in which the manufacture of earthenware is carried on. Worcester is also famed for fine Porcelain, as is Coal-port.

This trade is subdivided into a variety of branches: that is, the Stoneware Potter, the Delf Potter, the Maker of Portugal, or rather Brosely Ware, the common Earthenware Potter, the Maker of Queen's Ware, and many others; we can only give a general outline of the whole.

Clay and flints are the principal substances of which every kind of earthenware is made: clay alone shrinks and cracks, the flint gives it solidity and strength.

The wheel and the lathe are the chief instruments in the business of the pottery: the first is intended for large works, and the other for small; the wheel is turned by a labourer, as represented in the plate; but the lathe is put into motion by the foot of the workman.

When the clay is properly prepared and made into lumps, proportioned to the size of the cup, plate, or other vessel to be made, the potter places one of the lumps upon the head of the wheel before him, which he turns round, while he forms the cavity of the vessel with his finger and thumb, continuing to widen it from the middle, and thus turning the inside into form with one hand while he proportions the outside with the other, the wheel being kept the whole time in constant motion. The mouldings are formed by holding a piece of wood or iron, cut into the shape of the moulding, to the vessel while the wheel is going round; but the feet and handles are made by themselves, and set on by the hand; and if there be any sculpture in the work, it is usually made in wooden moulds, and stuck on piece by piece on the outside of the vessel. When the vessel is finished, the workman cuts it off from the remaining part of the clay, and sets it aside to dry; and when it is hardened sufficiently to bear removing without danger, it is covered with a glazing, made of a composition of lead, and put into a furnace where it is baked. Some sorts are glazed by throwing sea-salt into the furnace among the different pieces of pottery. The salt is decomposed, and its vapours form a glazing upon the vessels; which is not, however, much esteemed: it was introduced into England by two brothers from Holland, of the name of Elers, about the year 1700, who settled in the neighbourhood of the Staffordshire potteries.

English stone-ware is made of tobacco-pipe clay mixed with flints calcined and ground. This mixture burns white, and vessels of this kind were formerly all glazed with sea-salt. Wedgewood's queen's-ware is made of tobacco pipe-clay, much beaten in water. By this process the finer parts of the clay remain suspended in the water, while the coarser and all impurities fall to the bottom. The thick liquid is further purified by passing it through hair and lawn sieves, after which it is mixed with another liquid, consisting of flints calcined, ground, and suspended in water. The mixture is then dried in a kiln; and being afterwards beaten to a proper temper, it becomes fit for being formed at a wheel into dishes, plates, bowls, &c.

When this ware is to be put into a furnace to be baked, the several pieces of it are placed in cases made of clay, which are piled one upon another in the dome of the furnace; a fire is then lighted, and the ware is brought into a proper temper for glazing. By being baked, the ware acquires a strong property of imbibing moisture; in this state it is called *biscuit;* and when dipped into the glaze, consisting of water made thick with white-lead and ground flints, it absorbs it into its pores, and the ware presently becomes dry. It is then exposed a second time to the fire, and the lead forms a glossy coat on the surface, which is more or less yellow according as a greater or less proportion of that metal has been used.

The use of ground flints in the potteries was introduced in the following manner: about the year 1720, a potter travelling to London on horseback, had occasion to seek a remedy for a disorder in his horse's eyes: the hostler at the inn, by burning a flint-stone, reduced it to a fine powder, which he blew into them. The potter observing the beautiful white colour of the flint after calcination, instantly conceived the uses to which it might be applied in his art, and then introducing the white pipe-clay, found in the north of Devonshire, instead of the drossy clay of his own country, readily produced the white stoneware.

As a proof of the extent to which machinery is arrived in this country, we may mention here, that in the neighbourhood of Coal Port, in Shropshire, on the banks of the Severn is a water-wheel one hundred feet in diameter, which turns an apparatus for the purpose of reducing calcined flints to a powder for the making of English porcelain.

This is a business which is of so multifarious a kind, that it is not easy to give an idea either of the capital necessary to carry it on, or of the wages of the workmen employed in it. But the finer branches require considerable capital, and the best workmen earn good wages.

THE PRINTER.

The Printer takes off impressions from characters or figures moveable or immoveable, on paper, &c. by the aid of ink and a suitable apparatus.

There are several kinds of printing, one for copper-plates for pictures, which we have already described in page 103 of this work; another from blocks for printing calicoes, linens, &c. which will be found at page 65; our present article will treat of printing by moveable types, and the more recent introduction of stereotype, both employed for books.

Printing was discovered at Haarlem, in Holland, by Coster, and the first book was printed in the year 1430. It was a Dutch piece of theology, printed only on one side of the leaf, and in imitation of manuscript. The first attempts at printing were upon loose leaves, and the printed part was accompanied with cuts, somewhat in the manner of our present ballads. Coster's method was to cut out the letters upon a wooden block. He took for an apprentice John Fust, or Faustus, and bound him to secrecy. But Fust ran away with his master's materials, and set up for himself at Nantz. He had a servant called Peter Schoeffer, who first invented metal types. Fust seeing them, was so delighted, that he gave him, Schoeffer, his daughter in marriage, and made him his partner. The first book they printed is said to have been *Cicero de Officiis*,

Letter Press Printer.

which bears the date of 1495 ; but other books are mentioned with earlier dates, 1457, 1442. They printed a number of bibles in imitation of manuscript, and Fust carried them to Paris for sale. The Parisians, upon comparing the different copies, were confounded at the exact similarity which they bore in every part, a similarity so great, that the most exact copyist could not have attained it. They accused Fust of being possessed of some diabolical art. This at once obliged him to discover the secret, and gave the origin of the story of Dr. Faustus.

After the discovery of the art of printing, thus brought about at Paris, it quickly made its way over the whole of Europe. The first book printed in England is said to have been Rufinus on the Creed, printed at Oxford, in 1468.

At first the impression was taken off with a list coiled up, as the card-makers use at this day. But when they came to use single types, they employed stronger paper, with vellum and parchment. At last the press was introduced, and brought gradually to its present state. The same observation applies to the ink. At first the common writing-ink was employed, and the printing-ink of lamp-black and oil, at present used, was introduced by degrees. Rolling-press printing was not used in England till the time of king James the First; and then it was brought from Antwerp by the illustrious John Speed.

Letter-press printing is one of the most curious and important arts which the ingenuity of man has ever invented. It is to this art that we are indebted for our deliverance from ignorance and error; for the progress of learning,—the revival of the sciences,—and numberless improvements in the arts, which would have either been lost to mankind, or confined to the knowledge of a few persons only. " To the art of printing," says Dr. Knox, " we owe the Reformation." If the books of Luther had been multiplied only by the slow process of hand-writing, they must have been few, and would have easily been suppressed by the combination of wealth and power; but poured forth in abundance from the press, they spread over the land with the rapidity of an inundation, which acquires additional force from the efforts used to obstruct its progress. He who undertook to prevent the dispersion of books once issued from the press, attempted a task no less arduous than the destruction of the hydra. Resistance was in vain; religion was reformed; and we, who are chiefly interested in this happy revolution, must remember, amidst the praises bestowed on Luther, that his endeavours would have been ineffectual, unassisted by the invention of printing.

The art of printing, therefore, in whatever light it is viewed, claims the highest respect and attention. From the ingenuity of the contrivance it has ever excited mechanical curiosity; from its connection with learning, and its influence on the human character, it is certainly the most important invention with which the world has been benefitted; and young people should endeavour to go through a printing-office after they have read this account of the art.

The workmen employed in printing are of two kinds: *compositors*, who range and dispose the letters into words, lines, pages, &c. according to the copy delivered to them by the author; and the *pressmen*, who apply ink upon the same, and take off the impression. In the back-ground of the plate a compositor is represented at work, and a pressman is engaged at his business in the front.

The letters, or, as they are usually called, the *types*, are made of a mixed metal; (for the composition of which see the article Type-founder,) they are disposed in cases, with separate divisions, called boxes, for the different letters. There are two cases for the purpose of containing the types, called the upper and the lower case. In the upper are placed, in separate boxes, or divisions, the capitals, small-capitals, accented letters, figures, and the marks of reference; in the lower are placed the small letters, also the double letters, the stops, and the spaces which go between the words and fill up short lines. A pair of cases for the Roman types, and another for the Italic, are usually placed on each side the frame, and they stand sloping in such a manner as that every part shall be within the reach of the compositor. Having the letters properly distributed, he lays the written copy before him, and begins to compose. He has a small frame, made of iron, called a composing-stick, in his left hand, in which he places the first letter of the first word of the copy, and the second, and so on till the word is finished; he then puts a blank or space between that and the next word: in this manner he proceeds till he has finished the line, when he goes on to the next; but all the letters are reversed, that the impression may stand right on paper.

When the composing-stick, which holds several lines, is full, the compositor empties it carefully into a frame of wood, called a *galley*. He then fills and empties the composing-stick as before, till a complete page is formed, when he ties it up with a cord, or packthread, and setting it by, proceeds to the next, till the number of pages to be contained in a sheet is composed; this being done, he carries them to the imposing-stone, there to be ranged in order, and fastened together in a frame, called a *chase;* this is termed *imposing*. The chases are different, according to the number of pages contained in a sheet, that is, according as the work is in folio, quarto, octavo, &c.

To dress the chase is to range and fix the pages, leaving the proper margin between them; for this purpose the compositor makes use of a set of furniture, consisting of slips of wood of different dimensions; some of these are placed at the top of the pages, and called *head-sticks;* others at the sides, called *back-sticks* and *gutters.* The pages being placed at their proper distances, are secured by the chase and furniture, and fastened together by means of little wedges of wood, called *quoins,* driven between the chase and the foot and side-sticks, with a wooden mallet and a piece of hard wood. In this state the work is called a *form;* and as there are two forms required for every sheet, when both sides are to be printed, it is necessary that the distances between the pages in each form should be placed with such exactness, that the impression of the pages in one form shall fall exactly on the back of the pages of the other; this is called the *register.*

As mistakes will occur, a sheet, which is called a *proof,* is printed off, and given to the corrector of the press, who examines it while a boy reads the copy to him, making the requisite alterations in the margin; which being done, he gives the proof to the compositor to be corrected. This is done by unlocking the form upon the imposing-stone, loosening the quoins, and taking out the wrong or faulty letters marked in the proof, which he lays before him, with a slender sharp-pointed steel bodkin, and putting others in their places. After this another proof is taken; and having been again read by the corrector of the press, is sent to the author, who, if he wishes it, writes on it "*A revise,*" which signifies that another proof is to be sent to him, to see that all the mistakes marked in the last proof are corrected.

Here, then, the compositor's work is finished, and it is committed to the pressmen, whose business it is to work off the forms thus prepared and corrected; in doing which four things are required, viz. paper, ink, balls, and a press. To prepare the paper for use, it is first to be wetted by dipping several sheets together in water; these are afterwards laid in a heap over one another; and to make them take the water equally, they are all pressed down close with a weight at top. The ink is made of oil and lamp-black, well ground together. The balls by which the ink is applied on the forms, are a kind of wooden funnels with handles, the cavities of which are filled with wool, and this is covered with undressed sheep-skins, made extremely soft and pliable. The press-man takes one of these in each hand, and having applied one of them to the ink-block, works them together till the ink is equally distributed, and then he blackens the form, which is placed on the press, by beating the face of the letters with the balls.

The printing-press, represented in the plate, is a complex and a very curious machine, which will be readily understood by any person who is witness to the operation. Besides the machinery for pressing, there is a carriage, containing a large and polished stone, on which the form is placed; this is rolled backwards and forwards to receive the sheet, and deliver it when the impression is made.

The form being laid on the stone and inked, the pressman takes a sheet of paper from the heap, and spreads it straight on a frame, called a *tympan,* which confines a fold of blanket, or woollen cloth, between two sheets of parchment; this is necessary to take the impression of the letters upon the paper. To the tympan is added a thin frame of iron, called a *frisket,* which is covered with paper, cut in the necessary places, that the sheet, which is put be-tween the tympan and the frisket, may receive the ink without injuring the margins. To regulate the margins, a sheet of paper is fastened on the tympan, and on each side is fixed an iron point, which makes holes in the sheet, and the points are placed in the same holes when the impression is to be made on the other side.

The carriage containing the stone, form, paper,

&c. is now, by turning a handle, rolled under the screw, which, with two pulls of the handle, performs the business; it is then rolled out again, and the paper taken off and laid on one side. The form is then again inked, and another sheet laid on, as before; and this is continued till as many sheets are printed as the impression consists of. After one side of all the sheets is printed, another form, which contains the pages for the other side, is laid upon the press-stone, and printed off in the same manner.

In general there are two pressmen to each press; and then one man inks the form and the other does the rest of the work. When the required number of sheets are taken off, the form is to be separated, in order that the letters may be restored to their proper cases. The form is first washed in a strong ley, by means of a stout brush, and then with fair water. It is then laid on a board by the compositor, who unlocks it, and having loosened the lines, again washes it to free it completely from dirt. When he wants the type to compose another sheet, he takes out several lines at once upon a brass-rule, and taking a word or two at a time between his finger and thumb, replaces each letter into its proper division, and this is called *distribution*.

Besides the several sorts of letters used in printing, there are likewise *rules* for black lines, borders, and head and tail pieces. The rules for black lines are made of brass, and exactly the height of the letter. Borders, flowers, &c. are ornaments in the form of long bars, serving for the divisions of books, chapters, &c. Head and tail pieces are cut either in wood or brass, or cast in metal.

This is the usual method in which printing has been executed for a long period; but besides various improvements of a minor kind, and the performing of the operations of the printing-press by the assistance of the steam-engine, which we shall pass over, we cannot close our account of this important art without noticing the *Stereotype* printing, which has, for standard works, during the last fifteen years, been a good deal used.

We have not room to give a history of this curious process ; but it appears that it was attempted in the middle of the last century, and met with so much opposition from the trade, that it was discountenanced.

The mode of *stereotype* printing is this : first to set up a page in the usual way, and, when it is rendered perfectly correct, a cast of plaster of Paris, prepared from that which is found in Nottinghamshire, and said to be the best, being called gypsum-in-the-rock, is to be taken from it ; in this cast the metal for the stereotype is to be poured. The composition of the metal will be found under our article Type-founder. Each page is, therefore, cast separate ; and, if made in the first instance correct, it cannot, by any possibility, except wear or fracture, become incorrect, nor, of course, can any of the letters be displaced, as the whole page consists of one solid piece of metal. The principal advantage, besides correctness, in stereotype, is, that proprietors of voluminous works need not print any more copies at a time than they choose, and hence a large expence in the capital of paper is thereby avoided.

Journeymen printers, compositors and pressmen, will easily earn from thirty shillings to two guineas a week. The business of the pressman requires little genius, but a considerable portion of strength. A youth designed for a compositor ought to be well educated in his own language ; and he will find it of great advantage, in the course of his business, if he understands something of the modern and ancient languages.

THE ROPE-MAKER.

THE Rope-maker is a person who twists several
kinds of materials, and particularly hemp, into yarn,
and afterwards several strings of such yarn, assisted
by a wheel, into a larger and more compact cord.
When the article is of a small description it is called
a cord, when larger, a rope; the largest is called a
cable.

Ropes are made of many vegetable substances
that are sufficiently fibrous, flexible, and tenacious,
but chiefly of the bark of plants. The Chinese and
other orientals even make them of the woody parts
of several plants, such as certain bamboos, and
reeds, the stems of the aloes, the fibrous covering
of the cocoa-nut, the filaments of the cotton-pod,
and the leaves of some grasses, such as sparte.
The aloe and the sparte exceed all others in strength.
But the barks of plants are the most productive of
fibrous matter proper for this manufacture. Those
of the willow, the linden-tree, the bramble, and the
nettle, are frequently used; but hemp and flax are
the best; and of these hemp is preferred and employed in all cordage exceeding the size of a line,
and even in many of this denomination.

The trade of a Rope-maker is unquestionably
very ancient. As early as the fourteenth century,
in France the Rope-makers were formed into a company, and had statutes appointed for their regula-
tion. In this country, where the navy has obtained

The Rope Maker.

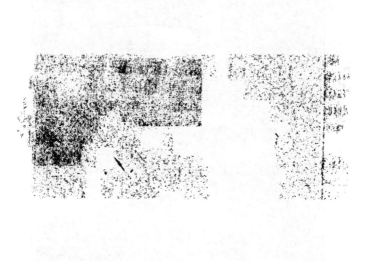

so much attention, a Rope-maker has, for a long period, been a trade of considerable importance.

Ropes of all kinds are generally made of hemp, twisted or spun, something after the same manner as the spinning of wool; and the places in which ropes are made are called rope-walks. These are sometimes a quarter of a mile or more in length, in the open air, and have a row or rows of trees planted beside them for shade, or are covered with a slight shed to keep the workmen from the inclemencies and changes of the weather.

At the upper end of the rope-walk is a spinning-wheel, which is turned round by a person who sits on a stool or bench for the purpose; the man who forms the rope or string, has a bundle of dressed hemp, such as that which lies on the truck in the plate, round his waist. From this he draws out two or more ends, and fixes them to a hook; the wheel is now turned, by which the threads are twisted, and as the spinner walks backward, the rope, or more properly the rope-yarn, is lengthened. The part already twisted draws along with it more fibres out of the bundle, and the spinner gives assistance to it with his fingers, supplying hemp in due proportion as he walks away from the wheel, and taking care that the fibres come in equally from both sides of his bundle, and that they enter always with their ends, and not by the middle, which would double them. The arrangement of the fibres, and the degree of twisting, depend on the skill and dexterity of the spinner. The degree of twist depends on the rate of the wheel's motion, combined with the retrograde motion of the spinner.

As soon as he has arrived at the lower end of the walk he calls out, and another spinner immediately detaches the yarn from the hook of the wheel, gives it to a third person, who takes it to the reel, and the second spinner attaches his own hemp to the wheel-hook. In the meantime the first spinner keeps fast hold of the end of his yarn, to prevent its untwist-ing, and as soon as the reeler begins to turn his reel, he goes slowly up the walk, keeping the yarn of an equal tightness all the way, till he arrives at the wheel, where he waits with his yarn in his hand till another has finished his yarn. The first spinner takes it off the wheel-hook, joins it to his own, that it may follow it on the reel, and begins a new yarn himself.

The fibres of hemp are thus twisted into yarns, and make a line of any length: down the rope-walk are a number of upright posts, with long pegs fixed in them at right angles; on these pegs the spinner throws the rope-yarn as he proceeds, to prevent its swagging.

As many fibres are made into one yarn, so many yarns are afterwards made into one rope, according to the use and strength required. By this process, which is called laying, it acquires a solidity and hardness which render it less penetrable by water, that would rot it in a short time.

Sometimes the union of several yarns is called a strand, and a larger rope is formed of two or more of these strands; in this manner many cables and other ground tackle are commonly made.

Cables and cords are frequently tarred, which is usually done in the state of yarn, this being the only method by which hemp can be uniformly penetrated. The yarn is made to wind off from one reel, and having passed through a vessel containing hot tar, it is wound upon another, and the superfluous tar is taken off by passing through a hole surrounded with spungy oakum; or it is sometimes tarred in skeins or hauls, which are drawn by a capstern through the tar-kettle, and through a hole formed of two plates of metal.

It is a fact, however, that tarred cordage is much weaker than white; it is also less pliable and less durable; but the use of tar is nevertheless necessary to defend the cordage from the action of the water.

Nets are made with small cords; larger cords are used for tying up packages; and ropes of all sizes and dimensions are used for shipping. A ship's cable is sometimes several hundred yards in length, and is worth a considerable sum of money.

Mr. Chapman has lately obtained a patent for making ropes and cordage, the machinery of which consists only of a spindle, divided into two parts, the upper containing apparatus to draw forward the hemp from the spinner, with twist sufficient to combine the fibres, which enables him to employ women, children, and invalids, and also to appropriate the rope-ground solely to the purpose of laying ropes. The remaining part of his invention consists chiefly in the giving from a stationary power the internal motion to a loco-motive machine, as to a roper's sledge, on which the strands and the rope itself are twisted, by which contrivance a water-wheel, or a steam-engine, is applied to the whole process of making ropes of all kinds whatever.

Other patents have been also obtained for improving this art; but we have not room to enumerate them.

The master Rope-maker requires a considerable capital to carry on business upon a large scale. A journeyman may earn with ease from a guinea to a guinea and a half a week, or even more if he be sober and industrious.

Yarn for sail-cloth is made of dressed-hemp, and spun in the same manner as rope-yarn is spun. The spinners of this make a good living; women are chiefly employed in it. The person who shapes and sews together the sail-cloth, is called a sail-maker; and is sometimes denominated a ship's-tailor.

THE SADLER.

MAKES seats adapted to the horse's back for the convenience of the rider ; he also makes bridles, girths, &c. The trade of a Sadler is also frequently joined to that of a Harness-maker.

In the early ages, when the horse was trained to the use of man, the rider sat on the bare back of the animal ; but in the course of time a covering was used, which consisted of a dressed or undressed skin of some slaughtered beast. Such coverings became afterwards very costly ; they were decorated with many ornaments, and made large enough to hang down nearly to the ground.

> Six lions' hides, with thongs together fast,
> His upper parts defended to his waist,
> And where man ended, the continued vest
> Spread on his back the house and trapping of a beast.
> DRYDEN.

But it was reckoned among the Romans more manly to ride on the bare back than upon coverings ; and Xenophon, in his Cyropœdia, reproaches the Persians for placing more clothes on the backs of their horses than on their beds ; and giving themselves more trouble to sit easily than to ride skilfully.

The origin of saddles is very ancient, if it be true that the *Selians*, an ancient people of Franconia, were the first inventors of them, as the name *Selle*, the French word for saddle, would seem to import.

Saddler.

However, it is certain, that neither saddles nor stirrups were in use amongst the early ages of the Roman Republic. Galen assures us, in many of his medical works, that the Romans were subject to frequent diseases of the hip, in consequence of their feet not being supported when they were on horseback; and Hippocrates has made the same observation relative to the Scythians. There is reason to believe, notwithstanding, about a century ago, a saddle used to be shown at Bern, as the same on which Julius Cæsar rode, that saddles were not used by the Romans till the year 340 of the Christian æra. Before this period square pannels were used, such as we see in the Capitol on the equestrian statue of Antoninus : it was also in this century that Theodosius forbad the use of saddles weighing more than sixty pounds.

A saddle consists of a wooden frame, called a saddle-tree, on which is laid a quantity of horsehair, wool, &c. and this is covered over with tanned leather, neatly nailed to the wooden tree. To keep the saddle steady on the horse, the crupper is used, which passes under the creature's tail; and girths to prevent it from turning round. To support the legs of the rider, a pair of stirrups is also added, one of which is very useful in assisting to mount the animal; to prevent the saddle galling the horse's back, a saddle-cloth is sometimes used.

The articles made use of in the manufacture of these things are more or less costly, according to the price which the purchaser pays for his goods.

Cutting-knives, hammers, and pincers, are the chief implements of the trade ; that is, of the person employed in the manufacture of saddles. To complete a single article in the business, the aid of many different artizans is required.

The tree-maker furnishes only the wooden part of the saddle ; this is, however, a very important branch of the business ; because upon the saddle-tree the fitting of the saddle depends; and in cases when gentlemen wish to have their saddles fit properly, it is as necessary to measure the horse's back as for the shoe-maker to measure his customer for boots or shoes. The saddle-tree maker requires no great strength or ingenuity.

The sadler's iron-monger furnishes him with the iron or steel stirrups, buckles of all kinds, bits for bridles, and other steel or brass furniture required for the harness of a horse, either for riding or drawing in a carriage. Many of these articles are originally made by the iron-founder.

There is also a distinct trade, called a horse's milliner, who makes roses for bridles, and other articles used in highly-ornamented caparisons. This tradesman should have an inventive genius, and a considerable share of taste, to set off the furniture belonging to a horse, and decorate it in a neat and elegant style.

The saddler makes all sorts of bridles, coach and chaise harness; of course, besides the trades already noticed as peculiarly belonging to his business, he employs the tanner, or leather-cutter, the currier, the embroiderer, who works devices, crests, and coats of arms, in gold, silver, or worsted. He buys broad-cloths and other woollens of the draper; velvet and silk of the mercer; ribbands of the weaver; gold and silver and livery lace from the lace-man; buckram, thread, &c. from the haberdasher. Of all these articles he should, for the sake of his customers, be a good judge.

A great number of saddles are exported to foreign parts, particularly to the East Indies; as English saddles are in great repute there.

There are many different kinds of saddles, as the hunting-saddle, the racing-saddle, ladies' saddles, called also side-saddles, &c.

The Sadler requires a considerable capital if he is in a large way, and called upon to give much credit; in general, however, this is not one of the trades which requires a very large stock.

The journeymen, in almost every branch of the saddlery business, work by the piece, and may earn a good living. They none of them require great strength; the men always work in the dry, and in most of the branches cleanliness, which is no small requisite in the mechanical arts, is a principal one.

THE SAWYER

Is a person who cuts the trunks of trees of various kinds into beams, planks, &c. for the use of carpenters and joiners for the purposes of building.

In the early periods of the world the trunks of trees were split by wedges into as thin pieces as possible by that mode; and if it were necessary to have them still thinner, they were hewn on both sides by hatchets till they were reduced to a proper size. The common saw, which requires only to be guided by the hand of the workman, was not known in America when it was discovered and subjugated by Europeans.

The saw is undoubtedly one of the most useful instruments in the mechanic arts ever invented. Among the Greeks, the inventor has been enrolled in their mythology among the gods, and honoured as one of the greatest benefactors of the human race. The invention is attributed to Icarius, the son of Dædalus, who is said to have taken the first hint from the spine, or back-bone of a flat-fish.

The saws of the Grecian carpenters had the same form, and were made in the like ingenious manner as ours are at present. This is fully shewn by a painting still preserved among the antiquities of Herculaneum.

Saws are of various kinds; the principal are the following:

The *pit-saw*, which is a large two-handed saw,

Sawyer.

used to saw timber in pits; this is chiefly used by the sawyers.

The *whip-saw,* which is also two-handed, used in sawing such large pieces of stuff as the hand-saw will not easily reach.

The *hand-saw* is made to be used by one man; there are various kinds of hand-saws: the *tenon-saw,* which, being very thin, has a back to keep it from bending; the *compass-saw,* which is very small, and its teeth usually not set; its use is to cut a round or any other compass-kerf; hence the edge is made broad and the back thin, that it may make room for it to be turned.

The best *saws* are of tempered steel ground bright and polished: the edge in which the teeth are is always thicker than the back. The teeth are cut and sharpened by a file. When filed the teeth are to be set, that is, turned askew, or out of a right line, (by an instrument called a *saw-set,*) to make the fissure wider, that the back may follow with ease. This is done by putting the instrument on every tooth, and giving it a little wrench or bend; one of the teeth is turned in one direction, and the other in a contrary one. The teeth are always set ranker for coarse cheap work than for that which is hard and fine.

The pit-saw, such as is represented in the plate, is a large two-handed saw, used to saw timber in pits. It is set rank for coarse stuff, so as to make a fissure of about a quarter of an inch wide.

The timber to be sawed is laid on a frame over an oblong pit, called a saw-pit, which is an improvement of modern times, as the power of a man standing in a pit must far exceed that which is exerted by him in a sitting posture. By means of a long saw, fastened in a frame, which is worked up and down by two men, one standing on the wood to be cut and the other in the pit, the operation of *sawing* is performed. As they proceed in their work, they drive wedges at a proper distance from the saw to keep the fissure open, which enables the saw to move with freedom.

The most beneficial and ingenious improvement is the *saw-mill*, which is worked either by water, by wind, or by steam. A saw-mill consists of several parallel saws, which are made to rise and fall perpendicularly by means of a mechanical motion. A very few hands are necessary to conduct this operation, to push forward the pieces of timber, which are either laid on rollers or suspended by ropes, in proportion as the sawing advances.

But the sawing-machines worked by steam in the block house in Portsmouth dock-yard, convey to the spectator the nature of mechanical operation in the completest manner possible. The manufacture of blocks in that place cannot fail to interest every one who has the slightest turn for mechanics; and a person must be devoid of all curiosity who can visit Portsmouth, and return without making every effort to be introduced into this part of the dock-yard.

This is a very laborious employment; yet two industrious men may earn from twelve to eighteen shillings a day.

Shipwright.

THE SHIPWRIGHT

Is a person who builds ships: a ship has been
defined a timber-building, consisting of various parts
and pieces, nailed and pinned together with iron
and wood, in such form as to be fit to float, and to
be conducted by wind and sails from sea to sea.

The word *ship* is a general name for all large
vessels with sails, adapted for navigation on the sea;
but by sailors the term is more particularly applied
to a vessel furnished with three masts, each of
which is composed of a lower-mast, a top-mast, and
a top-gallant-mast.

The first attempts which mankind made in navigation were beyond a doubt very ancient; but it was
not till after a long time, and considerable efforts
and labour, that they became enabled to construct
large floating houses, capable of encountering the
tempests of the winds and waves.

A thousand opportunities would of course present themselves to the eyes of mankind in the
earliest ages of the world to excite the idea of floating on the water, but nothing more readily than a
tree torn up by the winds, and floating down the
stream of a river. It would be easy afterwards to
collect a number of trees, or other floating pieces of
wood, and by proper ligatures form a *raft*. To the
raft most probably succeeded the *canoe,* composed
in the first place out of an old hollow tree; from the
facility with which the canoe can be managed,

canoes, among the most savage nations, have been
very early in use.

At what period the art of ship-building commenced it is not easy to determine; but the construction of boats must have preceded that of ships.
The ark of Noah is we believe the earliest record
which we have of any building made expressly to
float on the water. Ships are, however, since the
time of the deluge frequently mentioned in the
Scriptures. In the time of Homer, also, ships were
in great use : the catalogue of the Grecian ships
forms a considerable part of one of the Books of the
Iliad.

But there is great reason to believe that all the
ships of antiquity were comparatively of small dimensions : it has been reserved for modern times,
commercial speculation, and modern warfare, to
demonstrate the improved powers and capacities of
man for this extraordinary art.

The man of science and the practical ship-wright
have long lamented that, in the theory of the art of
ship-building, there are so few fixed and positive
principles established by demonstration, or confirmed by practice; thus the artist being left to the
exercise of his own opinion, in general resists theo-
retical propositions, however speciously formed, so
hard has it ever been found to overcome habitual
prejudices. The great neglect of the theory of
ship-building is much to be deplored in a country
like this, where the practical part is so well understood and executed. Mathematics, engineering,
and civil or house architecture, are sciences nourish-
ed and taught in our universities and other schools;
and to whatever degree of superiority scholars may
arrive in these, shew them shipping draughts, or
talk to them of the science of ship-building, and
they appear as much at a loss as though they had
never heard of such an art. This, however, is the

picture of a few years ago ; it is now begun to be studied under the denomination of naval architecture ; for the promotion of this science, a very respectable body of ingenious men have, for the last fifteen years, associated.

In ship-building three things are necessary to be considered ; first, to give the vessel such a form as shall be best adapted for sailing, and for the service for which she is designed ; secondly, to unite the several parts into a compact frame ; and thirdly, to provide suitable accommodations for the officers and crew, as well as for the cargo, furniture, provisions, guns, and ammunition.

The outside figure of the ship includes the bottom or the hold, and the upper works, which are also called the *dead-works ;* the first is that part which is generally under, the second are those which are usually above it when the vessel is laden.

To give a proper shape to the bottom of the ship, it is necessary to consider the service for which she is designed. A *ship of war* should be able to sail swiftly, and carry her lower tier of guns four or five feet out of the water ; a *merchant-ship* ought to be able to contain a large cargo of goods, and to be navigated with few hands ; both of these should be able to carry sail firmly ; to steer well ; and to sustain the shocks of the sea without being violently strained.

Ships are built principally with *oak-timber,* which is the stoutest and strongest wood we have ; and, therefore, best fitted both to keep sound under water, and to bear the blows and shocks of the waves, and the terrible strokes of cannon-balls. For this last purpose it is a peculiar excellence of the oak, that it is not so liable to splinter or shiver, as other wood ; so that a ball can pass through it without making a large hole.

The great use of oak for the structure of mer-

chant-ships, as well as for men of war, is referred to
by Mr. Pope:

> While by our oaks the precious loads are borne,
> And realms commanded which those trees adorn.

During the construction of a ship she is supported
in the dock, or upon a wharf, by a number of solid
blocks of timber, placed at equal distances from,
and parallel to, each other; in which situation she
is said to be *on the stocks.*

The first piece of timber laid upon the stocks is
generally the *keel,* which at one end is let into the
stern-post, and at the other into the *stem.* If the
carcase of a ship be compared to the skeleton of a
human body, the keel may be considered as the
back-bone, and the timbers as the ribs.

The *stern* is the hinder-part of the ship, near
which are the state-room, cabins, &c. To the
stern-post is fixed the iron-work that holds the
rudder, which directs the course of the vessel.

The *stem* is a circular piece of timber in the
front; into this the sides of the ship are inserted.
The outside of the stem is usually marked with a
scale, or division of feet, according to its perpendicular height from the keel; the intention of this
is to ascertain the draught of water at the fore-part,
when the ship is in preparation for a sea-voyage.

In the plate the shipwright is represented standing at the stern on a scaffold, and driving in the
wedges with his wooden trunnel. The holes are
first bored with the auger, and then the wedges
driven in; these are afterwards cut off with a saw.
At his feet lie his saw; his auger, which is used for
boring large holes; his axe; and punches of different sizes.

The caulking of a ship is a very important operation; it consists in driving oakum, (which is old
ropes untwisted, and the substance pulled or beaten

into loose hemp,) into the seams between the planks, to prevent the ship's leaking. It is afterwards covered with hot melted pitch or rosin, to prevent its rotting.

A mixture was formerly used for covering the bottom of ships, made of one part of tallow, one of brimstone, and three of rosin; this is called paying the bottom. The sides and bottom are now usually payed with coal-tar, the produce of England.

To enable ships to sail well, the outsides in contact with the water are frequently covered with copper.

The masts of ships are made of fir or pine, on account of the straightness and lightness of the wood. The length of the main-mast of an East India ship is about eighty feet. The masts always bear a certain proportion to the breadth of the ship; whatever the breadth may be, multiply that by twelve, and divide the product by five, which will give the length of the main-mast. Thus, a ship which measures thirty feet at the broadest part, will have a main-mast seventy-two feet long; the thickness of the mast is estimated by allowing one inch for every three feet in length; accordingly a mast seventy-two feet long must be twenty four inches thick. For the other masts different proportions are to be used. To the masts are attached the yards, sails, and rigging, which receive the wind necessary for navigation.

When a ship is finished building, it is next to be *launched;* that is, slipped off the stocks into the water. To render the operation of launching easy, the ship, when first begun to be built, is supported by two strong platforms, laid with a gradual inclination to the water. Upon the surface of this declivity are placed two corresponding ranges of planks, which compose the base of the frame, called the *cradle,* to which the ship's bottom is securely attached. The planes of the cradle and platform are well greased, and then the *blocks* and *wedges,* by

which the ship was supported, are driven out from
under the keel; afterwards the *shores*, by which she
is retained on the stocks, are cut away, and the ship
slides down into the water.

Ships of the first rate are usually constructed in
dry docks, and afterwards floated out, by throwing
open the flood-gates, and suffering the tide to enter,
as soon as they are finished.

In a dock-yard where ships are built, six or eight
men, called *quartermen*, are frequently entrusted to
build a ship, and engage to perform the business for
a certain sum, under the inspection of a master-
builder. These employ other men under them, who,
according to their different departments, will earn
from fifteen or twenty shillings to two or three
pounds per week.

Shoe Maker.

THE SHOE-MAKER

———

MAKES covering for the feet, usually of leather; but frequently also of other materials, as silk, jean, nankeen, &c. He also makes boots of various kinds, both for ladies and gentlemen.

There are few trades more useful than that of a shoe-maker, and, perhaps, not many that are more profitable, when it is carried on to a considerable extent. Some shoe-makers carry on a snug private trade, without any show; others have large shops, and exhibit in them shoes of all sorts for ladies and gentlemen, together with boots, gaiters, and spatterdashes.

It appears from history, that the Jews, long before the Christian æra, wore shoes made of leather or wood; those of their soldiers were sometimes formed out of brass or iron. The Egyptians wore a kind of shoe made of the papyrus. The Indians, the Chinese, and other nations, wore shoes made of silk, of rushes, of linen, of wood, of the bark of trees, of iron, of brass, and of gold and silver; and luxury has sometimes covered them with precious stones. The Greeks and Romans wore shoes of leather: the Grecian shoes generally reached to the middle of the leg: the Romans used two kinds of shoes; the *calceus*, which covered the whole foot, something in the shape of our shoes; and the *solea*, or slipper, which covered only the sole of the foot, and was fastened with leather thongs; the *calceus* was worn with the *toga* when a person went abroad, and slippers were put on during a journey, and at feasts. Black shoes were worn by the citizens of ordinary rank, and white ones by women. Red shoes were put on by the chief magistrates of Rome, on days of ceremony.

In Europe, about one thousand years ago, the greatest princes wore shoes having the upper part of leather, and the under of wood. In the reign of William Rufus, the shoes of the great had long sharp points, stuffed with tow, and twisted like a ram's horn. The clergy preached against these points; they continued, however, to increase till the reign of Richard the Second, when they were tied to the knees with chains of silver or gold. At length parliament interfered by an act in the year 1463, and prohibited the use of shoes or boots with pikes exceeding two inches in length : and the shoe-makers were forbidden, under severe penalties, to make them contrary to the statute.

To render this business profitable, a considerable degree of knowledge is required with regard to the properties of leather, and an accurate judgment to cut the leather in such a manner as to yield the greatest quantity with the least waste.

The master shoe-maker, or, if he be in a very large way, his foreman, measures his customers, and cuts out leather for his work-people to put together. In some instances, especially in the country, he is the leather-cutter to all the little traders in the sur-rounding villages. In this case, he buys the leather in skins and half-hides from the dresser, and cuts them out into soles and upper-leathers, which he either uses in his own business, or sells to those who cannot afford to go to a wholesale market.

In the *plate* is the representation both of the master and journeyman shoe-maker. The *former* is cutting out an upper-leather of a shoe to a paper pattern, which lies upon it. A small leaden weight is placed on the skin at the corner, to keep it from slipping : on his left lies the hammer, which he uses to beat down any rough parts which stand on the inside of the leather: and on his right hand is a pair of pincers, which are made with teeth, in order to hold the leather tight in the act of stretching it.

The journeyman is in the act of joining the upper-leather to the sole of the shoe: on his bench near him are his awl, his knife, and a stone with which he sharpens his tools. Before him, on his right, are the hammer and lap-stone, and on the other side, a tub of water, in which he keeps a quantity of wax in balls. These are the principal implements of his trade. He sews the leather with thread, waxed over, and thereby made a strong and durable substance; as, however, he makes no use of a needle, to the end of the thread is fastened a hog's-bristle, which guides the thread through the holes made in the leather with an awl.

Shoe-makers' wax is commonly made by melting together about equal parts of pitch and yellow rosin; but in warm weather it is necessary to have a greater proportion of rosin than in the winter, which proportion is best judged of by the workman himself. For ladies' light-coloured shoes, and other fine work, different wax is of course used.

The best and strongest thread for shoe-makers' stout and firm work is made of *hemp;* but latterly a good deal of flax has been used in the trade, which is by no means so strong or durable a material.

Shoes and boots are made on *lasts,* which are manufactured of some soft wood, by means of an engine, or knife, such as that which we have described in the brush-maker's trade. The same man that makes the *lasts* makes also the wooden heels for women's shoes. The last for shoes is made of a single piece of wood, to imitate the foot; but that for boots is slit into two parts, between which a wedge is driven when the boot-leg is desired to be stretched.

Shoe-makers use large quantities of Morocco-leather, which is the skin of a goat, dressed in su-mac; or gall, and coloured at pleasure.

Journeymen in this trade are distinguished into women's shoe-maker's and those who make shoes and boots for men. Few can follow both branches with advantage ; greater ingenuity is required in manufacturing women's shoes, because the seams must be neater, as the materials are much finer.

A journeyman shoe-maker, if he be a good hand, sober, and industrious, will earn thirty shillings a week.

Women are employed to bind shoes of all kinds, and to sew the quarters together of those that are made of silk, satin, stuffs, &c.

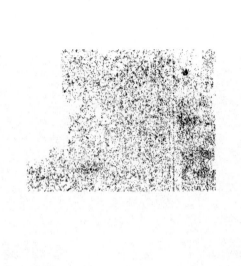

The Smith.

THE SMITH.

A Smith is one who works on iron, and who from that metal manufactures a vast variety of articles useful in the arts of life, and of great importance to domestic comfort.

The smith is one of those workmen whose assistance becomes necessary even in a rude state of society, and in the first dawnings of civilization: it is not easy to point out when the occupation of the smith was distinguished as a distinct branch of trade, but we learn from the scriptures, that such persons had existed at a very early period, for they are there distinguished as *workers in iron.*

There are at the present time several branches in this trade: some are called black-smiths; of this class is the man represented in the plate: others are called *white-smiths* or *bright-smiths;* these polish their work to a considerable degree of nicety; some include in their business bell-hanging, which is now carried to great perfection; others are chiefly employed in the manufacture of locks and keys.

In the Smith's shop there must be a forge, an anvil and block, a vice fastened to an immoveable bench, besides hammers, tongs, files, punches, and pincers of different sorts.

The *forge* is the most prominent article; it is represented in the plate on the left hand of the smith: The forge is a sort of furnace, intended for heating metals so hot as to render them malleable, and fit to be formed into their various shapes. The back of the forge is built upright to the ceiling, and is

o 4

enclosed over the fire-place with a *hovel* which leads into the chimney, to carry away the smoke. In the back of the forge, against the fire-place, is a thick iron plate, with a pipe fixed to it, to receive the nose of the bellows. The bellows is behind the forge, and is worked by means of a rocker, with a string or chain fastened to it, which the smith, or his labourer, pulls. One of the boards of the bellows is fixed, and by drawing down the handle of the rocker, the moveable board, which is also the upper one, rises, and by means of a weight on the top sinks again; and by this alternate motion, the fire is raised to the desired degree of heat.

In the front of the forge, but a little below it, is a *trough of water,* which is useful for wetting the coals to make them throw out a greater heat; the water serves also for cooling the tongs with which the smith holds the heated iron, and which in a short time becomes too hot for him to grasp: in this trough also the smith hardens his iron, by dipping it while red hot.

The Smith in the plate is represented in the act of forging a piece of iron which he has just taken from the fire with the tongs in his left hand.

Iron is hammered or forged two ways: either by the force of the hand, in which there are sometimes several persons employed, one holding and turning the iron, and hammering likewise, while the others hammer only with what are called sledge hammers, such as that which stands on the ground of the plate resting against the block: or it is done by the force of a water-mill, which raises and works several enormous hammers; under the strokes of these the men have only to present the large lumps of iron, which are sustained at one end by the anvils, and at the other by iron chains fastened to the ceiling of the forge. This last method is employed in the largest works, such as the making of anchors of ships, which weigh several thousand pounds.

In lighter works, such as we have in the plate, namely, in the making of stoves, shovels, gridirons, tripods, &c. &c. a single man is sufficient to hold, to heat, and to turn the iron with one hand, while he strikes it with the other.

The several heats given by smiths to their iron are called the *blood-red heat*, the *white heat*, and the *welding heat.*

The *blood-red* heat is used when the iron has already acquired its form and size, but wants hammering only to smooth and fit it for the file.

The *white* heat is used when the iron has not its form and size, but must be forged into both.

The *welding* heat is required when two pieces of iron are to be united.

The welding of cast steel and cast iron has been in this trade attended with considerable difficulty, and indeed has been by some persons deemed impracticable; but late experiments have demonstrated that not only cast steel may be welded to iron, but that cast iron may be united to itself, with much more ease than has been commonly imagined. The method now adopted for welding cast-steel to iron, is not to heat it to so *high* a temperature as it is necessary to heat iron for welding, as the welding heat of steel is considerably below that of iron. Cast iron bars, it is now found, can also be united by the use of a proper flux, glass of borax is usually preferred, their ends being previously enclosed in a wrought-iron tube, and heated to a proper degree, the tube serving as a mould to prevent the fixed cast iron from falling asunder during the operation.

The uppermost surface of the *anvil*, on which a smith hammers his iron, must be very flat and smooth, and so hard that no file will touch it. At one end of the anvil is a hole in which may be placed a strong steel chisel or spike; on this a piece of red hot iron may be laid, and cut in two with a single stroke of the hammer. Anvils are sometimes made of cast iron; but the best are those which are forged with the upper part made of steel. The whole is usually mounted on a firm wooden block.

The *vice* fixed to the bench serves to hold any thing upon which the smith is at work, whether it requires filing, bending, or riveting. There are hand vices and small anvils, which are occasionally used in the more delicate operations of this business.

Square and flat bars of iron are sometimes twisted for ornamental work; this is done by giving the metal a white heat, fixing it in the vice, and turning it with the tongs.

Iron rails before houses are generally made of cast-iron, which is run from the ore, and neither requires nor will bear the hammer: it is brittle and will not readily yield to the file. It is the business of the blacksmith to make the upper rail to receive these bars, and to fix them into the stone-work.

It would be impossible to enumerate all the articles manufactured by the smith; they are of all kinds, and of almost all values. Steel stoves have been made at Brodie's manufactory in Carey-street, of several hundred pounds value; and a more interesting sight cannot be well viewed, than the store-rooms of our large furnishing ironmongers.

A journeyman smith will earn from three to five shillings per day; but those who work on the fine polished articles will earn much higher wages.

The Soap Boiler.

THE SOAP-BOILER.

———

THE SOAP-BOILER makes the article called Soap,
which is composed of an oil and an alkaline salt,
for the purpose of washing linen, the hands, and
other domestic and manufacturing operations.

The combination of an oil with an alkali uniformly produces a compound, soluble in water, and
in which the characteristic properties of oils and
alkalies are destroyed or changed. But as combinations of soda and potash are only employed in
this business, we shall of course confine ourselves to
a particular consideration of them.

It is probable that ages must have elapsed before
mankind arrived at a knowledge of the composition
of soap. Saponaceous plants, argils, marls, fuller's-
earth, a species of argil, extensively, and in an early
period, known, and magnesia, appear all to have
been employed in cleansing linen and other cloths,
long before the discovery of soap. We even see
that some animal matters were employed with advantage for the same purpose. It is equally certain, that the use of ash-leys preceded the discovery
of soap. But the capability of combining oil with
alkali, so as to form a solid compound, soluble in
water, and which can dissolve spots of grease without changing the colour of the stuffs on which they
are found, is a discovery of inestimable value in the
arts. This discovery, successively improved, constitutes what is now termed the art of soap-making.

There is scarcely any substance manufactured
o 6

by the art of man more useful than that of soap : at first sight it may seem strange, that the article which is used to clean and whiten other substances, should itself be formed of grease or oil, and that the coarsest fat may be made into soap.

Soap is either hard or soft ; it is variously named, according to its colour : we have white, mottled, yellow soap, &c. But all the kinds are made with fat or oil, combined with either potash or soda ; but principally with soda, unless a soft soap is wanted, as potash liquifies upon exposure to atmospheric air, whereas soda effloresces, or, in other words, parts with the water which it contains, and therefore is the most proper for hard-soaps.

Potash is an alkaline salt, obtained from vegetables in the following manner : vegetable substances of any kind, burnt in the open air, and reduced to ashes, contain a certain proportion of salt, which is to be obtained from the ashes by mixing them with water : when the water is filtered, it is to be evaporated by heat, and the saline substance the potash, or if it be very fine and white, the pearl-ash, is left at the bottom of the vessel.

Soda is generally obtained in this country from an article imported from Spain called *barilla,* which consists of the ashes of a plant named soda, which grows plentifully in some parts of that country, particularly on the shores of the Mediterranean. Both potash and soda are called fixed alkalies, because they are not commonly dissipated by heat ; the *former* is also sometime denominated *vegetable* alkali ; the *latter, mineral* alkali ; distinctions which are neither correct, nor of any real use in science.

These alkalies, as they are usually found, cannot be employed in the manufacture of soap till they are deprived of their carbonic acid, and the earthy matters which they contain. This process is conducted in the following manner : into a vessel about eight feet square, and one foot deep, is introduced *quicklime*, in the proportion of one-fifth of the weight of oil intended to be converted into soap: water is slightly sprinkled over the quicklime, which then grows hot, cracks, smokes, and falls down into powder; after which the soda or barilla, previously pounded, must be carefully mixed with it by means of a shovel. In order to favour the operation, a little water is occasionally added. As soon as the mixture is accomplished, it is transferred into tubs. In small establishments the vessels are made of white wood; but in those which are on a larger scale, they are composed of stones, lined with bricks, formed on the spot, and sunk into a mortar made of puzzolana, or similar earths. These cisterns are usually about five feet by four, and one and a half in depth. They are perforated at the lower part of the side, next the workhouse, with two holes, which are closed by stop-cocks, or pegs of wood. Under each of these vessels are reservoirs, constructed with the same care, and intended for the reception and preservation of the leys, when the lime and soda is transferred to the tub, or to these cisterns, a quantity of water is poured on the mixture, sufficient to cover it to the height of a foot and a half. After leaving the water in this state for several hours, it is drawn off into one of the reservoirs. This ley marks from fifteen to twenty degrees of concentration, and is called the first ley. Water is to be again put upon the mixture, and to stand, and afterwards to be drawn off as before: this is termed the second ley: and the operation is repeated as long as ley of any power comes from the mixture.

In large manufactories, such as that represented in the plate, the ley is made no stronger than to be able to sustain a new-laid egg. The oil or tallow, is first boiled with a part of the ley, which may be diluted with water, till the whole is formed into a soapy compound. The stronger ley is then to be added, and kept slowly boiling, while a person, as represented in the upper part of the plate, assists the union by constant agitation. When it is sufficiently boiled, a separation will appear to be taking place; the soap being at top and the fluid below: to effect this separation completely, a quantity of common salt is added. The materials are usually boiled three or four hours, when the fire is withdrawn. The soap is found to unite at the top of the liquor, which is now called the waste ley, and being of no further use it is drawn off.

The soap is now melted with another ley, and when a little boiled it is cast into wooden frames, such as those represented in the plate. These frames are moveable, and range exactly one upon the other, and the soap is filled in from the bottom to the top. When it is perfectly set and cold, the workman takes off the upper frame, and with a piece of copper wire he cuts off the soap which that frame contained. In this part of the business, the man on the floor in the plate is represented as engaged. He then takes off another frame, and so on till he comes to within five or six of the bottom, and there he finds the ley has drained from the soap into the middle of the substance ; of course, from this height to the bottom, the cakes of soap have an oval hole left in them. This ley he takes carefully out with an iron ladle, and puts into the bucket which stands before him. By a like process he cuts the soap into narrow slices, as it is usually sold in the shops.

The tallow for making soap is reckoned very good if 13cwt. of it with alkali yield a ton weight of soap.

White soap is made of olive oil and soda. *Yellow* soap is made with tallow and yellow rosin, in the proportion of ten parts of tallow and three and a half of rosin ; these, if good, will, with alkali, yield twenty of soap.

Mottled soap obtains its speckled appearance by dispersing the ley through the soap towards the end of the operation, or by adding a quantity of sulphate of iron, which, by its decomposition, deposits its oxide through the soap, and gives it the appearance of streaked marble. Some manufacturers use oxide of manganese for the same purpose. We believe, however, that the colouring ingredient, in the mottled soap of London, is indigo. Certain it is, that the soap known in commerce by the name of *Castile soap*, (the best, however, of this sort is brought from Marseilles,) is an oil soap, united with a considerable quantity of the sulphate of iron, in the decomposition of which the beautiful marbling of that soap is effected.

In France a cheap soap is made by using woollen rags, old woollen cloths, and even the horns, &c. of animals, instead of oil. These substances are soluble in caustic ley, and by proper boiling form soap; but it has a very disagreeable smell.

Soap is easily and completely dissolved in water; but in hard water it curdles, or is only imperfectly dissolved; on this account, a solution of soap in spirits of wine is used to discover whether the water of any spring or pond be hard or soft; for if the water be soft, the solution will unite with it; but if it be hard, the soap will separate in flakes.

The soap-manufacturer is subject to the excise laws; and he pays a heavy duty for every pound of soap which he makes. His coppers, and even his furnace-doors, are furnished with locks and keys, and he dares not open them but in the presence of an excise officer, and he must give notice of twenty-four hours or more in writing to the officers before he begins making. His house is no longer an Englishman's castle, into which none may come but by his leave; the excise officers are required to enter it at all times, by day or by night; who may, between the hours of five in the morning and eleven

6

at night, unlock and examine every copper, and every part of the dwelling-house, none daring to obstruct them, without incurring very heavy penalties. To similar restrictions the tallow-chandler and other trades under the excise laws are subject.

The soap-manufacturer must also take out an annual licence from the excise-office, besides being subject to these fiscal regulations.

Spinner.

THE SPINNER.

THE SPINNER reduces silk, flax, hemp, wool, hair, &c. by means of a machine, into thread.

In many country villages the art of spinning is carried on by women and children in the open air.

The art of spinning wool and other materials is of the highest antiquity, and must of course have preceded the art of weaving.

The process of reducing cotton wool into yarn or thread, was for a long series of years performed by the hand, upon a machine which is called the *one thread wheel,* for the origin of which instrument we might possibly search in vain. In the reign of George the Second, several machines were constructed for facilitating the spinning of cotton, but without producing any material advantage, till about 1767, Mr. James Hargrave constructed a machine by which a great number of threads (from twenty to eighty,) might be spun at once, and for which he obtained his Majesty's letters patent. This machine is called a *Jenny,* and is considered as the best contrivance for spinning what is called *woof* or *shute,* that has hitherto appeared. It is now commonly constructed for eighty-four threads; and with it one person can spin a hundred English hanks in the day, each hank containing eight hundred and forty yards.

Spinning by hand is either performed by the distaff and spindle, or on the wheel; in the former case the person sits at her work; in the latter she stands, or rather runs backwards and forwards. We shall describe both methods. When the distaff and spindle are used, the flax or other substance is tied or fixed on a long stick: the spinner draws out a thread, which she fixes to a spindle; then with her left hand she turns the wheel, and with her right she guides the thread drawn from the flax, &c. round the spindle, or rather round a pole which goes on the spindle. When a sufficient quantity is wound on the pole it is taken off, thrown into the basket, and replaced by an empty one.

Spinning of wool is managed by a different process. Here the wool, in those fine slivers taken from the wool-comber, (which see under that article,) is held in the hand; a thread of it is fastened to the wheel, which the spinner turns with velocity, and runs backwards from it, thereby drawing out the thread to a considerable length. In either mode of spinning, when the spindle is filled, its thread is wound upon a reel, and taken off in the form of a skein or hank. The wool is delivered out to the spinner by weight, and when she returns it it is again weighed. Women must be very expert who can earn at this business one shilling in a day. Children at an early age are taught the art, and will soon earn from sixpence to one and sixpence a week.

Besides the above mode of spinning wool upon the wheel, a more ancient method is still practised in Norfolk with the distaff and spindle, which may be used either sitting or walking, while the spinner tends on cows, poultry, &c. The sliver of wool is braided round the distaff (or *rock*, as it is called by the Norfolk spinners,) from the slit end of which a thread is drawn and fastened to the slender spindle, which receives a whirling motion by being quickly rolled upon a piece of smooth leather, called the trip-skin, fastened upon the thigh of the spinner, who with one hand gently draws a few hairs from the tail of the sliver, while the other winds up the spindle and renews its whirling motion. In this way finer yarn is made than by any other method, but more than sixpence per day can seldom be earned.

Spinners are employed by the master *wool-combers*, for an account of whose art we refer to the article. Spinning wool into skeins is the next process: these are afterwards put into the hands of other women, called winders, whose business is, by means of a wheel and other simple apparatus, to wind two, three, or more of these skeins together, so as to make a compound thread of them. This thread is wound on two spoles or bobbins, for the convenience of having them fixed on spindles, which are turned round by mill-work, in order to twist the threads thus combined into a firm substance. When taken from the mill the worsted is washed, dyed, and dried; it is then done up in cruels and fit for sale.

The variety and importance of those branches of our manufactures, which are produced from cotton, wool, and flax, spun into yarn, have occasioned many attempts to render spinning more easy, cheap, and expeditious, by means of complicated machinery. Several of these have been very successful; particularly for cotton, by Sir Richard Arkwright; but the spinning-mill has not as yet been able to afford worsted yarn so cheap as that which is spun by hand.

THE STATUARY.

⸺

⸱'THIS Artist carves images and ornaments in stone, marble, &c.

The art is one of those in which the ancients surpassed the moderns. Phidias was the greatest statuary among the latter; and Michael Angelo, although he flourished in the sixteenth century, has not been often excelled by the statuaries of more recent times.

Dædalus has been celebrated as the inventor of statues, but it is certain that there were statuaries before his time. He was, however, the first person who found the method of making them appear as if they were alive. Till his time statues were made with their feet joined together: he formed his otherwise; he gave them the attitudes of people walking and acting.

The Parian marble is the most celebrated for statues: from this, which is of a most beautiful white, the greatest part of the Grecian statues were made. It is also called *statuary* marble, and is generally supposed to have had its name from the island of Paros, one of the Cyclades in the Ægean sea, where it was found: by others the name is derived from Agoracitus Parius, a famous statuary, who gave it celebrity by cutting a statue of Venus out of it.

Among the many statues of antiquity cut out of marble, was that of Laocoon and his two sons, which is mentioned by Pliny, and has escaped the

Statuary.

injuries of time: almost all white marbles now go under the name of Parian marble, and among the workmen they have the common name of alabasters, though they come from different places, as Spain, some parts of France, Italy, &c. Marble is also found in this country. Devonshire marble is now become well known; but we believe that no fine white marble has yet been discovered in England.

Statues are formed with the chisel, of several substances, as stone, marble, and plaster; they are sometimes cast of various kinds of metal, particularly gold, silver, brass, and lead.

When a statue is to be formed of stone, marble, &c. a drawing is first made of the subject intended to be carved; a model is next made by laying a mass of moist clay on a board, and reducing it to shape and form by knives and spattles. Sometimes a model is made without any previous drawing, and sometimes the stone is cut from a drawing without a model.

. The marble or stone is carved with steel chisels of different sizes, and a wooden maul or mallet, according to the representation in the plate. The statue is not made in a single piece, but of several, which, when finished, are fastened together with a cement of the powder of calcined alabaster, called plaster of Paris; this is mixed with water to the thickness of batter, which in a short time becomes as hard as the marble itself, and is as durable.

Statues are usually distinguished into four general kinds. The *first* are those less than life, of which kind are the statues of great men, of kings, and of the gods themselves. The *second* are those equal to the life; with these the ancients celebrated the deeds of men eminent for learning or valour. The *third* are those that exceed life; among which some surpassed the life once and a half; these were for monarchs and emperors, and those double the life for heroes. The *fourth* kind were still larger;

these were called colossuses or colossal statues. Of this last the most eminent was the colossus of Rhodes, one of the wonders of the world, a brazen statue of Apollo, so high that ships passed in full sail between its legs. It was the workmanship of Chares, who spent twelve years in making it.

Sculpture has with the other fine arts made considerable progress in England during the last century. The annual exhibition of the productions of this noble art at the Royal Academy, Somerset House, tend to excite a proper emulation and reward. The great collections of antique statues at the British Museum, must also, as models, have a considerable effect in improving the student, so as to produce that excellence which genius ever desires to attain.

The earnings of a statuary are of course as various as those of a painter. Princely and Patrician munificence has frequently enabled the artist to live like a gentleman, and mix in the first societies; a just and honourable reward for meritorious exertion.

Stocking Weaver.

THE STOCKING-WEAVER.

THE STOCKING-WEAVER makes a part of the covering of the body worn in cold climates, including
the foot, the leg, and a part of the thigh, commonly
called stockings: the principal use of which is to
defend those parts of the body from cold.

Formerly stockings were made of cloths, or of
milled stuffs, sewed together: but since the invention of knitting and weaving stockings of silk, wool,
cotton, thread, &c. the use of cloth stockings has
been entirely discontinued. In the year 1561,
Queen Elizabeth was presented with a pair of black
silk knit stockings, with which she was so much
pleased as to discontinue the use of those made of
cloth. Some years, however, previous to this, the
French historians inform us, that their Henry the
Second was the first person in the kingdom who
wore silk stockings, so that we might conclude the
custom passed from France to England about the
time of the death of that monarch, in 1559.

But it is said by Dr. Howel, in his History of the
World, that Henry VIII. commonly wore cloth
hose, except by accident he obtained a pair of silk
stockings. His son, Edward the Sixth, was presented with a pair of long Spanish silk stockings, by
Sir Thomas Graham, and the donation was highly
esteemed. Whether, therefore, the invention of
knit silk stockings came from France or Spain, is
a question which it is now impossible to decide.

William Rider was the first person who made them in England; and he, it is said, learned the art at the house of an Italian merchant, and knit a pair of worsted stockings, which he presented to William, Earl of Pembroke, in the year 1564.

Modern stockings, whether woven or knit, are formed of an indefinite number of little knots, called stitches, loops, or meshes, intermingled in one another.

Woven stockings are manufactured on a machine made of finely-polished iron or steel, such as that represented in the plate. It is of a structure too complex to admit of a description in this little work.

The invention of this machine is ascribed to William Lee, M.A. of St. John's College, Cambridge, in the year 1589. But by other persons, the credit of it is given to a student of Oxford, who was driven to pursuits of industry through mere necessity. This young man falling in love with an inn-keeper's daughter, married her, though she had not a penny, and he, by his marriage, lost his fellowship. They soon became miserably poor, and the only means by which they could support themselves, was the knitting of stockings, at which the woman was very expert. Sitting constantly together from morning to night, the young man observed, with great attention, the motion of his wife's fingers in the dextrous management of her needles, and, conceiving that it was possible to contrive a little loom, which might perform the work with more expedition, they soon began to make the experiment, which completely succeeded. Thus the stocking-loom was first invented, by which the inventor not only placed himself above want, but has rendered to his country great and important benefits, stockings being a considerable article of exportation from this to foreign countries.

This is the account given of the invention of the stocking-loom by our own historians; but the French say, that although the English boast of being the inventors of it, that it is in vain to attempt to deprive France of the glory of so useful an addition to our domestic arts. Every body, they say, knows that this surprising and useful machine was invented by a Frenchman, who, finding some difficulty in obtaining an exclusive privilege to establish it at Paris, went over to England, where his machine was admired, and where he was himself munificently recompensed.

The loom has, of course, received several improvements, so that, at length, stockings of all sorts can be made on it with great art and expedition. By means of some additional machinery to the stocking-frame, the turned ribbed stockings are made as well as those done with knitting-needles. These, together with the manner of making the open-work mills, a curious sort of lace aprons and handkerchiefs, as well as a great variety of figured goods for waistcoats, &c. have sprung from the same machine, and form now a considerable additional branch of the stocking trade.

Knit-stockings are made with needles of polished iron, which interweave the threads, and form the meshes, of which the stockings consist. This part of the invention, as it is now practised, is given by some to Scotland, and by others to France, though it probably originated in Spain. In Paris there is no great house without its porter, and these porters employ all their leisure moments in the knitting of stockings. In England, knitting is carried on as a trade in a singular manner. The wool-comber, in many parts of the country, appoints a day, generally once in a fortnight or three weeks, when he will meet his spinners and his *knitters,* to deliver out his wool and his worsted to be spun and knit. The poor women and girls of the village meet him on the day appointed with their work, return what they have spun or knit, and take other work instead. But the money which they obtain, either at spinning or knitting, is rarely more than six-pence or eight-pence a day. The wool-comber afterwards *dresses* the stockings, by stretching them on a wooden board, the shape of the leg and foot, having previously caused them to be scowered, or dyed, as the colour or colours require, and then he packs them up, either in a dozen or half-dozen pairs, for sale, as in the case of woven stockings.

Knit stockings are much more durable than those made in the loom; but the time required for this work, especially if the material be *very fine*, raises the price too high for common wearers. But such is their superior durability, that coarse knit stockings are preferred and worn by the common people in most parts of England, particularly by the men.

The Scotch are said to make the best knit stockings of any people in Europe, and they sell at enormously high prices, from thirty shillings to four or five pounds per pair.

A Stocking-weaver requires more genius than strength. It is a profitable business to the master; but journeymen must have considerable application to earn more than a guinea and a half a week. It is, however, clean neat work, and unexposed to the inclemencies of the weather. They are paid so much for each pair of stockings, and the price varies according to the fineness of the thread, cotton, silk, or worsted, of which they are manufactured: if, however, the workmen do not possess a loom of their own, they allow the master two shillings a week for the use of his. Looms will cost from fifty to a hundred and fifty guineas each.

The *hosier* purchases stockings, night-caps, socks, gloves, &c. from the manufacturer, and sells them again. Some of them employ looms, and are, in that respect, stocking-weavers. The business of the hosier consists in being able properly to appreciate the value of the goods in which he deals, an art which is easily acquired, and which ought to be reserved for the female sex, for whom, unfortunately, there are not a sufficient number of occupations appropriated.

THE STONE-MASON.

The business of a STONE-MASON consists in the art of hewing and squaring stone and marble, in cutting them for the purposes of building, and in being able to fix them in the walls of buildings with mortar.

This is one of the most ancient arts which exists in the world. The Pyramids of Egypt will ever remain monuments of the power, industry, and genius of man: although much has been written upon the construction of these massive piles, it is not known with certainty by whom or when they were erected, nor for what purpose they were designed. It is, we believe, pretty generally agreed, that they are at least three thousand years old.

If we look to Greece, and to Rome, before the Christian æra, we shall find that the art of the Stone-mason had arrived at such perfection that, at the present day, we seem to have little more to do than to become humble imitators of those grand and elegant remains of genius and of knowledge.

The tools principally used by masons, are the square, the level, the plumb-line, the bevel, the compass, the hammer, the chisel, the mallet, the saw, and the trowel; besides these, used by the hand, the master mason ought to possess powerful machines for raising or rearing large stones, or other great burdens, as levers, pullies, the wheel and axis, crane, &c.

The Stone Mason.

When the stones are large, the business of hewing and cutting them belongs to the stone-cutter, but these are frequently ranked with the masons, and so also are those who fashion the ornaments of sculpture, though they are, properly, carvers and sculptors in stone.

The Mason in the front of the plate is carving a stone with a *mallet* and *chisel;* before him, and on the block of the stone which supports the piece on which he is at work, lies the *bevel:* the two sides of the bevel move on a joint, so that they may be set to any angle. When masons or bricklayers speak of a *bevel* angle, they mean one which is neither forty-five nor ninety degrees.

In the back-ground of the picture there is a man sawing into thin pieces a large block of stone. The Stone-mason's saw is different from those used by other mechanics, it has no teeth, and being moved backwards and forwards by a single man, it cuts the stone by its own weight, and the friction occasioned by the motion. In the winter time, and in rainy or very sultry weather, the sawyer sits in a wooden box, not unlike a watchman's box, but without a front to it. These boxes are moveable, so that the workman may secure himself from the piercing blasts of winter, and the scorching sun-beam in summer.

Both marble and stone are dug out of quarries : the grain of marble is so fine as readily to take a beautiful polish. It is of course much used in ornaments of building, as columns, statues, altars, tombs, chimney-pieces, tables, &c.

There are an indefinite number of different kinds of marbles; and they take their name either from their colour, their age, their country, their degree of hardness, or their defects. Some are of one colour only, as black or white; others are streaked or variegated with stains, clouds, and veins; but almost all are opake, excepting white, which, when

P 3

cut into very thin slices and polished, becomes transparent.

Marble is polished by being first rubbed with free-stone, afterwards with pumice-stone, and lastly with emery or calcined tin. Artificial marble is real marble pulverized, and mixed with plaster; and from this composition are made statues, busts, basso-relievos, and other ornaments of architecture.

Few natural substances are less understood than marble; the people who are accustomed to work it know, from experience, and at first sight, that one sort will receive a high polish, that another is easily wrought, and a third refuses the tools. And men of science know little more.

Masons make use of several kinds of stone, but *Portland-stone* is the principal: of this there are vast quarries in the island of Portland, in Dorset-shire, from whence it is brought in large quantities to London. It is used for building in general; for copings at the tops of houses, and as supports for iron rails; for window-sills; for stone balusters; for steps, and paving, where great neatness is required.

This stone is very soft when it comes out of the quarry; it works easily, and becomes hard by length of time. The piers and arches of Westminster bridge are built with it; and so is the magnificent Cathedral of St. Paul.

Purbeck-stone comes from an island of that name, also in Dorsetshire; it is chiefly used in paving, making steps, and other rough work.

Yorkshire-stone is also used for paving, steps, coping, and other purposes in which strength and durability are required. There is also a stone which, when cut into slabs, is used for hearths, called *Rye-gate-stone*.

Stone-masons make use of mortar, plaster of Paris, and tarrass, for cementing or joining their works. The two former are used for dry work, and the latter for bridges and buildings exposed to the water.

Mortar is made of lime and sand, in about equal proportions, and after being sifted to a proper degree of fineness, is mixed with sufficient water to reduce them to a paste of the necessary consistence for use. The use of the sand is to supply the lime with the carbonic acid which it lost by being burnt; and thus be again converted into stone.

Plaster of Paris is made by exposing alabaster to a certain degree of heat, either in an oven, or in a common boiler, in order to discharge all the water which it contains; it being, for convenience, first reduced to a powder.

Tarrass is a coarse sort of plaster, or mortar, durable in wet: it is chiefly used to line basons, cisterns, wells, and other reservoirs of water. That which is called Dutch tarrass is made of a soft rock-stone, found near Cologne on the Rhine: it is burnt like lime, and reduced to powder by mills, and then carried to Holland, by which means it has acquired the name of Dutch tarrass. It is very dear, on account of the great demand there is for it in aquatic works.

An artificial tarrass is formed of two parts of lime, and one of plaster of Paris; and another consists of one part of lime, and two parts of well-sifted coal ashes. These are all used occasionally by the mason and bricklayer.

Stone-masons measure and charge for their work either by the superficial or cubic foot. They have extra charges for iron cramps, which fasten two or more stones together; for cutting holes in which iron rails are fixed, and for various other things.

A journeyman mason obtains usually about 4*s.* or 4*s.* 6*d.* per day, and the labourer has from 2*s.* 6*d.* to 3*s.* per day; but others who work by the piece, or who are employed in carving or other fine work, will earn more than double that sum.

THE STRAW-HAT MAKER.

THE STRAW-HAT MAKER, as a separate trade, is become of more importance than it formerly was : it is confined chiefly to the female sex, and engages them not only in the making of hats for females, but bonnets of every variety and shape.

The history of this trade is involved in the same obscurity as the generality of those trades whose commonness excites no attention from mankind; and where although, both for ornament and use, they become a source both of profit, convenience, and pleasure, yet their trivial nature are esteemed below the dignity of the historian and the philosopher.

The use of straw for various domestic purposes is unquestionably very ancient; and it is not difficult to suppose that after using straw and rushes for mats, that both would soon be converted to covering for the body, particularly the head, in a variety of ways and shapes.

We learn from undoubted authority, that the islanders of the South-seas, when first visited by Captain Cook, made use of mats of straw, or rushes, for the purposes of defence, and we think it is pretty evident that straw would offer, from its obviousness to man, a ready material, both ornamental and useful, in the earliest ages of society; and, indeed, we have no doubt that such was the case : but how it became improved to the present elegance and taste,

The Straw Hat Maker.

conjecture rather than fact is left to supply us with the history.

There are few manufactures in the kingdom in which so little capital is wanted, or the knowledge of the art so soon acquired, as in that of straw-platting. One guinea is quite sufficient for the purchase of the machine and materials for employing two persons several months.

The Straw-hat maker, represented in the plate, is employed in the making up of hats or bonnets, only after the straw is braided or platted.

The straw is cut at the joints; and the outer covering being removed, it is sorted of equal sizes, and made up into bundles of eight or ten inches in length, and a foot in circumference. These are then to be dipped in water, and shaken a little, so as not to retain too much moisture; and then the bundles are to be placed on their edges, in a box which is sufficiently close to prevent the evaporation of smoke. In the middle of the box is an earthen dish, containing brimstone broken in small pieces: this is set on fire, and the box covered over, and kept in the open air several hours.

It will be the business of one person to split and select the straw for fifty others who are braiders. The splitting is done by a small machine made principally of wood. The straws, when split, are termed splints, of which each worker has a certain quantity: on one end is wrapped a linen cloth, and they are held under the arm, and drawn out as they are wanted.

Platters should be taught to use their second fingers and thumbs, instead of the forefingers, which are often required to assist in turning the splints, and facilitate very much the platting; they should also be cautioned against wetting the splints too much. Each platter should have a small linen work bag, and a piece of pasteboard to roll the plat round. After five yards have been worked up, it should be wound about a piece of board half-a-yard wide, fastened at the top with yarn, and kept there several days to form it in a proper shape. Four of these parcels, or a score, is the measurement by which the plat is sold.

A good platter can make three score a week, and good work will always command a sale both in winter and summer. The machines are small; they may be bought for two shillings each, and will last for many years.

When the straw is platted it comes into the hand of the person represented in the plate; who sews it together into hats, bonnets, &c. of various sizes and shapes, according to the prevailing fashions. They are then put on wooden blocks for the purpose of hot-pressing; and, to render them of a more delicate white, they are again exposed to the fumes of sulphur.

There is also a kind of hats and bonnets called *Leghorn chip,* which is of a much more durable kind than our own straw, but not of so good a colour.

Persons who make up these hats will earn half-a-guinea a week: but braiders or platters, if very expert, will earn more.

The Tallow Chandler.

THE TALLOW-CHANDLER.

THE business of a TALLOW-CHANDLER consists in making candles of suet or fat, and in selling them after they are made. In the country the trade of a tallow-chandler and soap-boiler are frequently combined, in London more rarely.

In France, and in some other countries on the continent, the person who exercises the trade of a Tallow-chandler is called by the more appropriate name of candle-maker.

A candle is composed of a cotton-wick, loosely twisted, and covered with tallow, wax, or spermaceti, in a cylindrical figure, which being lighted at the end, serves to illuminate the place in the absence of the sun.

The history of the making of candles is not less obscure than the history of some of the other trades which we have had occasion to investigate. But that the tallow-chandler is a trade of ancient date we have every reason to believe: for in France, previous to the year 1450, the chandlers and grocers formed a united company, and were in that year separated into their distinct professions, the chandlers being forbidden to sell grocery, or any other article but those belonging to their particular trade. The grocers, however, continued to sell candles till the year 1459, when they also were prohibited from meddling with the trade of the chandler.

Of the origin of this trade we have no account; but we think that it is plainly discoverable at the present day in many remote country districts, where the farmers, for the commonest purposes, now use a dried rush, stripped of its exterior covering, and afterwards dipped in some melted fat. The *rush* is about twelve inches long, is lighted at one end like a candle; but instead of being placed perpendicularly in a candlestick, is put obliquely in a notch, or spring, fixed so as to hold it tight. One of such rushes will, perhaps, burn ten minutes or a quarter of an hour; and this, we doubt not, is the origin of candle-making.

The cotton used for dipped or common candles, is brought from Smyrna in the wool, which grows on trees in the shape of nuts, the shells inclosing the cotton. The cotton for moulded candles comes from Turkey and the adjacent countries.

The tallow-chandler employs women to wind the cotton into large balls; he then takes five, six, or eight of these balls, and drawing out the threads from each, cuts them into proper lengths, according to the size of the candles wanted. The machine for cutting the cotton is a smooth board, made to fixed on the knees, on the upper surface are the blade of a razor and a round piece of cane, placed at a certain distance from one another, according to the length of the cotton wanted; the cotton is carried round the cane, and being brought to the razor is instantly separated from the several balls.

The next operation is denominated *pulling th cotton*, by which the threads are laid smooth, al knots and unevenness removed, and, in short, the cotton is rendered fit for use. It is now spread, that is, placed at equal distances on rods about hal an inch in diameter, and three feet long; these ar called *broaches*.

A tallow candle to be good must be composed of sheep's and bullock's tallow. The wick ough to be pure, sufficiently dry, and properly twisted otherwise the candle will emit an inconstant vibra tory flame, which is both prejudicial to the eyes and insufficient for the distinct illumination of objects.

The Tallow-chandler's business in London is generally performed in a cellar, of which, with the stairs down to it, we have a representation in the plate.

There are two sorts of tallow candles; the one is dipped, the other moulded: the former are called common candles. The tallow is prepared by chopping the fat into small pieces, and then boiling it for some time in a large copper; when the tallow is extracted from the membranes by the boiling, the remainder is subjected to the operation of a strong iron press, and the cake that is left after the tallow is expressed from it, is called greaves; with this dogs are fed, and the greater part of the ducks that supply the London market.

When the tallow is in proper order, the workman holds three of the broaches, with the cotton properly spread between his fingers, and immerses the cotton into the vat, called a *mould*, containing the tallow; they are then hung on a frame and suffered to cool; and when cold they are dipped again, and thus the process is continued till the candles are of a proper size. During the operation the vat is supplied from time to time with fresh tallow, which is stirred frequently, and kept to the proper heat by means of a gentle fire under it.

Such was the laborious method universally adopted in making common candles till within these fifteen or twenty years, when an invention was introduced which is represented in the plate, and may be thus described. Three pulleys are let into a beam in the house; round these proper-sized ropes run, and are fixed to a machine, on which six broaches are placed. In the scale are weights sufficient to draw up the broaches; these are increased as the candles become larger and heavier. The workman, by means of this very simple and excellent contrivance, has only to guide the candles, and not to support the weight of them between his fingers.

In the left-hand corner of the plate is the mould, in which the moulded candles are cast. The frame is of wood, and the several moulds are hollow metal cylinders, generally made of pewter, of the diameter and length of the candle wanted. At the extremity of these is the neck, which is a little cavity in form of a dome, having a moulding within side, and pierced in the middle with a hole big enough for the cotton to pass through. The cotton is introduced into the shaft of the mould by a piece of wire being thrust through the aperture of the hook till it comes out of the neck; the other end of the cotton is so fastened as to keep it in a perpendicular situation, and in the middle of the candle; the moulds are then filled with warm tallow, and left to be very cold before they can be drawn out of the pipes.

Besides these, there are other candles made by Tallow-chandlers, intended to burn during the night, without the necessity of snuffing; the wick has been usually made of split rushes, but lately very small cotton wicks have been substituted for the rush; these are lighted much easier, are less liable to go out, and owing to the smallness of the cotton, do not require the aid of snuffers.

Large quantities of tallow are every year imported from Russia in casks, such as that which stands on the right-hand corner of the plate, from which are manufactured soap and inferior candles.

The price of candles in London used formerly to be regulated by the master and wardens of the Tallow-chandler's company, who met at their hall in Dowgate-hill every month for the purpose. But now the price of every article belonging to the trade is fixed at the weekly markets.

Common candles are subject to a duty of one penny per pound. Tallow-chandlers are obliged to take out an annual licence; and are also under a variety of revenue regulations, which are frequently not a little troublesome.

The *rush-lights* before-mentioned, as being only *once* dipped, are specifically exempted from the duties as candles.

Journeymen generally board in their master's house, and receive from twenty to thirty pounds a year, exclusive of board. There are also day-men, who work by the day, and are paid according to the number of candles made. Besides their common wages, it is the custom of the trade to allow *beer-money.*

THE TANNER.

———

THE art of the TANNER consists in converting the gelatinous part of the skins of animals into the substance called leather, by impregnating it with tannin, or the tanning principle, in such a way as to render it tenacious, durable, and impenetrable to water.

It is difficult to say at what period the art of tanning was discovered. It was doubtless known to the ancients in some degree of perfection; and it is highly probable that the skins of animals were employed by man as a covering, long before the art of tanning was known: but they would require, in this state, to be constantly kept dry, as moisture would soon bring them into a state of putrefaction.

The astringent matter which converts the skin into leather, abounds in so many vegetables in every country, that accident would soon lead to some method of producing the change. Independent, however, of vegetables, many earthy and metallic substances have the property of rendering skins incorruptible to a certain extent; and some mineral waters, containing copper or iron, will occasion this change. Hence we may conclude that some means of giving durability to the skins must have been known at a very early period.

Though there has been no radical alteration, or any great practical improvements in the art of tanning, yet for the last twenty or thirty years it has attracted the attention of many celebrated chemists

The Tanner.

and philosophers in all countries, who have investigated the subject with great accuracy and precision. Previous to this period we occasionally find some experiments and observations by men of science on the materials of tanning. A variety of patents has also been obtained in this country for improvements in the art of tanning, but we cannot speak of them as having effectuated much important advantage to the art. The last patent is one which promises, according to the specification, to shorten the time, and improve the process of tanning; and if the assertions of the Patentee, W. A. Ronalds, of Hammersmith, be correct, leather, by his process can be tanned in a few weeks. An account of this patent may be seen in the Monthly Magazine for July, 1818.

All tanned leather is classed, and universally known under two general denominations: namely, *hides* and *skins.* The former being commonly applied to the larger animals, as bulls, oxen, cows, &c. whose skins are chiefly intended for the soles of stout shoes, and other purposes, requiring very thick and solid leather; while the latter term is used for calves', seals's kins, &c. which being thinner and more flexible, are intended for the upper leather of shoes and boots, for saddles, harness, &c.

The stoutest and heaviest of the bull and ox hides are generally selected to make what are technically called *butts* or backs, and are manufactured in the following manner :

When the horns, &c. have been removed, the raw hides are laid in a heap for two or three days, and are then suspended on poles in a close room, called a smoke-house, which is heated somewhat above the middle temperature by a smouldering fire: this occasions incipient putrefaction, which loosens the epidermis, and renders the hair and other extraneous matter easy of separation from the true skin. This is effected by extending the hide on a wooden horse or beam of a convex form, and scraping it with a large two-handled knife, called a *fleshing-knife*, which is bent to suit the convexity of the beam. The hides are then immersed in a pit, containing water slighty impregnated with sulphuric acid. This operation, which is called *raising*, by distending the pores and swelling the fibres, prepares the hide for the reception of the tannin, and renders it more susceptible of its action.

When the hides are sufficiently *raised*, they are removed into a pit, in which they are laid smooth with a layer of oak bark, ground to a coarse powder, between each.

The pit is then filled with the tanning lixivium, or ooze, prepared from oak bark and water, and the hides remain a month or six weeks without being moved. At the end of this time the tanning principle being exhausted, the ooze and spent bark are taken out of the pit, and the hides put in again in the same way with fresh bark, and covered with fresh ooze as before. Here they remain about three months, when the same process is repeated at about the same intervals, three several times or more, according to the strength of the lixivium, and the substance of the hides. When sufficiently tanned, they are taken out of the pit, hung up in a shed to dry gradually, and being compressed with a steel instrument, and beaten smooth to render them fine and dense, the operation is complete; and having been numbered, and weighed and stamped by the excise officer, they are ready for sale, and are termed *butts* or backs.

Crop hides are thus manufactured. The horns having been removed, the hides are immersed in pits, containing a mixture of lime and water, where they remain three or four days, being occasionally moved up and down that every part may be uniformly exposed to the action of the lime-water. They are then taken out of the lime-pits, and the hair and other extraneous matter being scraped off, on a wooden beam as before described, are washed in water to free them from the lime and filth adhering. They are now immersed in a weak ooze, and by degrees are removed into other pits containing solutions, gradually increasing in strength during the time that they are taken up and put down, (technically termed *handling*,) at least once in every day, that all the parts of the hide may be acted upon by the tanning principle equally and uniformly. This is continued for about a month or six weeks, when they are put into other pits with stronger ooze, and a small portion of ground bark; whence as the tanning becomes exhausted, they are removed to other pits in regular succession, with fresh ooze and fresh bark for two or three months.

At the end of this period, the hides are put into larger vats called *layers*, in which they are laid smooth in a lixivium of greater strength, and with a larger quantity of ground bark between each fold. Here they remain about six weeks, when they are taken up and relaid in the same manner, with fresh bark and strong ooze for two months. This process is repeated with little variation once, twice, or thrice, at the discretion of the manufacturer, till the hides are thoroughly tanned; when they are taken out of the pits, suspended on poles to dry, and being compressed and smoothed nearly in the same manner as before described, are called *crop hides*, and form the principal sole leather of England.

The process of tanning calves' and seals skins, &c. is somewhat different. They are continued in the lime pits for ten or fifteen days; they are then deprived of their hair, and washed in water, after which they are immersed in an infusion of pigeons' dung, called a *grainer*, having the property of an alkali. In this they remain for a week or ten days, according to the state of the atmosphere, and other circumstances, during which time they are frequently handled and scraped on both sides upon a convex wooden beam. This scraping, or working as it is termed, with the action of the *grainer*, helps to discharge all the lime, oil, and saponaceous matter, and renders the skins soft and pliant, and fitted to imbibe the tanning principle. They are now removed into pits containing a weak solution of bark, where they undergo nearly the same process of handling, &c. as *crop hides;* but they are seldom placed in layers : and the time occupied in tanning them is usually from two to four months, according to their nature and substance. The skins are then dried and sold to the currier, who dresses and blacks them for the upper leathers of boots, shoes, for harness, and various other purposes.

The light and thin sort of cow-hides and horse-hides, undergo nearly the same process in tanning as calves' skins, and are applied to similar uses.

Tanners are obliged to take out an annual licence from the board of excise, and are besides subject to a variety of fiscal regulations and penalties, which, for the honour of a free state, and the advantages of trade, it would be well if they did not exist.

The trade of a tanner cannot be carried on without considerable capital; and a roomy yard, sheds, and pits, with plenty of water, are indispensable requisites.

The plate represents a tan-yard, as it is usually seen in the neighbourhood of the metropolis.

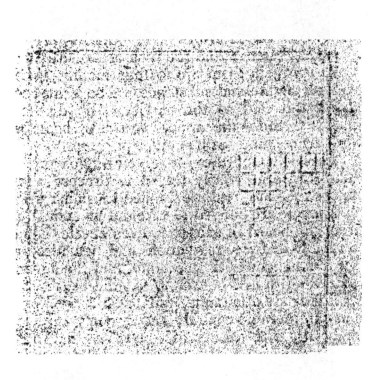

The Tailor.

THE TAILOR.

The Tailor makes clothes for men and boys, and riding habits for ladies.

The skins, with which mankind in the earliest ages of the world were clothed, were not in themselves very proper to dress the body, either exactly or conveniently. An art was, therefore, necessary to adjust them, and to unite many of them together. For this purpose thread was necessary, and the making of thread was for a long time unknown. We may judge of the means which the present civilized nations once used by those which many barbarous nations now employ. The dresses of the people of Greenland are sewed with thongs made from the gut of the sea-dog, or other fish, which they have the address to cut very fine, after having dried them in the air. The savages of America and of Africa employ for the same use the sinews of animals. Indeed, we ourselves used such in the earlier ages, and even now, for particular purposes of sewing, thongs are still in use.

With respect to the instruments proper for sewing well, pointed bones, fish-bones, and thorns, were doubtless the first articles used; afterwards awls, needles, and pins, the same as those now in use. The ancient inhabitants of Peru, which we may regard in many respects as a nation of considerable intelligence, knew neither pins nor needles. They used long thorns to sew and fix their clothes.

Mankind having acquired the art of preparing

wool, and, after many attempts, to make cloth of it, the art of cutting it out, and forming it into garments, became gradually known and perfected.

The Companies of *Merchant-Tailors*, a singular name, are well known to be very ancient, not only in France, but in some of the principal cities of England; and the tailors, as a body, have now in this country some rules and regulations in their numerous *houses of call*, as they are termed, particularly in London, which to the historian, who is desirous of marking the gradation of a people's character, are deserving of some attention ; but our limits forbid us from enlarging here.

In a tailor's shop, where much business is carried on, there are always two divisions of workmen : first, the foreman, who takes the measure of the person for whom the clothes are to be made, cuts out the cloth, and carries home the newly finished garments to the customers. The others are mere working tailors, who sit cross-legged on the bench, like the man near the window, represented in the plate ; of these very few know how to cut out, with any degree of skill, the clothes which they sew together.

The tools requisite in the business of a tailor are very few and unexpensive : the sheers for the foreman, who stands to his work ; for the others, a pair of scissors, a thimble, and needles of different sizes. In the thimble there is this peculiarity, that it is open at both ends. Besides these, there are required some long slips of parchment for measures, such as those represented hanging against the wall, and an iron, called a goose ; with this when made hot they press down the seams, which would otherwise take off from the beauty of the goods. The stand of iron is generally a horse-shoe, rendered bright from use. Before the foreman, or master, (for where the trade is not extensive the master cuts out, measures gentlemen, and carries home the

.clothes,) is an open box, this contains buckram,
tapes, bindings, trimmings, buttons, &c. with which
every master-tailor should be furnished, and from
which they derive very large profits. On the shelf
is a piece of cloth ready to be made into clothes,
and also a pattern-book.

The tailor in London purchases his broad-cloths
of the woollen-draper, who buys his goods from the
Blackwell-hall factory, or from the clothiers settled
in the west, or other parts of England. At Bristol
fair, which is held in September for fourteen days,
and also in March for the same period, an immense
quantity of broad-cloths are sold by the clothiers,
who assemble there, and hire shops as well as booths
for the purpose.

The tailor deals also with the mercer for fancy-
waistcoats and other articles of dress; with the
haberdasher for all his small wares; but when he
makes clothes for officers, he must go to the gold
and silver lace-maker for the necessary ornaments.

The wages of a journeyman tailor are regulated
by act of parliament, and he now has four shillings
and six pence a day: the trade is overstocked with
hands, although men that are sober, industrious,
and skilful in their business, are seldom out of employment. In times of general mourning for any
branch of the royal family, the wages of the men
are double; but they work more hours in the day.

A writer on this subject says, that a master-tailor
ought to have a quick eye to steal the cut of a
sleeve, the pattern of a flap, or the shape of a good
trimming, at a glance: any bungler may cut out a
shape when he has a pattern before him; but a good
workman takes it by his eye in the passing of a
chariot, or in the space between the door and a
coach: he must be able not only to cut for the
handsome and well-shaped, but bestow a good
shape where nature has not granted it: he must
make the clothes sit easy in spite of a stiff gait or

4

awkward air : his hand and head must go together : he must be a nice cutter, and finish his work with elegance.

The woollens in which the tailor principally deals is a vast branch of English manufacture. And so jealous are we of this trade, that, besides the precaution taken to use our own wools ourselves, we insist upon selling them ourselves, and of carrying them to the places where there is a demand for them.

A master-tailor in London, where a great number of hands are employed, requires considerable capital, as the weekly payments of wages are large ; and as he is obliged to give long credit, he cannot afford to do so without considerable profit; which is generally laid on to countervail the risk and time, with a handsome per centage for his indulgence.

The Tin Plate Worker.

THE TIN-PLATE WORKER.

TIN-PLATE, or tin sheets, as they are usually called, is a composition of iron and tin, not melted together, but the iron in plates is dipped into a vessel of melted tin, or the iron in bars is covered over with tin, and then flatted or drawn out by means of mills. The Tin-plate worker makes a great variety of culinary and other domestic utensils of this material, too well-known to need being described.

In the year 1681, tin-plates were made in England by Andrew Yarranton, who was sent into Bohemia to learn the art, although it was not brought to perfection for more than fifty years afterwards; but since the middle of the last century it has been carried on in these islands in so perfect a manner, that scarcely any have been imported from the continent. Our plates are of a finer gloss or coat than those made beyond sea. The latter being chiefly hammered, but ours, according to the plan of which we are now speaking, are always drawn out by the rolling mill.

On the affinity which there is between tin and iron, is founded the art of forming what is commonly called tin-plates, which is properly termed iron, or, as it is denominated in Scotland, and also on the Continent, *white-iron*. The process in manufacturing these plates is simply this: thin plates of malleable iron, thoroughly cleared from all rust, or oxide, are dipped into a vessel of melted tin, the

Q

surface of which fluid metal is protected from oxidation by the air, by a thin layer of melted tallow, the tin unites with the iron at each surface, but whether the two metals actually combine is not yet ascertained. The iron thus acquires a white colour, is rendered less liable to rust, and its durability is scarcely at all impaired; hence the plates can be easily bent, and from the alloy of tin at the surface can be easily worked. These plates have been sometimes called *latten,* and in remote districts of England the term is still in use.

The Tin-plate worker receives the tinned sheets in boxes, containing a certain number. It is his business to form them into various articles, which are represented in the plate, such as kettles, saucepans, canisters of all sorts and sizes, milk-pails, lanthorns, &c. &c.

The instruments that he makes use of are a large pair of shears, to cut the tin into a proper size and shape, a polished anvil, and hammers of various kinds. The joints of his work he makes with *solder,* which is a composition of what is called *block-tin* and lead; this he causes to unite with the tin by means of rosin, and the application of heat by an instrument of metal formed for the purpose.

The business of a tin-plate worker is very profitable to the master; and the journeyman, if sober and industrious, can with ease earn from thirty-five shillings to two guineas a week. The principal manufacturers in London, are Jones and Taylor in Tottenham-court-road, and Howard in Old Street. These seldom employ less than one hundred or a hundred and fifty men each. Those who manufacture tin-ware on a smaller scale, may be found in every part of the metropolis; and one of the chief sources of profit which these smaller tradesmen enjoy, is that of lamp lighting.

This business does not require great strength; but if a person would carry it on upon a large scale, it requires a very considerable capital: journeymen's wages may amount to between two and three hundred pounds a week: for on the Wednesday night a bell is rung, which announces to each workman that the master, or his chief clerk, is ready in the counting-house to lend money to those who cannot wait till Saturday-night. These plans are, however, rather overgrown exceptions, than the usual routine of the trade.

The large houses have constantly travellers in different parts of the kingdom; and as they cannot carry the articles of their trade in saddle-bags, they have drawings of all the works of taste, such as moulds for jellies, puddings, &c.

Although *tin* is not the immediate article under our consideration, perhaps it may be amusing, as well as instructive, to the juvenile reader, to be informed that tin in blocks resembles silver, but is darker. It is softer, less elastic and sonorous than any other metal, except lead. It is easily extended into leaves, and melts more readily than any of the metals. A composition of eight parts of bismuth, five of lead, and three of tin, will melt in boiling water. When tin is made pretty hot, it will break with a blow. In the ore tin is mixed with arsenic.

Tin being less liable to rust than iron, copper, or lead, is advantageously used for the inside covering of metallic vessels. An amalgam of tin and mercury is used to cover the back surface of looking-glasses.

The chief tin-mines in the known world are those in Cornwall. It is a fact well ascertained, that the Phœnicians visited these islands for the purpose of getting tin, some centuries before the Christian æra. In the time of King John, the Cornwall mines produced but little, the right of working them being at that period wholly in the king, as Earl of Cornwall. Their value has fluctuated at different periods: about a century ago they did not yield above thirty or forty thousand pounds per annum; but of late years they have produced five times that sum. The Prince of Wales, as Duke of Cornwall, receives four shillings upon every hundred weight of what is called *coined* white tin: this amounts to about ten thousand pounds per annum. The proprietors of the soil have one-sixth, and the rest goes to the adventurers in the mine, who are at the whole charge of working.

The tin being to be divided among the lords and adventurers, is stamped and worked at the mill, and is then carried, under the name of block-tin, to the melting-house, where it is melted and poured into blocks or bars, or carried to the coinage town.

The coinage towns are Leskeard, Lestwithiel, Truro, Helston and Penzance, being the most convenient parts of the country for the tinners to bring their tin to every quarter of a year.

Trunk Maker.

THE TRUNK-MAKER.

THE persons employed in this trade make trunks chests, portmanteaus, cases for holding plates and knives, and buckets; and sometimes the trade of a common box-maker is carried on in conjunction with the trunk-maker, by the same person.

This is one of those trades arising from the sub-division of labour, in consequence of a high degree of civilization: for there can be no doubt that this trade was originally a part of the occupation of a carpenter. How long a trunk-maker has been a separate trade we have not been able to ascertain, but we find that the trunk-makers in France, as early as the year 1596, formed a separate company, and had particular laws for their government. Amongst these, it was ordered, that a master trunk-maker should have but one apprentice at a time, and he was also forbidden, by the same laws, from beginning his work before five o'clock in the morning, or from continuing it after eight o'clock at night, that the neighbourhood might not be annoyed by the noise so inseparable from this trade.

Trunks, of which there are various shapes and sizes, are generally made of wood, and covered with leather, or the skins of horses or seals dressed with the hair on; and they are generally lined with paper. To some trunks, as that upon which the man is at work, represented in the plate, there are a number of thin iron cramps put on for the sake of strength. Those which are well finished are orna-

Q 3

mented with several rows of brass-headed nails, such as that which stands in the left-hand corner of the plate: that at the opposite corner, which is represented as open, is divided by several partitions, and lined with baize or cloth ; it is intended for holding a service of plate, which is usually sent to the banker's for safety, when the family to whom it belongs retire to their country residence. The trunks standing on the shelves, are intended either for holding linen at home, or carrying clothes on a journey. The upper one of the two on the lower shelf, is the best adapted as a travelling trunk. Travelling trunks are fastened either before or behind the carriage with leathern straps and buckles, or by means of chains. A patent was taken out some years since for a method of fastening trunks and portmanteaus to travelling carriages, so as to defy the art of robbers, who, in and near the metropolis, are ever on the watch to cut off trunks from coaches, as they come in or go out of town.

Portmanteaus are all of leather, and are adapted for the carriage, or may be placed behind the rider on his horse. These will contain a large quantity of linen clothes, and are very convenient for families.

The buckets hanging from the ceiling are formed also of strong and stout leather, soaked and boiled. They are very useful for conveying water to extinguish fires. Most large houses in the country have fifty or sixty of these, as well as a fire-engine, in case of accidents ; but it generally happens, through the inattention of servants, that if a fire breaks out, neither engine nor buckets are fit for use.

Trunk-makers often use, in very neat work, shagreen, which is a kind of grained leather, prepared from the skin of a fish, by exposing it to the weather, being first covered with bruised mustard seed, and afterwards tanned. The best shagreen comes from Constantinople, and is extremely hard ; but being soaked in water it becomes soft and pliable, and adapted to the use of the case-makers. It takes any colour, as red, green, black, &c. and is frequently counterfeited by morocco formed like shagreen; but morocco in wearing is apt to come off in scales, which is not the case with shagreen.

Journeymen, in this business, will earn a guinea or thirty shillings a week.

THE TURNER.

Turning is a very ingenious business, and the operation is very well represented in the plate.

The turning-lathe was well-known to the ancients, and the art of turning was carried by them to a great degree of perfection; at least many of the ancient writers tell us so, and amongst others Pliny, who says, that vessels of the most valuable kind were turned, and enriched with figures and ornaments, some of which are still to be found in the cabinets of the curious.

The art of turning is of great importance in a variety of trades and occupations, both useful and ornamental. The architect uses it for the ornaments both within and without highly-finished houses, and the mechanist and natural philosopher have recourse to it not only to embellish their instruments, but to adapt them to their different uses.

There are various kinds of lathes; that represented in the plate is as useful for small work as any. Some require the aid of one or two men to turn the wheel; but in this the wheel is turned by means of the treadle, by the same man who is employed in turning the wood. The thing to be turned is fixed on the lengthened axis of the smaller wheel, and upon the prop or rest, the chisel or other cutting instrument is supported; and being brought to touch the wood while it is swiftly turning round, it takes off shavings to the greatest nicety.

The piece to be turned should be rounded before

Turner,

it is put in the lathe; either with a small hatchet, such as that which stands just behind the man, or with a plane, &c. shaving it down till it is every where nearly of equal thickness, leaving it a little larger than it is intended to be when finished off.

The young Turner should endeavour to acquire a complete management of the gouge and chisel, which are the instruments by far the most frequently used, and the most necessary in this art; by them, of course of different sizes, almost all the soft woods are worked; and as to the harder materials, as box, ebony, ivory, &c. they are scarcely ever turned, except by shaving off. In that case gravers are used, with square, round, or triangular ends. These should be held horizontally while applied to the wood; but the gouge and chisel must be used obliquely.

When the work is completely turned, it is next to be polished. Soft woods, as the pear-tree, the hazel, and the maple, may be polished with fish-skin or Dutch rushes. Fish-skin, which is the skin of the shark, is always much better after it has been used, because, in its natural state, it is too rough to bring work to a proper degree of polish. The oldest plants of the Dutch rush are the best; but before they are used they must be moistened with water. When the work is finished in this way, it is to be rubbed up with a little wax or olive-oil. Ivory, horn, silver, and brass, are polished with pumice-stone, finely pounded, and put upon leather. Different methods, and different substances, are made use of for this purpose by different workmen.

According to Dr. Paley, not a man in a million knows how an oval frame is turned: it may be thus made: take two ovals of metals, exactly of the size of the oval wanted, fix them firmly on the spindle of the lathe, so as to turn round with it: fix between them the wood to be turned, and then it is readily

cut with chisels or other tools, as the lathe goes into
exactly the figure of the external ovals.

In fixing a lathe, great care should be taken that
it be placed in a light situation, near the window,
and neither so low as to oblige the workman to
stoop, in order to see his work, nor so high that the
chips should come in his eyes.

The lathe to which we have referred, is such as
is commonly employed by wood-turners, for whose
use it is well adapted; but for turning metal an iron
lathe is best; it is sometimes constructed in the
same form as a wooden one, only differing in the
size of the parts, which are of cast-iron; but this
form is unwieldy when applied to delicate and accurate work, such as is required by mechanics, clock-
makers, &c. ; for their use the *triangle-bar* lathe is
admirably adapted, as it is also for gentlemen who
make this interesting art an amusement, being the
most accurate and convenient of any kind of lathe.
But we must refer to larger works for a minut
description of this useful machine.

Ivory is much used by the turner; for a shor
account of which, and of the methods of dying i
of different colours, we refer the reader to the arti
cle *Comb-maker.*

A journeyman in this business may earn a guine
and a half a week; and those who work on toys an
smaller articles much more. The lathes used in th
nicer sorts of turning are very expensive, conse
quently the stock of a master is valuable; and n
lad should be brought up to the trade who has no
something of a mechanical genius, because there i
an almost endless variety in the trinkets made fo
sale, as may be seen in any large retail shop-window

The Type Founder.

———

THE business of a TYPE-FOUNDER consists in melting the metals which are used in the formation of the letters used in the art of printing, and casting the composition afterwards into suitable moulds for the various letters, figures, &c. &c.

The history of the type-founder is so closely connected with the history of printing itself, that we must refer to the article Printing for many particulars which we shall not now repeat. We will, however, observe, that it appears William Caxton was the first person in England who practised the art of printing with fusile types, and, consequently, the first who brought the metal types to perfection, which he is supposed to have done in the year 1474.

The first printers usually cast their own letters; but for some time past the type-founder has become a separate business.

The first part of the type-founder's business is, to prepare the metal, which is a composition of lead and regulus of antimony, melted together in a furnace. In large founderies this metal is cast into bars of about twenty pounds each, which are delivered to the workmen as occasion may require; this is a laborious and unwholesome part of the business, owing to the fumes which are thrown off. Fifteen hundred weight of this metal is cast in a day, and the founders usually cast as much at one casting as will last six months.

Q 6

We now come to the letter-cutter; that is, the person who cuts the moulds in which the letters are cast; he must be provided with vices, hammers, files, gravers, and gauges, of various kinds. He then prepares steel punches, on the face of which he draws or marks, the exact shape of the letter, and with pointed gravers and sculpters he digs out the steel between the strokes or marks which he made on the face of the punch, leaving the marks standing. Having shaped the inside strokes of the letter, he deepens the hollows with the same tools; for if a letter be not deep in proportion to its width, it will, when used at press, print black, and be good for nothing. He then works the outside with files till it is fit for the matrice.

A matrice is a piece of brass or copper, about an inch and a half long, and thick in proportion to the size of the letter it is to contain. In this metal is sunk the face of the letter intended to be cast, by striking the letter-punch. After this, the sides and face of the matrice must be cleared with files of all bunchings made by sinking the punch.

When the metal and other things are properly prepared, the matrice is fastened to the end of the mould, which the caster holds in his left-hand, while he pours the metal with his right; by a sudden jerk of the hand the metal runs into the cavity of the matrice, and takes the figure or impression. The mould consists of an under and upper half, of which the latter is taken off as soon as the letter is cast; he then throws the letter on a sheet of paper, laid for the purpose on a bench or table, and he is ready to cast another letter, as before.

When the casters have made a certain number of types, which are made much longer than they are wanted, boys come and break away the jets, or extra lengths, from the types; the jets are cast into the pot, and the types are carried to the man who is represented sitting at his work in the plate, who polishes their broad-sides. This is a very dexterous operation, for the man, in turning up the types, does it so quickly, by a mere touch of the fingers of the left-hand, as not to require the least perceptible intermission in the motion of the right upon the stone.

The caster, represented in the plate, is seen in the act of pouring the metal into the mould. He takes it up with a small ladle from the pan, which is constantly kept over the fire in a sort of stove under the brick-work. The iron plate on the right-hand of the caster is to defend him from the heat of the fire, and the screen between the two workmen is to prevent the man sitting from being injured by the metal, which is apt to fly about by the operation of casting. On the table near the newly-cast types are several blocks of the metal, with which the caster replenishes his pan as he casts the letters.

A type-founder will cast upwards of three thousand letters a day; the perfection of letters thus cast consists in their being all straight and square, of the same height, and evenly lined, without sloping one way or the other.

What is called a fount or font, of letters, is a quantity of each kind, cast by the letter-founder, and properly sorted. A complete fount includes, besides the running letters, all the single letters, double letters, points, lines, characters for reference, and figures.

Letter-founders have a kind of list, by which they regulate their founts; this is absolutely necessary, as some letters are much more frequently used than others, of course the cells containing these should be better stored than those of the letters which do not so often occur. Thus a fount does not contain an equal number of *a* and *b*, or of *c* and *z*. In a fount containing a hundred thousand characters, the *a* should have five thousand, the *c* three thousand, the *e* eleven thousand, the *i* six thousand, and the other letters in proportion.

Printers order their founts either by the hundred weight or by the sheet. If they order a fount of five hundred, they mean that the whole shall weigh about five hundred pounds. But if they require a fount of ten sheets, it is understood that with this fount they shall be able to compose ten sheets, or twenty forms, without being obliged to distribute. The founder reckons one hundred and twenty pounds to a sheet; but this varies with the nature of the letter.

We must not quit the type-founder without calling the reader's attention to the recent introduction of what is called *stereotype.* We mentioned the nature of it under the article printing; our confined limits prevent us from describing minutely the method of casting the plates, but a general outline is indispensable.

The page of any work is set up in the usual mode of printing, from which a mould of plaster of Paris is taken off, and from this mould a plate of type-metal is cast, from which the stereotype print is worked. Of course the plates are cast in *distinct* pages, which are to be put together in the usual way when a sheet is to be printed. The metal with which stereotypes are made, is a compound of regulus of antimony and hard lead, or tea-chest lead. The general method of mixing the metal is to take one hundred weight of regulus of antimony, and break it into small pieces, separating it from all dust and dirt, and then add to it from five to eight hundred weight of hard lead, according as the metal is required more or less hard. The lead is to be melted over a slow fire, and when melted, the scum is to be taken off, and the regulus is put in. To every hundred weight of lead may be added a pound or two of block-tin; but this is supposed by many persons not necessary.

In England, a person of the name of Ged appears to have been the inventor of this process, about the middle of the last century; which has been since much improved by Mr. Andrew Wilson. Didot, at Paris, the celebrated printer, is also eminent in stereotype.

THE WATCH-MAKER.

WATCH-MAKING is an employment so well known as to require no description, but it is usually combined, particularly in the country, with that of clock-making.

The ancients were contented with reckoning their time from the rising of the sun of one day to the rising of the sun on the next, as the Babylonians; or as the Romans, from the setting of the sun of one day to the setting of the sun of the next. This last method of dividing time is still in use at Rome, and many other cities of Italy. But it is productive of great inconvenience.

All the knowledge which the ancients appear to have had of measuring time, was confined to the sun-dial, to the clepsydra or water-clocks, and to hour-glasses. Till the twelfth century, the knowledge of reckoning time by means of wheels with teeth, regularly divided, was, most probably, unknown.

It is not known to whom we are indebted for the invention of the ingenious and useful art of making clocks of metal, for measuring time, and striking the hours. The first clock we hear of in England was placed in the old clock-tower which formerly stood opposite to the gate of Westminster Hall, and is said to have been purchased with part of a fine of eight hundred marks, or 520*l.* imposed upon Randolph de Hengham, chief-justice of the King's Bench, in 1288. Soon after this, another clock,

Watch Maker.

which cost no more than 30*l.* was set up in the Cathedral of Canterbury, 1292. These most ancient clocks were probably imported from abroad, or at least made by foreign artists.

About seventy years after this : King Edward the Third invited three clock-makers from Delft to come to England, and granted them a protection to exercise their trade in any part of the kingdom. By these means, before the end of the fourteenth century, clocks became common in our cathedrals and conventual churches. Chaucer, one of the best of our old poets, who lived at this time, compares the crowing of a cock to a church-organ for sweetness, and to a church-clock for exactness, as to time.

Of the *astronomical clocks,* one of the first was made by an abbot of St. Albans, in the reign of Richard the Second. It -represented the revolutions of the sun and moon, the fixed stars, and the ebbing and flowing of the sea. When he had finished it, so deficient were we at that time in the knowledge of mechanics, that he was obliged to compose a book of directions, for managing and keeping it in order, lest it should be ruined by the ignorance of the monks.

Watches were also made, or at least used, in England, not long after the beginning of the fourteenth century. One, which belonged to Robert Bruce, who was king of Scotland, from 1306 to 1309, is now in the possession of his Majesty ; and that which belonged to Oliver Cromwell, is still preserved in the British Museum. The King of Scotland's is not of a larger size than those which are used at this day ; Oliver Cromwell's, instead of a chain, winds up with cat-gut.

Pendulum watches were invented by Dr. Hooke, about the year 1688.

About a hundred years ago, Thomas Tompion was celebrated as the best watch-maker in Europe.

He was originally a farrier, and began the exempli-
fication of his great knowledge in the equation of
time, by regulating the wheels of a jack for roasting
meat. He was watch-maker to Queen Mary the
Second, and died Nov. 20th, 1713.

Although this business has not been known in
England more than a century and a half, yet the
best watches in the world are now made in London,
and an immense exportation trade in this article is
carried on here.

When watches were first made the whole business was performed by one man, who was then properly called a watch-maker; but the name is now
given to him who puts the various movements
together, adjusts their several parts, and finishes
the whole machine.

It is not above a century ago when watches went
upon cat-gut, instead of a chain; but cat-gut was
materially affected by every change in the atmosphere, and of course the watch could not measure
accurate time for two days together: but since the
invention of the chain, and the great improvement
in the temper of the springs, our watches are but
little affected by the weather in this climate.

Watches and clocks being adapted to the same
purpose, are made, or rather finished by the same
artisan. The *former* have such movements as *shew*
the parts of time ; the *latter* have such as *publish* it
by striking on a bell. But the name of watches is
usually appropriated to such as are carried in the
pocket; and that of clocks to the larger movements,
whether they strike the hour or not. Watches
which strike the hour are called repeaters.

Watches and clocks are composed of wheels and
pinions; in the former there is a balance or regulator, to direct the quickness and slowness of the
wheels, and a spring, which communicates motion
to the whole machine: but in clocks, instead of the
regulator and spring, there are a pendulum and two

weights. The spring of a watch is inclosed in a barrel, on the outside of which is wound a chain: one end of this chain is fixed to the barrel itself, and the other to the fusee, which is a piece of metal in the form of a cone.

When the watch is wound up, the chain which was upon the barrel, winds upon the fusee, and by this means the spring in the barrel is stretched: for the interior end of the spring is fixed to an immoveable axis, about which the barrel revolves. The spring being made of exceedingly elastic steel, endeavours to recover its former position, which forces the barrel to turn round; this motion obliges the chain, which is upon the fusee, to unfold and turn the fusee. The motion of the fusee is communicated to a wheel, which, by means of its teeth, connected with the pinion, turns another wheel, and so of the rest.

The parts of a watch are made by several mechanics. The *movement-maker* forges the wheels in solid metal to the exact dimensions; from him they go to the person who cuts the teeth. This part of the operation was formerly done by hand; and perhaps one of the greatest improvements which watches and clocks ever received, was the invention of engines for cutting the teeth. This has reduced the expense of workmanship and time to a mere trifle in comparison to what it was before, and has besides brought the work to a degree of exactness which no hand can imitate.

The wheels come back from the cutter to the movement-maker, who finishes them, and turns the corners of the teeth. The steel pinions are drawn at a mill, so that the watch-maker has only to file down the pivots, and fix them to the proper wheels.

The watch-springs form a trade of themselves: they are prepared by forming a very thin plate of steel into a double ring, binding it round with wire, and putting it in a proper furnace, to give it a suitable degree of heat. It is then dropped into oil or melted fat, which gives it a hardness equal to glass; it then undergoes several other operations, to bring it to that fine colour and polish which it possesses.

The chains are made principally by women, who cut them at a certain, and a small price per dozen.

It requires no great ingenuity to learn the art of making watch-chains; the instruments made use of render the work easy, which at first sight appears difficult.

There are workmen also, who make nothing else than the caps and studs for watches; others who make the cases; and others who cut and enamel the dial plates. A particular set of tradesmen are called watch tool-makers, because their whole business consists in forming implements used by watch and clock-makers.

When the watch-maker has obtained all the movements of the watch, and the other different parts of which it consists, he gives them to a finisher, who puts the whole together, and adjusts it to a proper time.

All the branches of this profession require a considerable share of ingenuity, and a light hand to touch those delicate instruments which are requisite in their trade. The watch-finisher not only wants a strong sight, but is obliged to make use of magnifying glasses, the frames of which are adapted to the shape of the socket of the eye. Few trades, if any, require a quicker eye or a steadier hand.

The trade in watches is very considerable; of course it employs a great number of hands, and the profits of master and men are considerable. A man, to be a scientific watch-maker, should understand the principles of mechanics, and something of the mathematics; a lad, therefore, intended for this business, should have a good education, particularly in these two last sciences.

Clock-making differs from watch-making principally in the size of the works; so that a person who is conversant in the latter, is equally fitted for the former.

Clocks with balances continued in use till about 1650, when a new improvement in the art commenced in the application of the pendulum as a regulator.

Bersard, a professor of astronomy at Oxford, of the last century, asserted that the Arabians used pendulums in Astronomy, long before the above period, as we know that Tycho, Lungrenus, Galileo, and several others did, though not in conjunction with wheel-work. According to Venturi, Sanctorius applied a pendulum to clock-work, some time before the year 1625; and Becker mentions a native of Switzerland, called Juste Birge, who did the same in 1597; but these experiments, if really made, were never sufficiently made public to benefit the world.

There are two very curious and celebrated clocks at Strasburg and Lyons. In the former a cock claps his wings, and proclaims the hour, and an angel opens the door and salutes the virgin. In the latter, two horsemen encounter, and beat the hour on each other; a door opens, and there appear in the theatre, the Virgin with Jesus Christ in her arms, the magi presenting their gifts, and two trumpeters to proclaim the procession.

There are many tradesmen in London, chiefly Germans, who make a good living by the manufacture of *wooden clocks*. In these every wheel as well as the sides, are made of wood, and, excepting some wire, and the striking-bell, there is nothing but wood that goes into the construction of those machines, which are sold as low as five shillings each; a very good one may be had for ten or twelve shillings. To these are often attached *alarums;*

they then become useful for servants, to awaken them in the morning.

Some years ago the minister imposed an impolitic tax upon watches, and although it has been long since repealed, we are assured that the injury then done to the trade by the measure is still felt.

Weaver.

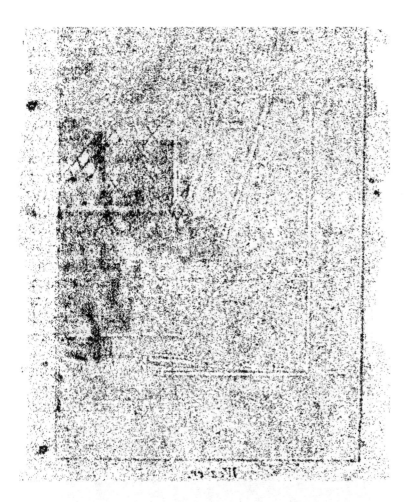

THE WEAVER.

WEAVING is the art of making threads into cloth. This art is of very ancient origin. The fabulous story of Penelope's web, and still more the frequent allusions to this art in the Sacred Writings, tend to shew, that the constructing of cloths from threads, hair, &c. is a very ancient invention. It has, however, like other useful arts, undergone an infinite variety of improvements, both as to the materials of which cloth is made, the apparatus necessary in its construction, and the particular modes of operation by the artist.

The arts of spinning, throwing, and weaving silk, were brought into England about the middle of the fifteenth century, and were practised by a company of women in London, called Silk-women. About 1480, men began to engage in the silk-manufacture, and the art of silk-weaving in England soon arrived at very great perfection. It has been generally supposed, however, that silk-weaving, and particularly that of figure-weaving, has never been brought to that perfection in England to which it has attained in other countries.

The art of cotton-weaving, in its present improved state, has not been long known, either in this or any other country. Wherever it originated, it is certain that most of our manufactures in this respect are unequalled in any part of the known world.

The art of weaving wool is of course anterior to both the forementioned, and was, in all probability, the art which was first learned relative to clothing the human body, and doubtless superseded the use of skins.

In the plate we have a good representation of a weaver engaged in his business. He sits at his work, and makes use of his feet as well as his hands. Weaving is a very extensive trade, and is divided into a number of different branches, such as the broad and narrow weavers. The broad-weaver is employed in stuffs, broad-cloths, woollen goods, &c.; the narrow-weaver in ribbons, tapes, and such other things: and there are engine-looms for making some of those narrow goods, by which ten or twelve pieces can be made at once; but goods made in this way are generally not so good as those made by hand, because it is not possible to find thread in every part equal; but the engines give an equal pressure upon all threads, while the workman, weaving by the hand, increases or diminishes the strength of his pull according to the quality of the thread, and by that method conceals all difference in the warp.

Linen and woollen cloth are both woven the same way; the one from thread, and the other from worsted. So also is silk, which, when taken from the silk-worm and wound, is called floss silk, and afterwards spun into sewing silk.

The *loom* is a machine by which several distinct threads of any kind are woven into one piece. They are of various structures, according to the several kinds of materials to be woven, and to the methods of weaving them. The other principal things to be noticed are, the *warp*, the *woof*, and the *shuttle*.

The *warp* is the threads, whether of silk, wool, linen, or cotton, that are extended lengthwise on the loom.

The *woof* is the thread which the weaver shoots across the warp, by means of a little instrument, called a *shuttle*.

The *shuttle* serves to form the woof, by being thrown alternately from right to left, and from left to right, across and between the threads of, the warp. In the middle of the shuttle is a cavity, called the eye, or chamber, and in this is enclosed the spole, or bobbin, on which the thread, or part of it, is wound.

The ribbon-weaver's shuttle is different from that of most other weavers, although it serves for the same purpose. It is made of box, and is six or seven inches long, shod with iron at both ends, which terminate in points that are crooked, one towards the right, the other towards the left.

In the front of the plate stands the reel, by means of which the thread is wound on the bobbins that lie in the wooden bowl ready for the weaver as he wants them. The thread for the warp is wound on a kind of large wooden bobbins, to dispose it for warping.

When the warp is mounted, the weaver treads alternately on the treadle, first on the right step, and then on the left, which raises and lowers the threads of the warp equally; between these he throws transversely the shuttle from one to the other; and every time that the shuttle is thus thrown, a thread of the woof is inserted in the warp. In this manner the work is continued till the piece is finished, that is, till the whole warp is filled with the woof; it is then taken off the loom, by unrolling it from the beam, on which it had been rolled in proportion as it was woven.

To give woollen stuff the necessary qualities, it is required that the thread of the warp be of the same kind of wool, and of the same fineness throughout.

The woof is of different matter according to the piece to be made. In taffety, both woof and warp are of silk. In mohairs, the woof is usually flax,

R

and the warp silk. In satins the warp is frequently wool, and the woof silk.

The common weaver requires but little ingenuity in carrying on his business; but weavers of flowered silks, damasks, velvets, &c. ought to be persons possessed of a considerable capacity: it is an advantage to them if they are able to draw and design their own patterns.

The silk-throwster prepares, by means of a mill, the raw-silk for the use of the weaver; he employs women chiefly. Spinning the hard silk and winding it, employ a great number of hands of almost all ages.

Journeymen weavers can, while in constant employ, make a good living. They will earn a guinea and a half or two guineas a week, according to the substance on which they are employed. It is a business that requires no great degree of strength, and a lad may be bound apprentice to it at twelve or thirteen years of age. Among weavers are found men of a thoughtful and literary turn. One of the first mathematicians of this country was Mr. Thomas Simpson, an industrious weaver in Spitalfields.

Wheelwright,

THE WHEELWRIGHT.

———

THIS artisan's employment embraces the making of all sorts of wheels for carriages which are employed in husbandry, as well as for those adapted to the purposes of pleasure. Road-waggons and other vehicles constructed for burden, are also the manufacture of the wheelwright.

In London this business is divided into two distinct branches of work; one of which being confined to the purpose of manufacturing wheels for carriages of pleasure, is an appendage to coach-making; the other to the making of the bodies, wheels, &c. of the different kinds of machines required for the transport of the various commodities for the purposes of trade, and the comfort and convenience of the people.

It will appear, by a very superficial examination, that such a business is of very great consideration, and must be undoubtedly of very great antiquity; as from the earliest dawn of civilization the transport of heavy bodies from one place to another, such as stones and timber, for the purpose of building, would suggest to man the use of rolling bodies for such conveyance, and as an improvement upon these, wheels for such purposes.

This trade contributes largely to the transfer and supply of many of our first necessities, by affording the means of ready transit for articles of all descriptions, as well as in offering a similar convenience of quick communication for ourselves. It is

pleasing to reflect, that amidst all the various improvements in arts and manufactures, this of car-
riage-wheels has been by no means neglected ; our
artizans in this line stand pre-eminent; our carriages are manufactured on better principles, as well
as more neat in the execution, than are to be found
in any other country.

The tools necessary in this business are many of
the same as those employed by the carpenter, and,
indeed, the carpenter and the wheelwright, in many
country places, are one and the same person.

The wheel is composed of several parts: as the
nave, which is the centre-piece ; the *spokes*, which
are inserted at one end of the nave, and at the other
into the *fellies*, which make up the outside rim or
circumference of the wheel. These three parts
constitute a wheel; but for the sake of giving
strength to the whole, some iron-work is used : this
we shall describe in its proper place.

The nave is that short thick piece of wood in the
centre of each wheel, which receives the axle-tree,
of which one is represented standing on its end in
the left-hand corner of the plate, with holes ready
to receive the spokes, which are made to fit accurately. When the spokes are fitted in the nave, the
rim, or fellies, are next put on the spokes. Each
felly is of sufficient length to receive two spokes, so
that if there be twelve spokes in a wheel, the rim
should consist of six pieces, or fellies.

The nave is bound at each end on the outside
with strong iron hoops, called *nave-bands :* within-
side also there is a ring of iron, called the *wisher*,
or *washer*, to prevent the hole from wearing by the
friction of the axle. To the outside rim, or fellies,
is an iron tire, fastened with very strong nails, or
spikes. The parts of the tire are made red-hot before they are put on the wheels, in order that they
may burn a small depth in the wheel, or, at least,
all that roughness which might hinder it from lying

flat with the wood ; besides, by being in this state, they may be easily bent, so as to conform most accurately to the curve of the wheel. Another advantage is, that iron, when hot, expands, and as it becomes cold it contracts into shorter length ; and as the tire of the wheel contracts, it must have a tendency to draw the several parts of the fellies closer together. To give the man power over his work, the wheel is placed in a sort of pit, made in the floor, on the sides of which the nave may rest, so little more than half of the wheel stands above the surface. The wheelwright, in the plate, is represented putting on the tire of the wheel ; and the smoke is made to pour forth from the burning of the wood. The large pincers at his feet enable him to bring the red-hot iron from the fire and place it on the wheel. The axe, resting against the other wheel, has a bended blade, and is used for hollowing out the fellies.

By thus scooping out the wood, the grain is often so much cut and injured as to weaken it in a great degree. To remedy this, a method has been invented of bending timber into a circular form, so that the whole rim of the wheel consists of not more than two pieces, which are covered with a tire in a single piece. By this mode of construction the circumference of the wheel is every where equally strong, and much more durable than wheels made in the usual form, although not more than half the quantity of wood is employed.

Elm, which is sometimes employed by wheelwrights for axle-trees, is also much in use for chopping-blocks, not being liable to split. But *Ash* is much more commonly used for axle-trees than Elm. The part of the axle-tree which is inserted into the wheel is either covered with two plates of iron, called a fore and hind *clout,* to prevent the wearing of the wood ; or a more common practice now, is to have what is called an *iron-arm,* fitted to the *iron-*

box, which is fixed tight in the nave of the wheel. The arms are screwed to the axle by stout screws. The wheel is secured by a pin, called a *linch-pin.*

Wheelwrights in the country are makers also of carts, and a variety of other carriages: the wood which they principally use is Elm, Ash, and Oak.

This business is a very laborious one, and requires that no lad should be brought up to it who does not possess a strong constitution: a journeyman will earn from a guinea to thirty shillings a week.

The Wire Drawer.

THE WIRE-DRAWER.

———

The Wire-drawer reduces rods of different metals into smaller sizes, in order to render them proper for use in various trades, and for manufactures, and also many other purposes.

When the wire-drawer became a distinct trade it is difficult to determine, but there is no doubt that the manufacture and use of wire is of some antiquity. Nor is it easy to say when attempts were originally made to draw into threads metal, cut or beaten into small slips, by forcing them through holes in a steel plate. It appears that as long as the work was performed by the hammer, the artists at Nuremberg were called wire-*smiths;* but that after the invention of drawing-iron, they were denominated wire-*drawers,* or wire-*millers.* Both these appellations occur in history, so early as the year 1351 ; therefore the invention must have been known in the fourteenth century. In France, a company of gold wire-drawers existed previously to the year 1583; and there were statutes in existence, a long time before this period ; one of which forbids the separation of the gold wire-drawer from the gold-beater.

At first threads exceedingly massy were employed for weaving and embroidery : it is not known when the *flatted* metal wire began to be spun round linen or silk thread. The spinning mill, by which the labour is now performed, is a contrivance of great ingenuity.

Metal wires are frequently drawn so fine as to be wrought with other threads of silk, wool, or hemp ; and thus they become a considerable article in the manufactures. The metals most commonly drawn into wire are gold, silver, brass, copper, and iron.

Silver wire and gold wire, so called, are the same, except that the latter is silver covered with gold.

There are also counterfeit gold and silver wires made of copper gilt, and silvered over.

The business of a wire-drawer is thus performed: If it be gold wire that is wanted, an ingot of silver is double gilt, and then by the assistance of a mill it is drawn into wire. The mill consists of a steel plate, perforated with holes of different dimensions and a wheel which turns the spindles. The ingot, which at first is but small, is pressed through the largest hole, and then through one a degree smaller, and so continued, till it is drawn to the required fineness; and it is all equally gilt, if drawn out as fine as a hair.

The next operation is that of the flatting-mill, which consists of two perfectly round, and exquisitely-polished rollers, formed internally of iron, and welded over with a plate of refined steel; these rollers are placed with their axes parallel, and their circumferences nearly in contact; they are both turned with one handle; the lowermost is about ten inches in diameter, the upper about two, and they are something more than an inch in thickness. The wire unwinding from a bobbin, and passing between the leaves of a book, gently pressed, and through a narrow slit in an upright piece of wood, called a ketch, is directed by a small conical hole in a piece of iron, called a guide, to any particular part of the width of the rollers, some of which are capable of receiving by this contrivance forty threads. When the wire is flatted between the rollers, it is wound again on bobbin, which is turned by a wheel, fixed on the axis of one of the rollers, and so proportioned, that the motion of the bobbins just keeps pace with that of the rollers.

Brass and copper wire is drawn in a similar manner to that already described. Of the brass wire, there are many different sizes, suited to different kinds of work. The finest is used for strings of musical instruments. Pin-makers also use great quantities of wires of several sizes to make pins.

Iron wire is made from bars of iron, which are first

drawn out to a greater length, to about the thickness
of half an inch in diameter, at a furnace, with a hammer gently moved by water. These thinner pieces
are bored round, and put into a furnace to anneal.
A very strong fire is necessary for the operation.

They are then delivered to the workmen, called rip-
pers, who draw them into wire, through two or three
holes, and then anneal them a second time: after which
they are to be drawn into wire of the thickness of a
pack-thread: after this, they are again to be annealed,
and then delivered to the small wire-drawers. The
plate in which the holes are is iron on the outside,
and steel on the inside surface, and the wire is anoint-
ed with oil to make it run easier. The first iron that
runs from the stone when melting, being the softest
and toughest, is usually preserved to make wire of.

The wire first spun about thread was round; and
the invention of first making the wire flat is probably
a new epoch in the history of the art; and it is a
curious fact, that three times as much silk can be
covered by flatted, as by round wire; so that various
ornamental articles are cheap in the same proportion. Besides, the brightness of the metal is
heightened in an uncommon degree, and the article
becomes much more beautiful.

The greatest improvement ever made in this art
was undoubtedly the invention of the large drawing
machine, which is drawn by water or by steam, and
in which the axle-tree, by means of a lever, moves a
pair of pincers, that open as they fall against the
drawing-plate; lay hold of the wire, which is guided
through a hole in the plate; shut as they are drawn
back; and in that manner pull the wire along with them.

Wire-drawing, in all its branches, is profitable to
the master and to the workman; it is a good business, being a trade that is not exposed to the weather; that can be carried on at all seasons of the
year; and by which the workman may earn from one
guinea to double that sum in a week.

THE WOOL-COMBER.

————

The Wool-Comber cleanses and prepares wool in a proper state to be spun into worsted, yarn, &c. for weaving and other purposes.

This is a very ancient trade in this country, wool having been long reckoned one of its staple commodities. The raw material, as is well known, is the hair or covering of the sheep, which when washed, combed, spun, and woven, makes worsted, many kinds of stuff, and other articles, adapted to the use, comfort, and even the luxuries, of life.

The invention of wool-combing is ascribed to Bishop Blaize, the patron saint of the trade, and also of the clothiers, in honour of whom a splendid festival is annually kept by the whole body of wool-combers in this kingdom, on the third of February. But, we think, there is more of fable than reality in this honour to the bishop.

While the wool remains in the state in which it is shorn from the sheep's back, it is called a fleece. Each fleece consists of wool of different qualities and degrees of fineness, which the wool-stapler, or the wholesale dealer in wool, sorts, and sells in packs, at different rates, to the wool-comber.

The wool which is obtained from the skins of sheep which are killed, and not shorn, is of a different quality, in regard to length, from the shorn wool, and is used by the wool-combers principally for making stockings, for which, from being longer,

The Wool Comber.

it is much better calculated; and hence one reason why knit-stockings are stronger than wove ones.

The attitude of the Wool-comber, in the plate, exhibits him in only one part of his business, the drawing out of the slivers. The wool intended for the manufacture of stuffs is brought into a state adapted for the making of worsted by the Wool-comber. He first washes the wool in a trough, and, when very clean, puts one end on a fixed hook and the other on a moveable hook, which he turns round with a handle, till all the moisture is drained completely out. It is then thrown lightly out into a basket, such as is seen in the plate. The Wool-comber next throws it out very lightly into thin layers, on each of which he scatters a few drops of oil; it is then put together closely into a bin, which is placed under the bench on which he sits: at the back of the wool-bin is another and larger one, for what is called the noyles, that is, the part of the wool that is left on the comb after the sliver is drawn out.

The shape of the comb is seen in the plate : there are in each comb three rows of teeth, parallel to one another. The best combs are manufactured at Halifax, in Yorkshire; the teeth are made of highly-tempered steel, and fixed into a very smooth stock, in which is inserted a handle, in nearly a perpendicular position. Each workman has two of these combs: these he makes pretty hot, by putting them into a jar, made of clay, *(see the plate,)* called a comb-pot, in which there is a fire, made of the best burnt charcoal.

When the combs are hot, he puts on each a certain quantity of wool, having first disentangled it from all knots and other obstacles that might impede the operation. He then combs the wool from off one comb on to the other, alternately, till it is exceedingly smooth ; when, having again heated the combs, he fixes each on an iron spike, placed in the wall for the purpose, as it is represented in the plate, and draws out the wool into a fine sliver, often- times five or six feet in length; what is left on the comb is called a noyle, and is fit only for the manu- facture of blankets and coarse cloth.

The business of the Wool-comber varies in differ- ent counties: some, as the Wool-combers in Hert- fordshire, prepare it only for worsted yarn, &c.; others, as those in and near Norwich, prepare it for weaving into camblets and other light stuffs.

Sometimes the worsted is required to be very white: in that case, before it is dry, after washing, it is hung up in a close room, in which a charcoal fire is burning; on the fire some finely-powdered roll-brimstone is thrown, and the room made air- tight, so as neither to admit the external air, nor suffer the vapour from the sulphur to escape.

In general, four Wool-combers work at the same pot, which is made large enough to admit of eight combs. There are, of course, four distinct benches and bins, of both kinds, in each shop. In almost every work-shop is an hour-glass, by which they measure the time; the care of this falls to the lot of a particular person. The small bottle underneath the comb is filled with oil, which is occasionally used. On the side of the wall are placed two ballads, of which, in general, there are several in the Wool- comber's shop.

The journeymen work by the piece, and will earn from sixteen to twenty shillings per week. Like people in many other trades, they often make holi- days in the early part of the week. They come on a Monday morning, and having lighted the fire in the comb-pot, will frequently go away, and, perhaps, return no more till Wednesday, or even Thursday. The men in this trade have a curious custom, the same with the hatters when out of work: they set out in search of a master, with a sort of certificate from their last place; this they call going on the

7

tramp; and at every shop where they call, and can get no employment, they receive one penny, which is given from a common stock, raised by the men of that shop. A spare bench is always provided in the shop, upon which people on the *tramp* may rest themselves.

Wool-combing is preparatory to the manufacture of worsted yarn, and is the first process towards the making of flannel, serges, stuffs, baize, kerseys, &c.

A pack of wool, which weighs two hundred and forty pounds, being made into stuffs, serges, &c. will employ two hundred persons. And when made into stockings, it will afford work for a week to one hundred and eighty-four persons, viz. ten combers, one hundred and two spinners, winders, &c. and sixty stocking-weavers, besides doublers, throwers, and a dyer.

APPENDIX,

CONTAINING

REPRESENTATIONS AND DESCRIPTIONS OF THE PRINCIPAL MACHINERY

USED IN THE

MANUFACTORIES OF GREAT BRITAIN.

IRON FOUNDRY.

THIS engraving represents the interior of one of the principal iron foundries in Colebrook Dale, Shropshire. The air-hole is visible at the end, and a man is employed drawing the dross from the liquid metal, which is represented to the right running from an orifice into a basin, where a man is lading it to pour into the moulds or matrices; two other men are also visible, similarly employed; and a fourth is emptying the metal into moulds.

To keep the moulds steady weights are commonly placed on them; but in the present case a cask of metal is suspended by a crane and let fall on the moulds, and by means of the crane shifted from mould to mould as occasion requires; such weights not only give precision to the casting, but prevent explosion from the expansion of the air and moisture within the moulds. The tarpauling in front is intended to be let down in case of wet

An Iron Foundry.

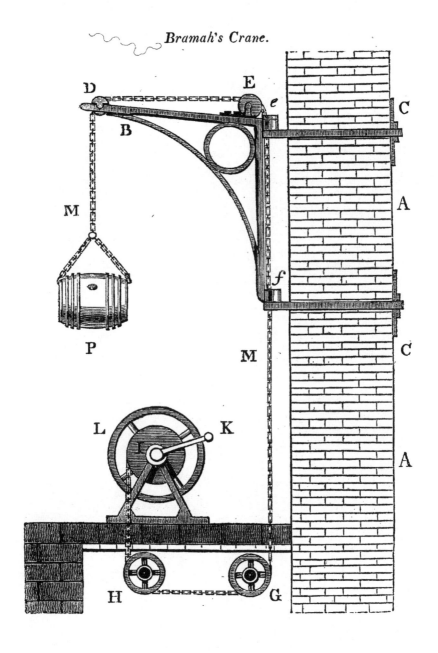

Bramah's Crane.

A Water Mill.

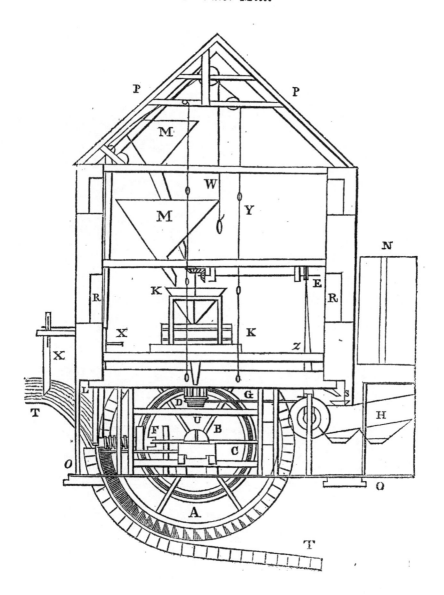

weather, as rain to windward would spoil the
moulds, and explode in contact with the liquid
metal. The chimney of the furnace is represented
to the left, and the intensity of the fire is maintained
by means of double-blast bellows, the noise of
which exceeds the conception of those who never
heard them.

BRAHMAH'S CRANE.

A, supporting wall	I, cylinder and fly
B, the arm or jib	K, winch
C, C, attaching bolts	M, chain of suspension
H, leading rollers	P, weight

In this crane, which is the contrivance of the
celebrated machinist and engineer, Mr. Bramah,
the advantages are facility of management, a great
accession of power, freedom from danger to the
operators, and considering the complication of the
mechanical arrangement, great rapidity of work.

A WATER-MILL.

A, the water-wheel	L, trough conveying flour to S
B, the supporting framing	M, M, hoppers
C, cog wheel	N, the building
D, lantern pinions	O, ground floor
E, E, bevel gear driving by the strap Z, Z, the bolting machinery	P, P, roof of the mill
F, a pinion on a cylinder, with which is connected the sack tackles W	Q, V, throwing sack tackle into and out of gear
	R, windows
	S, flour hopper
G, connecting the lantern pinion D, with the bolters	T, steam
	U, supporting beams
H, bolter binns	V, regulator
K, mill stones	X, X, water-gates

THE figure represents a vertical section of a mill,
5

in which the driving power is an under-shot water-wheel A, which, by the cog-wheel C, and the lantern pinion D, drives the mill stones K, to which the corn or material to be ground is delivered by the hopper K, to which again it is brought from the different floors or apartments respectively by the hoppers M, M. The flour, as it is delivered from the stones K, is collected in the leading trough L, and conveyed at S, to the bolting apparatus at H, where it receives the final operation.

THE CIRCULAR SAW.

A, B, saws
C, B, leading rollers for
E, F, driving band
G,

H, substances cut by the operation
I, a receiving trough

CIRCULAR saws are those which revolve on an axis, and thus act on the substance to be cut; the saw remaining without locomotion, while the substance on which it operates is moved to it by mechanical arrangements suited to the intent and scale of the operation, and the nature of the material.

The references explain the several parts of this arrangement. The pieces to be cut into the required form, are introduced by the operator into a channel, in which they are brought under the action of the saws A and B in succession; the saws receive a rapid motion by a driving band, from a large turning wheel, which cannot be shewn in our drawing.

A Circular Saw.

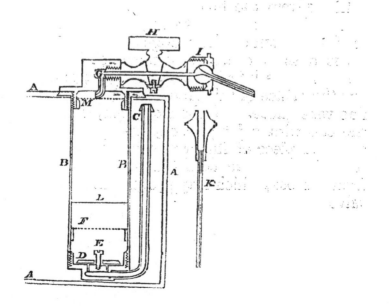

THE OXY-HYDROGEN BLOW-PIPE.

THE oxy-hydrogen blow-pipe is one of the most powerful instruments in chemistry.

A, B, is a deal screen, so constructed, that A opens as a door, whilst B remains fixed. C, pump for exhausting the common air, and condensing the gases. D, the metallic box of the blow-pipe, for containing the condensed mixed gases. E, the bladder, containing the gaseous mixture for compression. F, the stop-cock of the jet, on the outside of the screen. G, H, a glass or brass tube for the jet. I, the spirit lamp for igniting the gases.

A, A, A, the box for the gases. B, B, a brass tube, closed at the bottom, called the trough, which is fixed air-tight into the box. C, is a small tube in the interior, inserted into the bottom of the trough; two or four holes are made from the trough into this tube, and open a communication to the gases in the box. D, is a circular flat valve, lined with oiled silk or leather. E, is a central pin, which covers the holes, and prevents the passage of any thing from the trough into the box. F, is an intersection of the trough, by fine wire gauze. G, is a small chamber, communicating by a fine tube with the interior of the trough; and just below the orifice of this tube, is a second piece of very fine wire gauze. H, the stop-cock, which connects the cap with a jet pierced, having a circular motion. A piece of fine wire gauze covers the end of the tube at C, to stop the passage of any thing from the box, which may prevent the action of the valve.

THE WATCH.

THE term watch is well known to apply only to those time-keepers which are of form and shape admitting them to be carried in the pocket. Dr. Hook, about the year 1650, first rendered the machinery for registering time of sufficient portability, by adapting the spiral spring to the balance; by the vibrations of which, the action of the pendulum in the clock is produced in a compressed form. The great principle of the watch thus improved, this most curious and useful machine, was brought to a state of practical accuracy by Tompion.

Parts of a Watch.

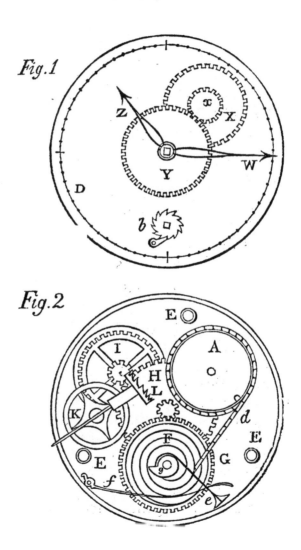

Fig.1

Fig.2

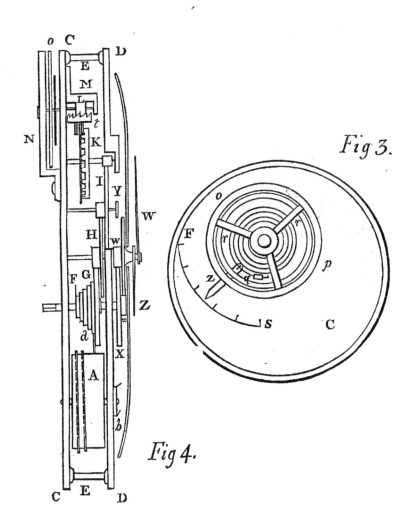

Fig 3.

Fig 4.

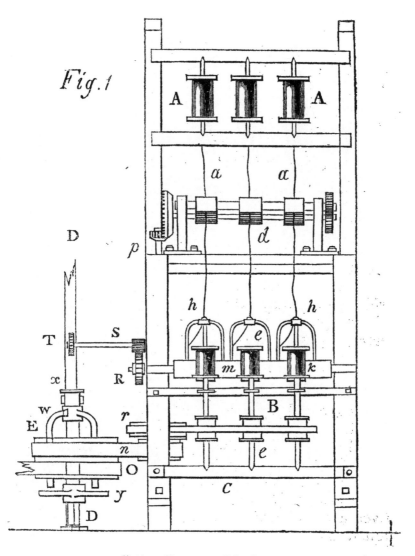

Fig.1

A   **A**

a   *a*

d

p

D

h   *h*

e

S

T

x

m   *k*

R

w

r

E

B

n

O

e

y

D

C

Cotton Spinning Machine.

A, A, the bobbings for rovings
b, c, d, rollers
E, spindle band
e, e, spindles
B, c, spindle frames
h, h, supporting forks
k, k, thread bobbins
m, supporting rail
D, D, verticle spindle
E, drum
n, spindle driving strap

r, wheel
P, pinion to face wheel
S, spindle,
R, wheel
T, wheel driving spindle S
w, a bolt for throwing out of gear
x, lifting sockets of bolt w
o, power driving strap
Y, locking bar

In the figure A represents the bobbings filled with rovings to be spun into thread; they are set up in a frame over-head, and are conducted down at a, a, through rollers d, which extend it in length, ten, twelve, or sixteen times, according as the yarn to be spun is to be finer or coarser. This is delivered out to the spinning apparatus or spindles: these are straight steel arbors, on the lower end of which the pulleys receive bands for turning them. These spindles are mounted in a frame common to them all, which consists of two rails B, C, the lower one supporting the points or toes of the spindles, and the other having bearings for the cylindrical parts of each spindle, and a wire is fixed over each to keep them up to their bearings. Above this bearing, the spindle is only a straight cylindrical wire, and on the upper end of it the fork or flyers h are fastened, either by screwing on, or they they are stuck fast by friction, which is sufficient to carry it about. The two arms or branches of the flyer are sufficiently distant from them, to revolve round clear about the bobbin k, which is fitted loosely upon the spindle, and with liberty to slide freely up and down upon it. The weight of the bobbin is supported by resting on a piece of wood attached to a rail M, which has a slow rising and falling motion, equal in extent to the length of the bobbin between its shoulders, by which means the thread as it comes through the eye is formed at the ends of either of the branches h, of the flyer, and is wound by the motion thereof upon the bobbin. It becomes equally distributed throughout its length, giving it a cylindrical figure instead of keeping all the thread at one part like a barrel.

The motion of the whole machine is communicated in the same manner as the roving frame, by a vertical spindle D, to a drum E, which receives a strap n, for one frame, and another o, for a similar one. The former of these straps extends the whole length of the machine, turning all the vertical spindles p, on both sides of the frame, by means of pulleys on the lower ends of them. Each of these vertical spindles puts in motion four spindles and the rollers belonging to them; the former by the bands f, which go round the wheel r, upon the spindles P, and the rollers it turns by a pinion at the top of each roller.

COTTON WEAVING MACHINE.

Figures 2, 3, and 4.

d, d, e, e, heddle rods	k, k, pickers
r, connecting pulley	I, I, troughs
D, E, treddles	P, pecker handle
y, z, yarns	Fig. 4, shuttle
A, cloth beam	m, eye of shuttle
B, yarn beam	n, n, shuttle rollers
H, the shuttle race	G, G, upright of the batton
M, the seat	k, the bobbin
G, the batton	R, the weight
R, cane frame	F, G, the batton
T, T, separating rods	

THIS figure represents a side-view of a cotton-

Cotton Weaving Machine.

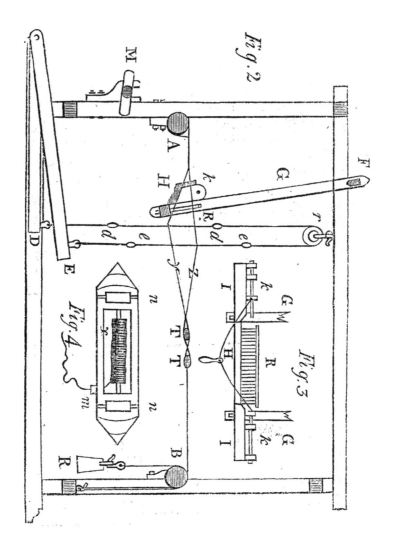

Fig. 2

Fig. 3

Fig. 4

weaving machine. The ends of the yarn are made fast to a beam A, called the cloth-beam, and upon which they are rolled up after being made into cloth; d, d, are two sticks connected together by several threads, the number of which is equal to half the number of yarns upon the warp; this system of threads is called a heddle; e, e, is another similar heddle. Behind the former, and in the middle of each thread composing the heddle, is a loop through which the yarns of the warp are passed, one half of them going through the loops of the heddle e, e, and the other half passing between the threads of the heddle e, e, and afterwards through the eyes of the other heddle d, d. The two heddles d, d, and e, e, are connected together by two small cords going over pulleys r, suspended from the top of the loom, so that when one heddle is drawn down, the other will be raised up, as shewn in the figure; the heddles receive their motion from levers or treddles D, E, moved by the weaver's feet, the yarns of the warp being passed alternately through the loops of the heddles, so that by pressing down one treddle, as D, all the yarns y, belonging to the heddle d, are drawn down, and by means of the cords and pulleys r, the other heddle e, with all the yarns z. belonging to it, are raised up, leaving a space of about two inches between the two sets of yarn.

F, G, G, H, I, is a frame called the batton, suspended by its upper bar F, from the upper rail of the loom, so that it can swing backwards and forwards. The bottom bar H, has boards shewn separate in figure 3, is much broader than the rails G, G, and projects before their plane about an inch and a half, forming a shelf, called a shuttle-race. The end of the bar H, has boards nailed on each side of it, and at the ends, to form two short troughs I, I, in which pieces of wood k, k, called pickers or drivers, are guided by two small wires fixed at one end to the uprights G, G, and at the other ends to the end pieces of the troughs I, I. Each picker has a string fastened to it, which is tied to a handle P, which the weaver holds in his right hand when at work, to pull the picker backwards and forwards. The shuttle figure 4, is a small piece of wood pointed at each end, about six inches long, having an oblong mortice in it, containing a small bobbin K, on which is wound the thread for the woof, and at the end of it comes through a small hole m, in the shuttle called the eye.

GAS-LIGHT APPARATUS.

A, the fire-place. B the cast-iron retorts in which the coal for distillation is deposited. C, the brick furnace. D, E, the iron pipe for conducting the gas from the retorts at B, to the receiver or tank F, S. N, the tar vessel. G, the gasholder or gasometer. K, the pipe for conveying the gas to the purifier at H, filled with lime-water. I, a vessel for receiving the refuse. L, pipe for conveying the purified gas to the tank, where it ascends into G. V, V, balance-wheels, over which is suspended the weight W, and the gasometer G. T, the pipe for conveying away the refuse.

The mode of lighting streets, houses, &c. with gas from coal, is an invention of the nineteenth century. The light afforded by the street-lamps previous to the year 1810, hardly enabled us to find our way. The case is now different, for the gas-lamps afford a light little inferior to day-light, and the streets are consequently divested of many disagreeables, formerly borne with, because they were inevitable.

The gas with which these lamps are supplied is

Gas-Light Apparatus.

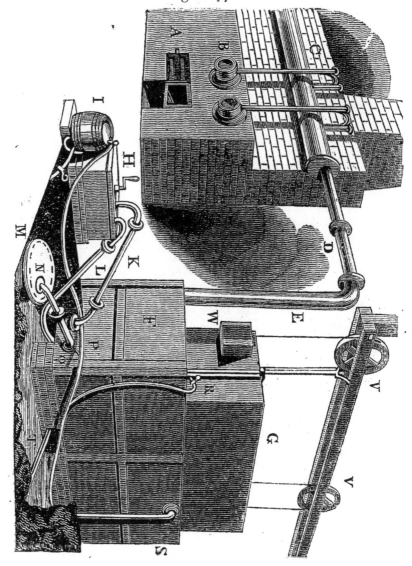

not generated on the spot, but in many cases at a very great distance. For the supply of several districts in London, and other towns, the gasometer and other apparatus for producing and purifying gas from coals, are situated in some convenient place, from whence the gas is conveyed in metallic pipes to the lamps, where it is destined to undergo combustion.

THE STILL.

A, is the furnace on which the still is placed; B, the head or capital; c, the refrigeratory, or cooler, containing the worm; and d, the vessel for receiving the distilled or condensed product.

THE SAFETY LAMP.

To obviate the destructive effects of carburetted hydrogen gas, Sir Humphrey Davy constructed the safety-lamp, since called by the miners "*the Davy,*" The apertures in the gauze should be one-twentieth of an inch square. As the fire-damp cannot be inflamed by ignited wire, the thickness of the wire is of no importance; but wire of one-fortieth to one-sixtieth of an inch in diameter, is most convenient: but the thicker the wire, the more will the light be intercepted; for the size of the apertures must never be more than one-twentieth of an inch square.

When the wire-gauze safety-lamp is lighted and introduced into an atmosphere mixed with fire-damp, the effect will increase the length and size of the flame. When the inflammable gas forms as much as one-twentieth of the volume of air, the cylinder becomes filled with a feeble blue flame; but the flame of the wick appears burning brightly within the blue flame, and the light of the wick continues until the fire-damp increases to one-sixth or one-fifth, when it is lost in the flame of the fire-damp, which in this case fills the cylinder with a pretty strong light. As long as any explosive mixture of gas exists in contact with the lamp, so long it will give light; and when it is extinguished, (which happens when the foul air constitutes as much as one-third of the volume of the atmosphere,) the air is no longer proper for respiration.

The figure represents the wire-gauze safety-lamp. A, is the cistern which contains the oil; B, the rim in which the wire-gauze cover is fastened to the cistern by a moveable screw; C, an aperture for supplying oil, fitted with a screw or a cork; D, the receptacle for the wick; E, a wire for raising, lowering, or trimming it, and which passes through a safe tube; F, the wire-gauze cylinder, which should not have less than 625 apertures to a square inch; G, the second top, three-quarters of an inch above the first; H, a copper-plate, which may be in contact with the second top; I, I, I, I, thick wires surrounding the cage, to preserve it from being bent; K, K, are rings to hold or hang it by.

THE END.

Printed by R. GILBERT, St. John's-square, London.

SD - #0009 - 190923 - C0 - 229/152/30 - PB - 9780282311520 - Gloss Lamination